Windows Forensic Analysis DVD Toolkit

Harlan Carvey

KEY	SERIAL NUMBER
001	HJIRTCV764
002	PO9873D5FG
003	829KM8NJH2
004	BPOQ48722D
005	CVPLQ6WQ23
006	VBP965T5T5
007	HJJJ863WD3E
008	2987GVTWMK
009	629MP5SDJT
010	IMWQ295T6T

PUBLISHED BY
Syngress Publishing, Inc.
Elsevier, Inc.
30 Corporate Drive
Burlington, MA 01803

Windows Forensic Analysis DVD Toolkit

Printed in the United States of America
1 2 3 4 5 6 7 8 9 0

ISBN 10: 1-59749-156-X
ISBN 13: 978-1-59749-156-3

Publisher: Amorette Pedersen
Acquisitions Editor: Andrew Williams
Technical Editors: Jesse Kornblum, Dave Kleiman
Cover Designer: Michael Kavish

Project Manager: Gary Byrne
Page Layout and Art: Patricia Lupien
Copy Editor: Darlene Bordwell
Indexer: Michael Ferreira

For information on rights, translations, and bulk sales, contact Matt Pedersen, Commercial Sales Director and Rights, at Syngress Publishing; email m.pedersen@syngress.com.

To Terri

Author Acknowledgments

First, I'd like to thank God for the many blessings He's given me in my life, for which I am immensely and eternally grateful. My life has been a wonderful bounty since I accepted Jesus into my heart and my life.

I'd like to thank the love and light of my life, Terri, and her beautiful daughter, Kylie, for their patience and understanding in supporting me while I wrote a second book (as if the first one wasn't enough!). I know that I've left them both wondering as I've stared off into space, reasoning and turning over phrases in my mind as I attempted put them down on "paper." It can't be easy for either of these two wonderful women to be living with a nerd.

I'd also like to thank a number of other people for their contributions, both big and small, to this effort. Jesse Kornblum deserves a special thanks, not only for being the technical editor for this book but also for being a friend and sounding board for a number of ideas—many of which have been off the wall. I'd also like to thank Jesse for his many contributions to the field of computer forensics, from his FRED disk to his hashing tools to the many papers that he's authored. I'd like to thank Cory Altheide, as he was the one who approached me with the idea of tracking artifacts left on Windows systems by the use of USB removable storage devices. I'd like to thank Andreas Schuster for his many current and future contributions to the field, including the area of Windows memory analysis. Others who have contributed to the field, and hence this book, in one way or another include Aaron Walters, the coauthor of FATKit; Bill Harback, General Dynamics—Advanced Information Systems; George M. Garner, Jr., President, GMG Systems, Inc.; Detective Richard F. McQuown, Milwaukee Police Department; Detective Jon Evans, Gwent Police Hi-Tech Crime Unit; and Don Lewis, Computer Forensic Analyst for the Lakewood, CO, Police Department.

Lead Author

Harlan Carvey (CISSP), author of the acclaimed *Windows Forensics and Incident Recovery*, is a computer forensics and incident response consultant based out of the Northern VA/Metro DC area. He currently provides emergency incident response and computer forensic analysis services to clients throughout the U.S. His specialties include focusing specifically on the Windows 2000 and later platforms with regard to incident response, Registry and memory analysis, and post-mortem computer forensic analysis. Harlan's background includes positions as a consultant performing vulnerability assessments and penetration tests and as a full-time security engineer. He also has supported federal government agencies with incident response and computer forensic services.

Harlan holds a bachelor's degree in electrical engineering from the Virginia Military Institute and a master's degree in electrical engineering from the Naval Postgraduate School.

Harlan would like to thank his wife, Terri, for her support, patience, and humor throughout the entire process of writing his second book.

Technical Editors

Jesse D. Kornblum is a Principal Computer Forensics Engineer with ManTech SMA. He currently develops new computer forensics tools and techniques for members of the Intelligence Community. Based in the Washington, DC, area, he has pioneered several areas of the field, including automated incident response, fuzzy hashing, and Windows memory analysis. In addition, he is the author of several widely used computer forensics tools, such as md5deep and fore-most. Jesse currently sits on the Editorial Board for the journal *Digital Investigation* and is a major contributor to the ForensicsWiki Project. His background includes serving as a Computer Crime Investigator with the U.S. Air Force Office of Special Investigations.

Dave Kleiman (CAS, CCE, CIFI, CISM, CISSP, ISSAP, ISSMP, MCSE) has worked in the information technology security sector since 1990. Currently, he is the owner of SecurityBreach Response.com and is the Chief Information Security Officer for Securit-e-Doc, Inc. Before starting this position, he was Vice President of Technical Operations at Intelliswitch, Inc., where he supervised an international telecommunications and Internet service provider network. Dave is a recognized security expert. A former Florida Certified Law Enforcement Officer, he specializes in computer forensic investigations, incident response, intrusion analysis, security audits, and secure network infrastructures. He has written several secure installation and configuration guides about Microsoft technologies that are used by network professionals. He has developed a Windows operating system lockdown tool, S-Lok (www.s-doc.com/products/slok.asp), which surpasses NSA, NIST, and Microsoft Common Criteria Guidelines.

Dave was a contributing author to *Microsoft Log Parser Toolkit* (Syngress Publishing, ISBN: 1-932266-52-6). He is frequently a speaker at many national security conferences and is a regular contributor to many security-related newsletters, Web sites, and Internet forums. Dave is a member of several organizations, including the International Association of Counter Terrorism and Security Professionals (IACSP), International Society of Forensic Computer Examiners® (ISFCE), Information Systems Audit and Control Association® (ISACA), High Technology Crime Investigation Association (HTCIA), Network and Systems Professionals Association (NaSPA), Association of Certified Fraud Examiners (ACFE), Anti Terrorism Accreditation Board (ATAB), and ASIS International®. He is also a Secure Member and Sector Chief for Information Technology at The FBI's InfraGard® and a Member and Director of Education at the International Information Systems Forensics Association (IISFA).

Technical Reviewer

Troy Larson is a Senior Forensic Engineer in Microsoft's Network Security team, where he enjoys analyzing Microsoft's newest technologies in a constant race to keep forensics practice current with Microsoft technology. Troy is a frequent speaker on forensics issues involving Windows and Office, and he is currently focused on developing forensic techniques for Vista and Office 2007. Prior to joining Microsoft's forensics team, Troy served tours of duty with Ernst & Young's national forensics practice and Attenex, Inc. Troy is member of the Washington State Bar and received his undergraduate and law degrees from the University of California at Berkeley.

Contents

Preface

The purpose of this book is to address a need. One thing that many computer forensic examiners have noticed is an overreliance by investigators on what forensic analysis tools are telling them, without really understanding where this information is coming from or how it is being created or derived. The age of "Nintendo forensics" (i.e., loading an acquired image into a forensic analysis application and pushing a button) is over. As analysts and examiners, we can no longer expect to investigate a case in such a manner. Cybercrime has increased in sophistication, and investigators need to understand what artifacts are available on a system, as well as how those artifacts are created and modified. With this level of knowledge, we come to understand that the absence of an artifact is itself an artifact. In addition, more and more presentations and material are available regarding anti-forensics, or techniques used to make forensic analysis more difficult. Moreover, there have been presentations at major conferences that discuss the anti-forensic technique of using the forensic analysts' training and tools against them. This book is intended to address the need for a more detailed, granular level of understanding. It attempts not only to demonstrate what information is available to the investigator on both a live Windows system and in an acquired image but also to provide information on how to locate additional artifacts that may be of interest.

My primary reason for writing this book has been so that I can give back to a community and field of endeavor that has given so much to me. Since I started in the information security field over 10 years ago (prior to that, I was in the military and involved in physical and communications security), I've met a lot of great people and done a lot of really interesting things. Over time, people have shared things with me that have been extremely helpful, and some of those things have served as stepping stones into further research. Some of that research has found its way into presentations I've given at various conferences, and from there, others have asked questions and provided insight and answers that have helped push that research forward. The repeated exchanging of information and engaging in discussion have moved the interest and the level of knowledge forward, thus advancing the field.

This book is intended to address the technical aspects of collecting and analyzing data during both live and post-mortem investigations of Windows systems. It does not cover everything that could possibly be addressed. There is still considerable room for research in several areas, and a great deal of information needs to be catalogued. My hope is that this book will awaken the reader to the possibilities and opportunities that exist within Windows systems for a more comprehensive investigation and analysis.

Intended Audience

This book focuses on a fairly narrow technical area, Windows forensic analysis, but it's intended for anyone who does, might do, or is thinking about performing forensic analysis of Windows systems. This book will be a useful reference for many, and my hope is that any readers who initially feel that the book is over their heads or beyond their technical reach will use the material they find as a starting point and a basis for questions and further study. When I started writing this book, it was not intended to be a second or follow-on edition to my first book, *Windows Forensics and Incident Recovery*, which was published by Addison-Wesley in July 2004. Rather, my intention was to move away from a more general focus and provide a resource not only for myself but also for others working in the computer forensic analysis field.

In writing this book, my goal was to provide a resource for forensic analysts, investigators, and incident responders. My hope is to provide not only useful material for those currently performing forensic investigations but also insight to system administrators who have been faced with incident response activities and have been left wondering, "What should I have done?" On that front, my hope is that we can eventually move away from the misconception that wiping the hard drive and reinstalling the operating system from clean media are acceptable resolutions to an incident. Even updating the patches on the system does not address configuration issues and in many cases will result in reinfection or the system being compromised all over again.

This book is intended for anyone performing forensic analysis of Windows systems—be they corporate or government investigators, law enforcement officers, or consultants. My hope is that this book will also serve as a useful reference for those developing or attending computer forensic programs at colleges and universities.

Throughout this book, the terms *investigator, first responder, examiner*, and *administrator* are used interchangeably because the same person often may be wearing all of these hats. In other cases, the investigator may come into the corporate infrastructure and work very closely with the administrator, even to the point of obtaining an administrator-level account within the domain in order to perform data collection. In some cases, the administrator may escort the investigator or first responder to a compromised system, and the user account may have administrator privileges on that system. Please don't be confused by the use of the terms; they are synonymous in most cases.

Reading through this book, you'll likely notice a couple of things. First, there is a heavy reliance on Perl as a scripting language. There's nothing magical about this choice: Perl is simply a very flexible and powerful scripting language that I like to use because I can make changes to the code and run it immediately without having to recompile the program. And with regard to compiling, if you're not familiar with Perl and have never used it, you have nothing to worry about. With only a few exceptions, the Perl scripts presented in the book and provided on the accompanying DVD have been "compiled" into standalone Windows executable files using Perl2Exe. These executable files enable you to run the Perl scripts without having to install Perl (the version of Perl used throughout this book is freely available from ActiveState.com) or anything else. Simply extract the necessary files from the archive on the DVD and run them. Another useful feature of Perl is that, with some care, Perl scripts can be written to be platform independent. Many of the Perl scripts included on the DVD perform data extraction (and to some degree, analysis) from binary files, and where possible, I have tried to make them as platform independent as possible. What this means is that the Perl script (and the accompanying Windows executable) will run on the Windows platform, but the Perl script itself can be run on Linux or even Mac OS X. Many of the Perl scripts on the DVD (although admittedly not all) have been tested and run successfully within the Perl environment on Linux. Therefore, the examiner is not restricted to any particular analysis platform. Some of the scripts will require the installation of additional modules. You can install these modules by using the Perl Package Manager (PPM) application. PPM is part of the ActiveState distribution of Perl, which is available for Windows, Linux, Mac OS X, and a number of other platforms. Another very useful aspect of using Perl is to meet the needs of automation. I often find myself doing the same sorts of things (data extraction, translation of binary data into something human-readable, etc.) over and over again, and like most folks, I'm bound to make mistakes at some point. However, if I can take a task and automate it in Perl, I can write the code once and not have to be concerned with making a mistake regardless of how many times I perform that same task. It's easy to correct a process if you actually have a process—I find it extremely difficult to correct what I did if I don't know what it was that I did!

You'll notice that the forensic analysis application used throughout this book is ProDiscover Incident Response Edition, from Technology Pathways. Thanks to Chris Brown's generosity, I have worked with ProDiscover since Version 3, and I have found the interface to be extremely intuitive and easy to navigate. When it comes to examining images acquired from Windows systems, ProDiscover is an excellent tool to use. It has many useful and powerful features. Chris and Alex Augustin have been extremely responsive to questions and updates, and Ted Augustin has been an excellent resource when I've met him at conferences and had a chance to speak with him (Chris, Alex, and Ted are with Technology Pathways). ProDiscover itself is an excellent analysis platform, and the Incident Response Edition has made great strides into the live response arena, providing an easy, effective means for collecting volatile data. Also, in my opinion, Chris made an excellent decision in choosing Perl as the scripting language for ProDiscover because Perl enables the investigator to perform functions (e.g., searches, data extraction, a modicum of data analysis, etc.) within the image via Perl "ProScripts." The accompanying DVD contains several ProScripts that I've written and used quite regularly during examinations (please note that though the ProScripts are Perl scripts, they are not "compiled" with Perl2Exe, as the ProScripts must be scripts to be used with ProDiscover).

Organization of This Book

This book is organized into seven chapters.

Chapter 1: Live Response: Data Collection

This chapter addresses the basic issues of collecting volatile data from live systems. Because of several factors (an increase in sophistication of cybercrime, increases in storage capacity, etc.), live response has gained a great deal of interest. This increase in interest has not been restricted to consultants (such as myself) either; law enforcement professionals are also beginning to see the need for collecting volatile information from live systems in order to support an investigation. This chapter lists tools and methodologies that you can use to collect volatile information. It also presents the current incarnation of the Forensic Server Project.

Chapter 2: Live Response: Data Analysis

I've separated data collection and data analysis as I see them as two separate issues. In many cases, the data that you want to collect doesn't change, as you want to get a snapshot of the activity on the system at a point in time. However, how you interpret that data is what may be important to your case. Also, it's not unusual to approach a scene and find that the initial incident report is only a symptom of what is really happening on the system or has nothing to do with the real issue at all. During live response, how you analyze the data you've collected, and what you look for, can depend on whether you're investigating a fraud case, an intrusion, or a malware infection. This chapter presents a framework for correlating and analyzing the data collected during live response in order to develop a cohesive picture of activity on the system and make analysis and identification of the root cause a bit easier and more understandable.

Chapter 3: Windows Memory Analysis

Windows memory analysis is an area of study that has really taken off since its formal introduction to the community during the summer of 2005. In the past, if the contents of physical memory (i.e., RAM) were collected from a live system, they were searched for strings (i.e., passwords), IP addresses, and e-mail addresses. The contents were then archived. Unfortunately, any information found in this manner had little context. Thanks to research that has been done since the DFRWS 2005 Memory Challenge, methods of obtaining RAM dumps have been investigated, and data within those RAM dumps can be identified and extracted on a much more granular level, even to the point of pulling an executable image out of the dump file. This chapter discusses the issues of collecting and parsing RAM dumps, as well as extracting the memory used by a specific process from a live system.

Chapter 4: Registry Analysis

The Windows Registry maintains a veritable plethora of information regarding the state of the system, and in many cases, the Registry itself can be treated like a log file because the information that it maintains has a time stamp associated with it in some manner. However, because of the nature of how the data is stored, searches for ASCII or even Unicode strings do not reveal some of the most important and useful pieces of information. This chapter presents the structure of the Registry to the readers so that they'll be able to recognize Registry artifacts in binary data and unallocated space within an acquired image. The chapter then discusses various artifacts (Registry keys and values) at great length, describing their usefulness and value to an investigation, as well as presenting a number of tools for extracting that information from an acquired image.

Chapter 5: File Analysis

Windows systems maintain a number of log files that many examiners simply are not aware of, and those log files often maintain time-stamp information on the entries that are recorded. In addition, there are a number of files on Windows systems that maintain time-stamp information within the files themselves that can be incorporated into your timeline analysis of an event. Many of these time stamps are maintained by the application and are not immediately obvious. Various files, file formats, and file metadata are discussed in detail, and tools are presented for extracting much of the information that is discussed.

Chapter 6: Executable File Analysis

Executable files represent a special case when it comes to file analysis. For the most part, executable files follow a known and documented structure because they need to be launched and run on various versions of Windows. However, malware authors have discovered ways to obfuscate the structure in order to make their malware more difficult (albeit not impossible) to analyze. By understanding the format of these files and what they *should* look like, examiners can go further in their investigations in determining which files are legitimate, in addition to what effect the suspicious files have on a Windows system. Using the techniques and information presented in this chapter, the examiners can determine which files are legitimate, as well as what artifacts to attribute to a particular piece of malware.

Chapter 7: Rootkits and Rootkit Detection

The final chapter of this book addresses the topic of rootkits in the hopes of piercing the veil of mystery surrounding this type of malware and presenting the administrator, first responder, and forensic analyst (remember, these could all be the same person) with the necessary information to be able to locate and recognize a rootkit. Rootkits are being used increasingly not only in cyber-crime but also in "legitimate" commercial applications. An understanding of rootkits and rootkit detection technologies is paramount for anyone working with Windows systems, and this chapter presents a great deal of the information that an investigator will need.

DVD Contents

The DVD that accompanies this book contains a great deal of useful information and tools. (An icon appears before sections in the book that contain references to material that is on the DVD.) All the tools provided are grouped into the appropriate directory based on the chapter in which they were presented. There is a directory on the DVD for each of the chapters that contain code or sample files for that chapter (with the exception of Chapter 7). In addition, there is a bonus directory containing several tools that were not specifically discussed in any chapter, but I developed them to meet a need that I had, and I thought that others might find them useful.

All the tools available on the DVD are Perl scripts. However, almost all the Perl scripts have been "compiled" into stand-alone Windows executables for ease of use. The Perl scripts themselves are, for the most part, platform independent and can be run on Windows, Linux, and even Mac OS X (note that there are some exceptions), and providing Windows executables simply makes them easier for those without Perl installed to use. Several of the chapters also contain ProScripts, which are Perl scripts specifically written to be used with the ProDiscover forensic analysis application from Technology Pathways (www.techpathways.com). These Perl scripts are launched via ProDiscover and are not "compiled."

In addition, several of the chapter directories contain sample files that the reader can use to gain a familiarity with the tools. This is particularly the case for Chapter 5, "File Analysis." It's one thing to have a tool or utility and an explanation of its use, but it's quite another thing to actually use that tool to derive information. Having something immediately available to practice with means that the readers can try out the tools anywhere they have a laptop, such as on a plane, and not have to wait until they're able to get copies of those files themselves.

Finally, I have included several movie files on the DVD that I use to explain certain topics. These video (.wmv) files describe the use of some of the tools presented and discussed in the book. These tools are also available on the DVD itself. In the past, I wrote an appendix to explain the setup and use of the Forensic Server Project, but I've found that listening to podcasts and watching movies can be much more educational than reading something in a book.

All the tools provided on the DVD are provided "as is," with no warrantee or guarantee of their use. All the tools, with the exception of those located in the bonus directory, were mentioned or described in the book. Therefore, you will have some idea of how the tools are used. In all cases, the Perl scripts from which the EXEs were derived are also provided. All the tools are command-line-based (CLI) tools. Double-clicking the icon won't produce any interesting results. Most of the tools require at least a file name (including the full path) to be entered at the command line. If you have any questions or concerns about the tools, start by looking at the Perl script. Or try typing either the command or the command followed by "-h" at the command line. If you're still having issues, e-mail me at keydet89@yahoo.com with a concise, complete description of the issue, and we'll see if we can work it out.

Because of licensing issues, third-party tools produced by others are not provided on the DVD. Instead, I've provided links to the tools in the text of the book itself.

Thanks, and I hope you enjoy and find some use from the book. Please feel free to drop me a line with any comments you might have.

—Harlan Carvey, keydet89@yahoo.com

Chapter 1

Live Response: Collecting Volatile Data

Solutions in this chapter:

- **Live Response**
- **What Data to Collect**
- **Nonvolatile Information**
- **Live-Response Methodologies**

☑ **Summary**

☑ **Solutions Fast Track**

☑ **Frequently Asked Questions**

Introduction

More and more, investigators are faced with situations in which the traditional, accepted computer forensics methodology of unplugging the power from a computer and then acquiring a bit-stream image of the system hard drive is, quite simply, not a viable option. Investigators and incident responders are also seeing instances in which the questions they have (or are asked) cannot be answered using the contents of an imaged hard drive alone. For example, I've spoken with law enforcement officers regarding how best to handle situations involving missing children who were lured from their homes or school via instant messages (IMs).

These questions are not limited to law enforcement. In many cases, the best source of information or evidence is available in computer memory (network connections, contents of the IM client window, memory used by the IM client process, and so on), since an IM client does not automatically create a log of the conversation, for example. In other cases, investigators are asked if there was a Trojan or some other malware active on the system and whether sensitive information was copied off the system. First responders and investigators are being asked questions about what activity was going on while the system was live. Members of IT staffs are finding anomalous or troubling traffic in their firewall and IDS logs and are shutting off the system from which the traffic is originating before determining which process was responsible for the traffic. Situations like these require that the investigator perform *live response*—collecting data from a system while it is still running. This in itself raises some issues, which we will address throughout this chapter.

Live Response

There are a number of issues facing investigators today where unplugging a system (or several systems) and acquiring an image of the hard drive(s) might not be an option. As the use of e-commerce continues to grow, system downtime is measured in hundreds or thousands of dollars per minute, based on lost transactions. Therefore, taking a system down to acquire a hard drive image has a serious effect on the bottom line. Also, some companies have service-level agreements (SLAs) guaranteeing "five nines" of uptime— that is, the company guarantees to its customers that the systems will be up and operational 99.999 percent of the time (outside of maintenance windows, of course). Taking a system with a single hard drive offline to perform imaging can take several hours, depending on the configuration of the system.

The Information Superhighway is no longer just a place for joy riders and pranksters. A great deal of serious crime takes place in cyberspace, and criminal activities are becoming more and more sophisticated. There are software programs that can get into your computer system and steal your personal information (passwords, personal files, income tax returns, and the like), yet the code for some of these programs is never written to the hard drive; the programs exist only in memory. When the system is shut down, all evidence of the program disappears.

In April 2006, Seagate introduced the first 750GB hard drives. (For more information go to www.seagate.com/cda/newsinfo/newsroom/releases/article/0,1121,3153,00.html.) Imagine a RAID system with five or eight such hard drives, topping out at 6 terabytes (TB) of storage. How long would it take you to image those hard drives? With certain configurations, it can take investigators four or more hours to acquire and verify a single 80GB hard drive. And would you need to image the entire system if you were interested in only the activities of a single process and not in the thousands of files resident on the system?

In some cases, before stepping off into a more traditional computer forensics investigation, we might want to collect some information about the live system before shutting it down and acquiring a bit-stream image of the hard drive or drives. The information you would be most interested in is *volatile* in nature, meaning that it ceases to exist when power is removed from the system. This volatile information usually exists in physical memory, or RAM, and consists of such things as information about processes, network connections, the contents of the clipboard, and so on. This information describes the state of the system at the time you are standing in front of it or sitting at the console. As an investigator, you could be faced with a situation in which you must quickly capture and analyze data (covered in the next chapter) to make a determination of the nature and scope of the incident. When power is removed from the system in preparation for imaging the hard drive in the traditional manner, this information simply disappears.

We do have options available to us—tools and techniques we can use to collect this volatile information from a live system, giving us a better overall picture of the state of the system as well as providing us with a greater scope of information. This is what "live response" entails: accessing a live, running system and collecting volatile (and in some cases, nonvolatile) information.

There is another term you might hear that is often confused with live response: *live acquisition*. Live response deals with collecting volatile information from a system; live acquisition describes acquiring the hard drive while the system is still running and creating an image of that hard drive. In this chapter, we start by discussing tools, techniques, and methodologies for performing live response. When we talk about performing live response, we need to understand *what* information we want to collect from the system and *how* we should go about collecting it. In this chapter, we will walk through the *what* and *how* of collecting volatile information from a system; in the next chapter, we will discuss how to analyze this data. Following that, we will examine some solutions for performing a live acquisition. Analysis of the image collected during live acquisition will be covered in the remaining chapters of this book.

Before we start discussing live response tools and activities, we need to address two important topics: Locard's Exchange Principle and the order of volatility. These concepts are the cornerstones of this chapter and live response in general, and we will discuss them in detail.

Locard's Exchange Principle

In performing live response, investigators and first responders need to keep a very important principle in mind. When we interact with a live system, whether as a user or as an investigator, changes will occur on that system. On a live system, changes will occur simply due to the passage of time, as processes work, as data is saved and deleted, as network connections time out or are created, and so on. Some changes happen when the system just sits there and runs. Changes also occur as the investigator runs programs on the system to collect information, volatile or otherwise. Running a program causes information to be loaded into physical memory, and in doing so, physical memory used by other, already running processes may be written to the page file. As the investigator collects information and sends it off the system, new network connections will be created. All these changes can be collectively explained by *Locard's Exchange Principle*.

In the early 20th century, Dr. Edmond Locard's work in the area of forensic science and crime scene reconstruction became known as Locard's Exchange Principle. This principle states, in essence, that when two objects come into contact, material is exchanged or transferred between them. If you watch the popular *CSI* crime show on TV, you'll invariably hear one of the crime scene investigators refer to *possible transfer*. This usually occurs after a car hits something or when an investigator examines a body and locates material that seems out of place.

This same principle applies to the digital realm. For example, when two computers communicate via a network, information is exchanged between them. Information about one computer will appear in process memory and/or log files on the other (see the "Locard and Netcat" sidebar for a really cool demonstration of this concept). When a peripheral such as removable storage device (a thumb drive, an iPod, or the like) is attached to a Windows computer system, information about the device will remain resident on the computer. When an investigator interacts with a live system, changes will occur to that system as programs are executed and data is copied from the system. These changes might be transient (process memory, network connections) or permanent (log files, Registry entries).

Tools & Traps…

Locard and Netcat

Simple tools such as *netcat* can be used to demonstrate Locard's Exchange Principle[1] If you're not familiar with netcat (nc.exe on Windows systems), suffice it to say that netcat is an extremely versatile tool that allows you to read and write information across network connections.

For this example, you will need three tools: netcat (nc.exe), pmdump.exe[2] and strings.exe[3] or BinText (once available from the Foundstone.com Web site; you might need to Google for it). You can run this example using either one or two systems, but it works best when two systems are used. If you're using one system, create two directories, with a copy of netcat in each directory.

Start by launching netcat in listening mode with the following command line:

```
C:\test>nc –L –d –p 8080 –e cmd.exe
```

This command line tells netcat to listen on port 8080, in detached mode, and when a connection is made, to launch the command prompt. Once you've typed in the command line and pressed **Enter**, open the Task Manager and note the process identifier (PID) of the process you just created.

Now open another command prompt on the same system or go to your other system and open the command prompt. Type the following command line to connect to the netcat listener you just created:

```
C:\test2>nc <IP address> 8080
```

This command line tells netcat to open in client mode and connect to the IP address on port 8080, where our listener is waiting. If you're running the test on a single system, use 127.0.0.1 as the IP address.

Once you've connected, you should see the command prompt header that you normally see, showing the version of the operating system and the copyright information. Type a couple of commands at the prompt, such as **dir** or anything else, to simply send information across the connection.

On the system where the netcat listener is running, open another command prompt and use pmdump.exe (discussed later in this chapter) to obtain the contents of memory for the listener process:

```
C:\test>pmdump <PID> netcat1.log
```

Continued

This command will obtain the contents of memory (both physical memory as well as the page file) used by the process and put it into the file netcat1.log. You may also dump the process memory of the client side of the connection, if you like. Now that you have the process memory saved in a file, you can exit both processes. Run strings.exe against the memory file from the listener or open the file in BinText and you will see the IP address of the client. Doing the same thing with the client's memory file will display information about the system where the listener was running, demonstrating the concept of Locard's Exchange Principle.

Programs that we use to collect information might have other effects on a live system. For example, a program might need to read several Registry keys, and the paths to those keys will be read into memory. Windows XP systems perform application prefetching, so if the investigator runs a program that the user has already run on the system, the last access and modification times of the prefetch file (as well as the contents of the file itself) for that application will be modified. If the program that the investigator runs hasn't been used before, a new prefetch file will be created in the Prefetch directory (assuming the contents of the Prefetch directory haven't reached their 128 .pf file limit … but more on that later in the book).

Investigators not only need to understand that these changes will occur, they must also document those changes and be able to explain the effects their actions had on the system, to a reasonable extent. For example, as an investigator you should be able to determine which .pf files in the XP Prefetch directory are a result of your efforts and which are the result of user activities. The same is true for Registry values. As with the application prefetching capabilities of Windows XP, your actions will have an effect on the system Registry. Specifically, entries may appear in the Registry, and as such the LastWrite times of the Registry keys will be updated. Some of these changes might not be a direct result of your tools or actions but rather are made by the shell (i.e., Windows Explorer), due simply to the fact that the system is live and running.

By testing and understanding the tools you use, you will be able to document and explain what artifacts found on a system are the result of your efforts and which are the result of actions taken by a user or an attacker.

Order of Volatility

We know that volatile information exists in memory on a live system and that certain types of volatile information can be, well, more volatile than others. That is, some information on a live system has a much shorter shelf life than other information. For instance, network connections time out, sometimes within several minutes, if they aren't used. You can see this by browsing to a specific site or making some other network connection and viewing that connection via netstat.exe. Then shut down the client application you're using and the state of the network connection will change over time before it eventually disappears from the output of netstat.exe. The system time, however, changes much more quickly, while the contents of the clipboard will remain constant until either they are changed or power is removed from the system. Additionally, some processes, such as services (referred to as *daemons* in the UNIX realm) run for a long time, whereas other processes can be extremely short lived, performing their tasks quickly before disappearing from memory. This would indicate that we need to collect certain information first so that we can capture it before it changes, whereas other volatile data that happens to be more persistent can be collected later.

A great place to go for this information is the request for comment (RFC) document 3227, *Guidelines for Evidence Collection and Archiving* (www.faqs.org/rfcs/rfc3227.html). This RFC, published in February 2002, remains pertinent today, since core guiding principles don't change as technologies change. The RFC specifies such principles for evidence collection as capturing as accurate a picture of the system as possible; keeping detailed notes; noting differences between UTC, local time, and system time; and minimizing changes to data as much as possible. We'll keep these principles in mind throughout our discussion of live response.

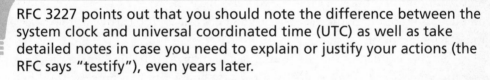

TIP

RFC 3227 points out that you should note the difference between the system clock and universal coordinated time (UTC) as well as take detailed notes in case you need to explain or justify your actions (the RFC says "testify"), even years later.

Of specific interest in this RFC document is section 2.1, "Order of Volatility," which lists certain types of volatile information in order, from most to least volatile. Those items that are apt to change or expire more quickly due to the passage of time, such as network connection status, should be collected first, whereas less volatile information, such as the physical configuration of the system, can be collected later. Using these guidelines, we can see what types of information we need to collect from a system, where to look for that information, what tools to use to retrieve it, and even how to get that information off the system, thereby minimizing the impact to the "victim" system while at the same time collecting the information we need to perform our analysis.

When to Perform Live Response

Perhaps the most prominent question on the minds of investigators and first responders is, "When should I consider live response?" In most instances today (for example, criminal or civil cases, internal corporate investigations), there is no predefined set of conditions that define conditions for live response. In fact, there are many situations in which live response and subsequently volatile information aren't considered. The decision to perform live response depends on the situation, the environment (taking into consideration the investigator's intent, corporate policies, or applicable laws), and the nature of the issue with which you have been presented.

Let's look at a couple of examples. Say that you've been contacted by a system administrator reporting some unusual network traffic. She received an alert from the intrusion detection system (IDS), and in checking the firewall logs, found some suspicious log entries that seemed to correlate with the IDS alerts. She says that there seems to be some odd traffic coming from one particular system that sits on the internal network. She already has the IDS alerts and network logs, but you decide to perform a more comprehensive capture of network traffic. In doing so, you realize that you have the network traffic information, but how do you associate it with a particular system? That's pretty easy, right? After all, you have the system's IP address (as either the source or destination IP address in your network capture), and if you've also captured Ethernet frames, you also have the MAC address. But how do you then associate the traffic you see on the network with a particular user and/or process running on the system?

To definitively determine the source of the suspicious traffic (which process is generating it), you'd have to collect information about running processes and network connections from the system prior to shutting it down. Other information collected during live response might show you that someone is logged into the system remotely, via a network logon or a backdoor, or that a running process was launched as a Scheduled Task.

What other types of situations might suggest or even require a live response? How about the "Trojan defense," in which illicit activity is attributed to a Trojan or backdoor? In October 2002, Julian Green was found to have several (some reports stated over 170) illicit images on his system. A forensic examination of his system found that his system had several Trojans that would access illicit sites whenever he launched his Web browser. He was found innocent of all charges.

The following year, Aaron Caffrey claimed that Trojans allowed others to control his computer and launch attacks against other systems, for which he'd been accused. Caffrey's defense argued that although no Trojan had been found on his system during a forensic examination, still, a Trojan *could* have been responsible. His argument was sufficient to get him acquitted.

In cases such as these, hindsight tells us that it would have been beneficial to have some information about running processes and network connections collected at the time the systems were seized, particularly if they were running when the investigator arrived on the scene. This information might have told us whether there were any unusual processes running at the time and if anyone had connected to the system to control it and upload files, direct attacks against other systems, or the like.

As discussed previously, another reason for performing live response is that the system itself cannot be taken down without good (and I mean *really good*) reason. On larger critical systems, such as those used in e-commerce, down time is measured in lost transactions or hundreds (even thousands) of dollars per minute. As the process of acquiring an image from the hard drives (most systems of this nature use more than one hard drive, in a RAID configuration) can often take considerable time, it's preferable to have some solid facts to justify taking the system offline and out of service, if that is what is necessary. Doing so might not simply be a matter of a system administrator justifying these actions to an IT manager but one of a CFO justifying them to the board of directors.

Yet another factor to consider is legislation requiring notification. Beginning with California's SB 1386, companies that suffer security breaches in which sensitive information has been compromised must notify their customers so that those customers can protect themselves from identity theft.[4] At the time of this writing, other states have begun to follow California's lead, and there is even talk of a federal notification law. What this means is that companies that store and process sensitive information cannot simply remain silent about certain types of security breaches. The corollary is that those same companies are going to want to know definitively whether sensitive information has been compromised during a security breach. After all, alerting customers that their personal information is now in the hands of some unknown individual (or, as could be the case, multiple unknown individuals) will have a significant, detrimental impact on the company. Customers could discontinue service and tell their friends and family in other states what happened. New customers might decide to sign up with a competitor. The loss of current and future revenue will change the face of the company and could lead to bankruptcy. So why would a company simply suspect that it's been breached and sensitive data stolen and dutifully notify its customers? Wouldn't the company first want to know for sure that sensitive personal information about its customers has been compromised? Wouldn't you?

Take, for example, an incident in which an "anonymous" individual on the Internet claims to have stolen sensitive information from an organization. This person claims that he broke into the organization over the Internet and was able to collect customer names, Social Security numbers, addresses, credit card data, and more. The organization's senior management will want to know if this was, in fact, the case, and if it was, how this person was able to do what he claimed he'd done. Investigators will need to perform live response and examine systems for volatile information, such as running processes and network connections. They might also be interested in locating malware that is present in memory but doesn't have any information or even an executable image written to disk.

What Data to Collect

At this point, we're ready to look at the types of volatile information we can expect to see on a live system and learn about the tools we could use to collect that information during live response.

When we're performing live response, it's likely that one of the first things we'll want to collect is the contents of physical memory, or RAM. When we take Locard's Exchange Principle into account, it's pretty clear that by collecting the contents of RAM first, we minimize the impact we have on in the contents of RAM. From that point on, we know that the other tools we run to collect other volatile information are going to be loaded into memory (as is the tool that we use to collect the contents of RAM), modifying the contents of memory. However, collecting and analyzing the contents of RAM is a relatively new area of study (as of Summer 2005), and as such it deserves its own chapter. (For a detailed discussion of this topic, see Chapter 3, "Windows Memory Analysis.")

That being said, specific types of volatile information we'll look at in this chapter are:

- System time
- Logged-on user(s)
- Open files
- Network information
- Network connections
- Process information

- Process-to-port mapping
- Process memory
- Network status
- Clipboard contents
- Service/driver information
- Command history
- Mapped drives
- Shares

For each of these types of volatile information, we will look at some tools that we can use to retrieve it from a Windows system. You will most likely notice that throughout this chapter there is a tendency toward using command-line interface (CLI) tools over those with a graphical user interface (GUI). Some would think that this is because CLI tools have a smaller "memory footprint," meaning that they consume less memory, rely on fewer dynamic link libraries (DLLs), and have less impact on the system. This is partially the case, but keep in mind that the actual "footprint" of any particular tool can be determined only through thorough testing of the tools you use.

WARNING

One should never make assumptions about a tool and its "memory footprint" when run on a system. Without thorough examination and testing (see Chapter 6, "Executable File Analysis," for information that pertains to examining executable files), you'll never know the kind of footprint an executable has on a system or the kind of artifacts it leaves behind following its use.

The primary reason we focus on the use of CLI tools is that they are usually very simple, perform one simple, specific function, and are much easier to automate through the use of batch or script files. CLI tools can be bound together via batch files or scripting languages, and their output is usually sent to the console (i.e., STDOUT) and can be redirected to a file or a socket. GUI tools, on the other hand, predominantly require you to save their output to a file, since they pretty much all have a File menu item with Save and Save As... entries in the drop-down menu.

Most programmers of GUI tools don't necessarily develop them with incident response or forensics in mind. One of our goals is to minimize the impact of our investigative measures on a system (particularly for follow-on imaging and forensic analysis activities), so we want to avoid writing files to the system, in addition to getting the data we need off the system as quickly and efficiently as possible.

Now, this is not to say that GUI tools absolutely cannot be used for live-response activities. If there's a GUI tool that you find absolutely perfect for what you need, then by all means, use it. But consider ahead of time how you're going to get that data off the system.

Regardless of the tools you decide to use, always be sure to check the license agreement before using them. Some tools can be used as you like, but others require a fee for use in a corporate environment. Reading and heeding these agreements in advance can help you avoid major headaches at the wrong time.

System Time

One of the first pieces of information you want to collect when you're investigating an incident is the system time. This will give a great deal of context to the information collected later in the investigation and will assist in developing an accurate timeline of events that have occurred on the system.

The most well-known means of displaying the system time is illustrated in Figure 1.1.

Figure 1.1 Displaying the System Date and Time on Windows XP

Notes from the Underground…

Getting the System Time

The investigator can get the system time using a simple Perl script, such as:

```
print locatime(time)."\n";
```

This script displays the system time in local format, based on the time zone and daylight savings information that the system has set, but the time can also be displayed in GMT format using a script such as:

```
print gmtime(time)."\n";
```

The systime.pl Perl script located on the CD that accompanies this book demonstrates how the system time can be retrieved using the Windows application programming interface (API). The systime.exe file is a stand-alone executable compiled from the Perl script using Perl2Exe.

Another method for retrieving this information is to use WMI to access the Win32_OperatingSystem class and display the *LocalDateTime* value.

Not only is the current system time important for the investigator, but the amount of time that the system has been running, or the *uptime*, can also provide a great deal of context to the investigation. For example, noting the amount of time that the system has been running compared to the amount of time a process has been running can provide you with an idea of when an exploit or compromise attempt might have been successful. (More on retrieving information about processes later in this chapter.)

In addition, the investigator should also record the real time, or *wall time*, when recording the system time. Having both allows the investigator to later determine whether the system clock was inaccurate. Information about the "clock skew" provides a better understanding of the actual time at which events recorded in log files occurred. This information can be invaluable when you're trying to combine timestamps from more than one source.

Another piece of time-related information that could be important is the time zone settings for the computer. Windows systems using the NTFS file system store file times in UTC (analogous to GMT) format,[5.] and systems using the FAT file system store file times based on the local system time. This is more important during post-mortem analysis (discussed later in this book), but it can become extremely important when you're performing live response remotely.

Logged-on Users

During an investigation, you will want to know which users are logged on to the system. This includes people who are logged on locally (via the console or keyboard) as well as remotely (such as via the *net use* command or via a mapped share). This information allows you to add context to other information you collect from a system, such as the user context of a running process, the owner of a file, or the last access times on files. This information is also useful to correlate against the Security Event Log, particularly if the appropriate auditing has been enabled.

Psloggedon

Perhaps the best-known tool for determining logged-on users is psloggedon.exe.[6] This tool shows the investigator the name of the user logged on locally (at the keyboard) as well as those users who are logged on remotely, such as via a mapped share.

As shown in Figure 1.2, psloggedon.exe shows users logged onto the system remotely. To set up this demonstration, I logged into a Windows 2000 system (Petra) from my Windows XP system and then ran the command on the Windows 2000 system.

Figure 1.2 Output of Psloggedon.exe on Windows 2000

```
Users logged on locally:
     10/13/2006 2:34:30 PM      PETRA\Administrator

Users logged on via resource shares:
     10/13/2006 2:36:26 PM      <null>\ADMINISTRATOR
```

Net Sessions

The *net sessions* command can be used to see not only the username used to access the system via a remote login session but also the IP address and the type of client from which they are accessing the system. Figure 1.3 illustrates the output of the *net sessions* command run on a Windows 2003 system.

Figure 1.3 Output of the *net sessions* Command on Windows 2003

```
Command Prompt                                                    _□×

C:\tools>net sessions

Computer              User name          Client Type      Opens Idle time
-------------------------------------------------------------------------
\\192.168.1.25        ADMINISTRATOR      Windows 2002 Serv    0 00:02:06
\\192.168.1.28        ADMINISTRATOR      Windows 2002 Serv    0 00:01:49
The command completed successfully.
```

The *net sessions* output illustrated in Figure 1.3 shows two Windows XP systems logged into a Windows 2003 system using the Administrator account. Neither session has any files open, but neither has been active for very long (as illustrated by the times listed in the "Idle time" column of the output).

Logonsessions

Logonsessions.exe is a CLI tool available from SysInternals.com that lists all the active logon sessions on a system.[7] Figure 1.4 illustrates a portion of the output of logonsessions.exe on a Windows XP system (the system name is Ender).

Figure 1.4 Output of the *logonsessions* on Windows XP

```
[6] Logon session 00000000:000478c7:
     User name:    ENDER\Harlan
     Auth package: NTLM
     Logon type:   Interactive
     Session:      0
     Sid:          S-1-5-21-1606980848-308236825-682003330-1004
     Logon time:   2/6/2006 4:19:42 PM
     Logon server: ENDER
     DNS Domain:
     UPN:
       304: C:\WINDOWS\system32\wscntfy.exe
      1372: C:\WINDOWS\Explorer.EXE
      1828: C:\Program Files\CyberLink\PowerDVD\DVDLauncher.exe
      1252: C:\WINDOWS\BCMSMMSG.exe
       892: C:\Program Files\Synaptics\SynTP\SynTPLpr.exe
       788: C:\Program Files\Synaptics\SynTP\SynTPEnh.exe
      1000: C:\WINDOWS\System32\spool\drivers\w32x86\3\hpztsb07.exe
      1016: C:\Program Files\Viewpoint\Viewpoint Manager\ViewMgr.exe
      1932: C:\Program Files\QuickTime\qttask.exe
       108: C:\Program Files\Real\RealPlayer\RealPlay.exe
       552: C:\Program Files\Mozilla Firefox\firefox.exe
```

Logonsessions.exe provides a great deal more information than the other tools, as illustrated in the output excerpt displayed in Figure 1.4. For example, it lists the authentication package used (it might be important to your investigation that the Kerberos authentication package was used instead of LanManager), type of logon, active processes, and so on.

TIP

The logonsess.txt file located in the \ch1\dat directory on the accompanying DVD contains the output of *logonsessions* from the Windows 2003 system illustrated in Figure 1.3.

Another useful utility you'll find handy is netusers.exe, a free utility from Somarsoft.com. Using the *-local* and *-history* switches with netusers.exe, you can retrieve a brief report of the last time all local users logged onto the system. The last logon time is maintained in the Registry; specifics of this Registry information are discussed in Chapter 4, "Registry Analysis." Netusers.exe allows you to retrieve this information from a live system.

Keep in mind, however, that these tools will not show you if someone is logged on via a backdoor. Backdoors and Trojans such as the infamous SubSeven[8] allow users to "log in" to the Trojan via a raw TCP connection, bypassing the Windows authentication mechanisms. As such, these connections will not show up when you're using tools such as psloggedon.exe. Having the output of these tools, however, can be instrumental in showing that a user you discover later on did not show up in the list. It can be used to demonstrate hidden functionality, even if the mechanism for that functionality is never found.

Open Files

If the output of psloggedon.exe shows the investigator that there are users logged into the system remotely, she will also want to see what files they have open, if any. Many times when someone accesses a system remotely, they might be looking for something specific and opening files. A user in a corporate environment could have a share available and allow other users to view images, download songs, and so on. Poorly protected Windows systems, such as Windows 2000 systems that are connected to the Internet with no Administrator password (and no firewall), can be "visited" and files searched for, accessed, and copied. The *net file* command, psfile.exe,[9] and the openfiles.exe[10.] tools (native to Windows XP Pro and Windows 2003) will show files that are opened remotely on a system.

Network Information (Cached NetBIOS Name Table)

Sometimes when intruders gain remote access to a system, they want to know what other systems are available on the network and can be "seen" (in the network-centric sense) by the system they've compromised. I've seen this happen quite often in investigations, in a variety of ways; sometimes batch files have been created on the system and executed, and other times the intruder has launched *net view* commands via SQL injection (by using a browser to send commands to the system through the web and database servers). When connections are made to other systems using NetBIOS[11.] communications (the same as are used for logins, connecting to shares, and the like), the systems will maintain a list of other systems they've "seen." By viewing the contents of the cached name table, you might be able to determine other systems that have been affected.

Let's take a look at an example. My home "network" consists of one laptop and several VMware sessions that appear as stand-alone systems on a virtual network. To demonstrate the caching of NetBIOS names, I started my Windows 2000 VMware session and logged in to view the IP address that was assigned via DHCP. I then went back to the host operating system (Windows XP Pro SP2) and in a command prompt, typed **nbtstat –A 192.168.1.22** to view the "remote" system's name table. I then typed **nbtstat –c** to view the cached NetBIOS names on the host operating system. What I saw appears in Figure 1.5.

Figure 1.5 NetBIOS Name Table Cache

```
Wireless Network Connection:
Node IpAddress: [192.168.1.8] Scope Id: []

                    NetBIOS Remote Cache Name Table

         Name              Type         Host Address      Life [sec]
    ---------------------------------------------------------------------
    PETRA         <20>  UNIQUE            192.168.1.22          440
```

You might be thinking at this point, "So what? Why is this important?" Well, if I were an attacker and had gained access to one system, I might be interested in gaining access to other systems as well. To do so, I would need to see what systems are on the network and what vulnerabilities they have. Essentially, I'd be looking for easy targets. Now, if I were to start scanning for vulnerabilities, I might alert someone to what was going on. Also, to scan for vulnerabilities, I would need to copy my tools to the system I had already compromised, and that could alert someone to my activities. However, I can use nbtstat.exe to locate potentially vulnerable systems. For example, Figure 1.6 shows the output of the command I ran to populate the NetBIOS name cache.

Figure 1.6 Output of *nbtstat –A 192.168.1.22*

```
Wireless Network Connection:
Node IpAddress: [192.168.1.8] Scope Id: []

          NetBIOS Remote Machine Name Table

     Name               Type         Status
     ---------------------------------------------
     PETRA         <00>  UNIQUE      Registered
     PETRA         <20>  UNIQUE      Registered
     WORKGROUP     <00>  GROUP       Registered
     PETRA         <03>  UNIQUE      Registered
     WORKGROUP     <1E>  GROUP       Registered
     INet~Services <1C>  GROUP       Registered
     IS~PETRA......<00>  UNIQUE      Registered
     WORKGROUP     <1D>  UNIQUE      Registered
     .._MSBROWSE__.<01>  GROUP       Registered
     ADMINISTRATOR <03>  UNIQUE      Registered

     MAC Address = 00-0C-29-EC-6B-96
```

From the output of the *nbtstat* command displayed in Figure 1.6, we can see that the administrator is logged in, and we can see that the system is running the IIS Web server. Penetration testers and attackers alike will use the information in the NetBIOS name table on any system they are able to compromise, to locate other vulnerable systems. The MS KB articles 163409[12] and 119495[13] provide a great deal of information regarding the information available in the name table.

Network Connections

As soon as possible after an incident is reported, the investigator should collect information regarding network connections to and from the affected system. This information can expire over time, and if too much time passes, that information will be lost. An investigator might approach a system and, after an initial look, determine that the attacker is still logged into and accessing the system. Or she could find that a worm or an IRCbot is communicating out from the system, searching for other systems to infect, updating itself, or logging into a command and control server. This information can provide important clues and add context to other information that the investigator has collected. Not every system will have a firewall installed, particularly not one configured to log successful connections into and out of the system. Nor will every system have an application such as Port Reporter[14] installed to record and log network connection information. The investigator must be prepared to react quickly and collect the information he or she needs in an efficient, timely manner.

I've been involved in several cases where I have been provided with image files acquired from a system, and the client has asked, "Was sensitive data copied from the system?" Without at least some network-based information, the answer will invariably be "There's no way to tell." I have also been in numerous situations where having some information about network connections would greatly reduce what I have to look for, particularly when what alerted the client to the incident in the first place really had nothing to do with the compromise we ended up discovering. In one particular situation, a timeline analysis of the system image showed that the intruder was accessing the system via a backdoor at the same time that two different administrators were accessing the system to remediate two separate issues. Having information about network connections going to and from the system would have been extremely helpful in locating the core intrusion.

Netstat

Netstat is perhaps the most well-known tool for collecting information regarding network connections on a Windows system. This CLI tool is straightforward and simple to use and provides a simple view of TCP and UDP connections and their state, network traffic statistics, and the like. Netstat.exe is a native tool, meaning that it is provided as part of the operating system distribution.

The most common way to run *netstat* is with the *-ano* switches, which tell the program to display the TCP and UDP network connections, listening ports, and the identifiers of the processes (PIDs) using those network connections. Figure 1.7 illustrates the output of the *netstat −ano* command.

Figure 1.7 Excerpt from the Output of the *netstat –ano* command on Windows XP

```
C:\>netstat -ano

Active Connections

  Proto  Local Address          Foreign Address        State           PID
  TCP    0.0.0.0:135            0.0.0.0:0              LISTENING       1344
  TCP    0.0.0.0:445            0.0.0.0:0              LISTENING       4
  TCP    127.0.0.1:1026         0.0.0.0:0              LISTENING       1992
  TCP    127.0.0.1:1031         127.0.0.1:1032         ESTABLISHED     2536
  TCP    127.0.0.1:1032         127.0.0.1:1031         ESTABLISHED     2536
  TCP    192.168.1.25:139       0.0.0.0:0              LISTENING       4
  TCP    192.168.1.25:1310      216.239.51.104:80      ESTABLISHED     2536
  TCP    192.168.1.25:1323      209.18.34.78:80        ESTABLISHED     2536
  TCP    192.168.1.25:1326      209.18.34.41:80        ESTABLISHED     2536
  TCP    192.168.1.25:1327      209.18.34.41:80        ESTABLISHED     2536
  TCP    192.168.37.1:139       0.0.0.0:0              LISTENING       4
  TCP    192.168.206.1:139      0.0.0.0:0              LISTENING       4
```

TIP

Under normal circumstances, Windows 2000 does not respond to the -o switch when running netstat.exe. However, MS KB article 907980 provides access to a hotfix that allows the version of netstat.exe on Windows 2000 to list the PID for the process that "owns" the network connection listed in the output.

The output of the *netstat –ano* command illustrated in Figure 1.7 shows the active network connections, the state of each connection, and, on the far right, the PIDs of the processes using the ports. What you're looking for in the output of *netstat* are any unusual connections. For example, it is not unusual on many user systems to see connections going out from a high client port to a remote system, connecting on port 80. The PID of the process using this connection will usually map back to a Web browser. However, the investigator can be easily fooled. I have investigated cases where the tool wget.exe was used to connect to remote systems on port 80 and download malware and hacker utilities. By themselves and without further scrutiny, these connections would look to the investigator (and to an IDS) like legitimate Web-surfing traffic.

TIP

MS KB article 137984[15.] is older but provides descriptions of the states listed in the output of netstat.exe.

Using *netstat* with the *-r* switch will display the routing table and show you whether any persistent routes are enabled on the system. This could provide some very useful information to an investigator or even simply to an administrator troubleshooting a system. I've seen systems that have been set up to transfer files to another location as part of a business process, and the only way that process would work was if there was a persistent route enabled on the system, since the persistent route redirected certain traffic out over a VPN connection rather than through the normal routes out of the infrastructure. In troubleshooting an issue that really wasn't making much sense to me, I ran across a persistent route and told one of the system engineers about it. This information jogged his memory a bit, and we were able to track down and resolve the issue.

Process Information

An investigator will *always* want to know what processes are running on a potentially compromised system. Note that *always*. When viewing the running processes in the Task Manager, you can see some information about each process. However, there's much more information that's not visible in Task Manager that you will want to collect during an investigation. You will want:

- The full path to the executable image (.exe file)
- The command line used to launch the process, if any
- The amount of time that the process has been running
- The security/user context that the process is running in
- Which modules the process has loaded
- The memory contents of the process

The Task Manager view provides some of this information, but it does not provide everything. For instance, some malware installs itself under the name svchost.exe, which is the name of a legitimate process on Windows systems (see the "Svchost" sidebar). The executable image for this process is located in the system32 directory and is protected by Windows File Protection (WFP) (see the "Windows

File Protection" sidebar for more information). This means that as long as WFP is running and hasn't been tampered with, attempts to replace or modify a protected file will cause the new file to be automatically replaced by a "known good" copy from the cache and an Event Log entry to be generated.

Why is this important? If you're looking at the list of processes in Task Manager, how are you going to tell which process is "suspicious"? An easy way to find "suspicious" processes is to view the full path to the executable image file (svchost.exe running from something other than C:\Windows\system32 is going to be suspicious) and/or the command line used to launch the process, as inetinfo.exe launched with the arguments -L −d −p 80 −e cmd.exe should be suspicious to most administrators and investigators; this command line is indicative of the use of netcat as a backdoor. Many bits of malware disguise themselves by using names of legitimate files. For example, the W32/Nachi[16] worm places a copy of a TFTP utility in the C:\Windows\System32\Wins directory and names it svchost.exe. When this program is running, there is no way in Task Manager to really distinguish it from the legitimate version of svchost.exe.

Are You Owned?

Windows File Protection

Windows File Protection, or WFP, was added to Windows in Windows 2000 and is present in Windows XP and 2003 as well. In a nutshell, WFP protects critical system files from being modified or deleted accidentally. Assuming that the system hasn't been compromised to the point where WFP can be subverted, if an attempt is made to modify or delete a protected file, the system will "wake up" and automatically replace that file with a known good copy from cache. An event ID 64001[17] is then generated and written to the Event Log.

MS KB article 222193,[18] *Description of the Windows File Protection Feature*, provides a more in-depth explanation of the feature along with various Registry keys associated with WFP.

Now let's take a look at some tools you can use to view more detailed information about processes.

Tlist

Tlist.exe, included as part of the MS Debugging Tools,[19] displays a good deal of information about running processes. For example, the -*v* switch will display the session identifier, PID, process name, associated services, and command line used to launch the process for the investigator, as follows:

```
0   344 svchost.exe      Svcs:  LmHosts,SSDPSRV,WebClient
      Command Line: C:\WINDOWS\System32\svchost.exe -k LocalService
```

Other switches will show this information in isolation. The -*c* switch will show just the command line used to launch each process (similar to cmdline.exe,[20] which only displays the command line for each process), whereas the -*s* switch will show the associated services (or the window title, if there are no services associated with the process). The -*t* switch will display the task tree, listing each process below its parent process, as follows:

```
System (4)
  smss.exe (628)
    csrss.exe (772)
    winlogon.exe (1056)
      services.exe (1100)
        svchost.exe (1296)
        svchost.exe (1344)
        svchost.exe (1688)
          wscntfy.exe (1184)
```

Tlist.exe also allows you to search for all processes that have a specific module loaded, using the -*m* switch. For example, wsock32.dll provides networking functionality and is described as the Windows Socket 32-Bit DLL. To list all the processes that have this module loaded, type the following command:

```
D:\tools>tlist —m wsock32.dll
```

This command returns the PID and name for each process, such as:

```
WSOCK32.dll - 1688 svchost.exe
wsock32.dll -  344 svchost.exe
WSOCK32.dll - 1992 alg.exe
WSOCK32.dll - 1956 explorer.exe        Program Manager
wsock32.dll -  452 ViewMgr.exe         AXTimer
WSOCK32.dll -  480 realplay.exe
```

Tasklist

Tasklist.exe, a native utility included with Windows XP Pro and Windows 2003 installations (it is noticeably absent from Windows XP Home), is a replacement for tlist.exe.[21.] The differences in the two tools are subtle, mostly being the name and the implementation of the switches. Tasklist.exe does provide options for output formatting, with choices between table, CSV, and list formats. The /v (or *verbose*) switch provides the most information about the listed processes, including the image name (but not the full path), PID, name and number of the session for the process, the status of the process, the username of the context in which the process runs, and the title of the window, if the process has a GUI. The investigator can also use the /svc switch to list the service information for each process.

Pslist

Pslist.exe displays basic information about running processes on a system, including the amount of time each process has been running (in both kernel and user modes).[22.] The -x switch displays details about the threads and memory used by each process. Pslist.exe launched with the -t switch will display a task tree in much the same manner as tlist.exe. Pslist.exe can also show detailed information about threads or memory used by a process. However, it does not provide information about a process in regard to the path to the executable image, the command line used to launch the process, or the user context in which the process runs.

Listdlls

Listdlls.exe shows the modules or DLLs a process is using.[23.] Listdlls.exe will show the full path to the image of the loaded module as well as if the version of the DLL loaded in memory is different from that of the on-disk image. This information can be extremely important to an investigator because each program loads or "imports" certain DLLs. These DLLs provide the actual code that is used, so application developers don't have to rewrite common functions each time they write a new application. Each DLL makes certain functions available, listing them in their export table, and programs access these functions by listing them the DLL and the functions in their import tables. This allows you to "see" (using an appropriate tool) which DLLs the program loads or accesses. However, some programs can load additional DLLs that are not part of the import table; for example, the IE browser can load toolbars and browser helper objects for which the code is listed in DLLs. Spyware, Trojans, and even rootkits use a technique called *DLL injection* to load themselves into the memory space of a running process so that they will be running and executing but won't show up in a process listing because they are actually part of another process. This is different from a child process (as illustrated in the output of tlist.exe run with the -t switch) because the executing malware does not have its own process identifier (PID).

Part of the output displayed by listdlls.exe includes the command line used to launch each process, excerpted as follows:

```
svchost.exe pid: 1292
Command line: C:\WINDOWS\system32\svchost -k DcomLaunch
```

Using listdlls.exe (with the -d dllname switch), you can also list the processes that have loaded a specific DLL, in a manner similar to tlist.exe. This can be extremely useful if you've identified a specific DLL and want to see if it has been loaded by any other processes.

Handle

Handle.exe shows the various handles that processes have open on a system.[24.] This applies not only to open file handles (for files and directories) but also to ports, Registry keys, and threads. This information can be useful for determining which resources a process accesses while it is running. Figure 1.8 illustrates an excerpt of the output from running handle.exe, without any switches, on a Windows XP SP2 system.

Figure 1.8 Excerpt of Output of Handle.exe

```
svchost.exe  pid: 1288 NT AUTHORITY\SYSTEM
    C: File               C:\WINDOWS\system32
   64: File               C:\WINDOWS\WinSxS\x86_Microsoft.Windows.Commo
5b64144ccf1df_6.0.2600.2180_x-ww_a84f1ff9
   B8: File               C:\WINDOWS\Sti_Trace.log
  168: File               C:\WINDOWS\wiaservc.log
  1C4: File               C:\WINDOWS\wiadebug.log
  1D8: File               C:\WINDOWS\Sti_Trace.log
```

Figure 1.8 illustrates some of the handles opened by svchost.exe—in this case, several log files in the Windows directory. While I was writing this chapter, for example, one of the handles opened by winword.exe includes the full path to the MS Word document.

Handle.exe has several switches that could be of use, such as -a to show all handles and -u to show the owning username for each handle.

Tools & Traps...

Processes and WMI

The Perl script *proc.pl*, located in the \ch1\code directory on the accompanying
CD, illustrates how Perl can be used to implement WMI and retrieve process
information via the Win32_Process[25.] class. Both the script and the stand-alone
executable named proc.exe (compiled from the Perl script using Perl2Exe, also
available on the accompanying CD) display the PID and name of the process,
the user context of the process, the PID of the parent process, the command
line of the process (if available), the path to the executable image to the process (if available), and the service information for the process.

Both the script and the executable can be run locally or against a remote
system. Simply type the name of the executable to run it on a local system. The
syntax to run the executable against a remote system is as follows:

```
C:\tools>proc <system> <user> <password>
```

An example of this would appear as follows:

```
C:\tools>proc WebSvr Administrator password
```

An excerpt of the output of proc.exe appears as follows:

```
PID        : 668
Name       : spoolsv.exe
User       : NT AUTHORITY\SYSTEM
Parent PID: 1100 [services.exe]
CmdLine    : C:\WINDOWS\system32\spoolsv.exe
Exe        : C:\WINDOWS\system32\spoolsv.exe
Services   : Spooler
```

The script can be easily modified to display its output in another format,
such as comma-separated values, which is suitable for opening and analysis in
a spreadsheet.

The procmon.pl Perl script (and the accompanying executable,
procmon.exe) located in the same directory is an interesting demonstration of
the use of WMI to monitor the creation of processes on the local system.
Simply launch procmon.exe from the command prompt, and while it is run-

Continued

ning, it will report on the PID, user context, and executable path (and command line) of the new process, as illustrated in the following:

```
PID    USER            PROCESS
----   ----------      ----------------

3208   Harlan          C:\WINDOWS\system32\cmd.exe
("C:\WINDOWS\system32\cmd.exe")
1768   Harlan          C:\WINDOWS\system32\ping.exe (ping 192.168.1.1)
3100   Harlan          C:\WINDOWS\system32\sol.exe (sol)
```

Tools such as procmon.exe are extremely useful in that they can be used to augment auditing of process creation as well as provide insight into processes created during the installation of applications and malware.

It should be clear by now that no single tool or utility displays all the information you might want to know about processes that you find during an investigation. You might want to run only one tool for a quick overview (tlist.exe or tasklist.exe would be good candidates), or you might want to run more than one tool; for example, you could run pslist.exe with the -x switch and the listdlls.exe utility. Depending on the level of detail you need for your investigation, you might want to run handle.exe as well. The level of granularity of information that you want to obtain will depend on your investigation. This topic is discussed in more detail later in this chapter as well as in Chapter 3, when we address issues of correlating and analyzing data.

Tools & Traps…

Svchost

Svchost is a process that appears quite often on Windows 2000, XP, and 2003 systems. It appears several times in the Task Manager, as many as two times (or more) on a default Windows 2000 system installation (with no other applications installed), five times on a Windows XP system, and seven times on a Windows 2003 system. Each instance of svchost.exe is running one or more services, as seen when you use *tasklist /svc* on Windows XP Pro and 2003 systems and *tlist −s* on Windows 2000 systems.

MS KB article Q314056[26] provides more information regarding svchost.exe on Windows XP systems, and KB article Q250320[27] provides similar information with regard to Windows 2000.

Continued

In a nutshell, svchost.exe provides a generic process for running services from DLLs. Each instance of svchost can run one or more services. On startup, svchost reads the Registry key in order to obtain the groupings of services it should run:

```
HKEY_LOCAL_MACHINE\Software\Microsoft\Windows
NT\CurrentVersion\Svchost
```

Several Trojans and backdoors try to copy themselves to the victim system using the filename svchost.exe. Backdoor.XTS[28] and Backdoor.Litmus[29] are examples of malware that attempt to hide themselves as svchost.exe, most likely due to the fact that administrators and investigators should not be surprised to see multiple copies of svchost listed in the Task Manager. On Windows systems, copying the bogus svchost.exe to the system32 directory proves to both a just plain bad idea, since the file is protected by WFP on Windows 2000, XP, and 2003.

TIP

Pulist.exe[30] is a Resource Kit utility that lists the processes running on a system as well as the user context (the user account that the process is running under) for each process.

Process-to-Port Mapping

When there is a network connection open on a system, some process must be responsible for and must be using that connection. That is, every network connection and open port is associated with a process. Several tools are available to the investigator to retrieve this process–to–port mapping.

Netstat

On Windows XP and Windows 2003, the netstat.exe program offers the -o switch to display the process ID for the process responsible for the network connection. Once you've collected this information (refer back to the *netstat –ano* command), you will need to correlate it with the output of a tool such as tlist.exe or tasklist.exe to determine the name (and additional information) of the process using the connection.

As of Service Pack 2, Windows XP has an additional -b option that will "display the executable involved in creating each connection or listening port." This switch is also included in netstat.exe in Windows 2003 SP1 and can provide more information about the process using a particular port. In some cases, the output will also show some of the modules (DLLs) used by the process. Figure 1.9 illustrates an excerpt from the output of the command run on a Windows XP SP2 system.

Figure 1.9 Excerpt of Output from *netstat –anob* from a Windows XP SP2 System

```
TCP     192.168.1.8:1036      205.188.69.61:5190    ESTABLISHED    1976
[AOLSoftware.exe]

TCP     192.168.1.8:1038      64.12.189.249:443     ESTABLISHED    1976
[AOLSoftware.exe]

TCP     192.168.1.8:1039      64.12.25.220:5190     ESTABLISHED    3624
[aim6.exe]

TCP     192.168.1.8:2702      199.45.62.18:80       TIME_WAIT      0
TCP     192.168.1.8:2703      199.45.62.18:80       TIME_WAIT      0
TCP     192.168.1.8:2706      213.200.97.206:80     TIME_WAIT      0
TCP     192.168.1.8:2707      213.200.109.28:80     TIME_WAIT      0
TCP     192.168.1.8:2709      213.200.109.28:80     TIME_WAIT      0
UDP     0.0.0.0:1182          *:*                                  1752
C:\WINDOWS\system32\mswsock.dll
c:\windows\system32\WS2_32.dll
c:\windows\system32\DNSAPI.dll
c:\windows\system32\dnsrslvr.dll
C:\WINDOWS\system32\RPCRT4.dll
[svchost.exe]
```

Tip

Another extremely useful utility to have available is tcpvcon.exe, one of the utilities available from Microsoft.[31] The output of tcpvcon.exe is similar to that of netstat.exe in that it provides the state of the connection and endpoint information. On Windows XP and 2003, tcpvcon.exe also provides the PID and path to the executable image for the process responsible for the network connection.

Fport

Fport.exe has long been one of the tools of choice for obtaining the process-to-port mapping from a Windows system.[32] The output of the tool is easy to understand; however, the tool needs to be run from within an Administrator account to obtain its information. This can be an issue if you're responding to a situation in which the user's logged in account is, well, a user account and does not have Administrator privileges.

Openports

Openports.exe is probably the best tool for retrieving the process-to-port mapping information from a Windows system.[33.] Openports.exe allows for multiple output formats (including netstat-style, fport-style, and CSV) and does not require that an Administrator account be used. Openports.exe, run with the *-fport* switch to provide an fport-style output, displays the PID, the name of the process, the number of the port, the protocol (TCP or UDP), and the path to the executable image, as illustrated in the following:

```
4       SYSTEM          -> 139   TCP   SYSTEM
4       SYSTEM          -> 139   TCP   SYSTEM
168     alg             -> 1025  TCP   C:\WINDOWS\System32\alg.exe
1340    svchost         -> 135   TCP   C:\WINDOWS\system32\svchost.exe
1568    firefox         -> 1037  TCP   C:\Program Files\Mozilla
Firefox\firefox.exe
1568    firefox         -> 1038  TCP   C:\Program Files\Mozilla
Firefox\firefox.exe
```

TIP

If the system you're responding to is a Windows 2000 system that does not have the hotfix mentioned earlier in the chapter installed so that netstat.exe is capable of listing the PID for each network connection, an excellent alternative is to use openports.exe with the *-netstat* switch.

As each entry is placed on a line, this output is easily parsed by automation tools (to be addressed in Chapter 2, "Live Response: Data Analysis").

Using the *-netstat* switch, openports.exe displays its output similar to that of netstat.exe, so only the process IDs are displayed and not the path to the executable image. To get a more complete view of each network connection, you will want to correlate the output of openports.exe with that of netstat.exe; this is something that will be thoroughly addressed in Chapter 3.

In several instances, I have run both fport.exe (version 2.0) and openports.exe (version 1.0) on the same system, from an Administrator-level account. The output of openports.exe showed the path to the executable image for the process for several connections, where that information was not available in the fport.exe output. I strongly encourage you to perform your own testing before deciding which tool to use. Also, before using either tool in a corporate environment, be sure to read the license agreement for each one. (*Note:* You should do this with every third-party tool you use.)

That being said, you may also opt to use a port scanning tool such as *nmap*[34] to remotely gather information on open ports from a potentially compromised system. In doing so, you could find a number of ports open in listening mode, awaiting connections; authentication services, Web servers, and FTP servers do this, but so do backdoors. If you scan a system and find certain ports open but neither *netstat* nor any other tool that shows network connections or process-to-port mappings shows the same port open, you definitely have a mystery on your hands. At that point, you should double-check your scan results and ensure that you scanned the correct system. (Hey, it happens!) If the issue persists, you could have a rootkit on your hands. (See Chapter 7, "Rootkits and Rootkit Detection," for more information regarding rootkits.)

Process Memory

A live system will have any number of running processes, and any one of those processes could be suspicious or malicious in nature. When a process is executed on a system, it is most often given the same name as the file where the executable image resides, and on Windows systems in particular, a file can be named just about anything. The bad guys simply aren't so helpful as to name their malicious code something easily recognizable, like badstuff.exe. More often than not, they will rename the file to something less conspicuous, or they could try to disguise the intent of the program by using the name of a program usually found on Windows systems (see the "Svchost" sidebar).

Once you've used the tools we've discussed and found what you determine to be a suspicious process, you might then decide that you want more information about what that process is doing. You can get this information by dumping the memory used by the process. There are several tools you can use to accomplish this task. As stated previously, a detailed discussion of collecting the contents of RAM (as well as the memory used by specific processes) can be found in Chapter 3, "Windows Memory Analysis."

Network Status

Getting information about the status of the network interface cards (NICs) connected to a system can be extremely important to an investigation. For instance, today many laptops come with built-in wireless NICs, so you might not know just by looking at the desktop whether or not the system is connected to a wireless access point and if so what IP address it is using. Knowing the status of the NICs prior to a system being acquired can provide insight into a follow-on investigation.

Ipconfig

Ipconfig.exe is utility native to Windows systems that the investigator can use to display information about NICs and their status.[35] The most useful switch for investigators is */all*, which is used to display the network configuration of the NICs on the system. This information includes the state of the NIC, whether DHCP is enabled or not, the IP address of the NIC, and more.

You might find this information useful during an investigation, because you might have network traffic logs to examine, and the IP address of the system could have been modified at some point. Also, many Web-based e-mail services (such as Yahoo! Mail) record the IP address of the system from which an e-mail was drafted (this information is retrieved by the browser) in the headers of the e-mail. I took part in one particular investigation in which a former employee was sending annoying (not harassing) e-mails to our company. Looking at the e-mail headers, we were able to determine from where he was sending the e-mails. Several of them had been sent from a local copy shop and others from a local public library. With the gracious help of admins from the copy shop and the county, we were able to narrow the locations even further; in the case of the public library, we were able to pinpoint the branch of the library and the fact that the system he was using was on the second floor. Needless to say, he was shocked when confronted with this information and stopped sending the e-mails. Had he not been fired and had he been sending the e-mails from his work system via Yahoo! Mail, we would have been able to determine his location as well.

Promiscdetect and Promqry

Sometimes compromised systems will have a "sniffer" installed to capture network traffic, such as login credentials to other systems, or to develop a picture of what other systems are on the network and what services they are running. Some malware payloads include this capability, or it can be a follow-on download installed by an attacker. For the NIC to capture network traffic in this manner, it has to be placed in "promiscuous" mode. This isn't something an administrator or investigator will see, because there is nothing obvious to indicate that the NIC is in promiscuous mode. There's no system tray icon or Control Panel setting that clearly indicates to the investigator that the system is being used to "sniff" traffic.

There are tools available to tell you if the NIC is in promiscuous mode. One such tool is promiscdetect.exe.[36.] The other is promqry.exe,[37.] written by Tim Rains. The primary difference between the two tools is that promqry.exe can be run against remote systems, allowing an administrator to scan systems within the domain for systems that might be sniffing the network.

Tools & Traps…

Promiscuous Mode

The Perl script ndis.pl, located in the \ch2\code directory on the accompanying DVD, implements WMI code to determine the settings for a NIC. Specifically, it was designed to be used to determine whether a NIC is in promiscuous mode and capable of "sniffing" packets from the network.

The file ndis.exe in the same directory is a stand-alone executable version of this script, provided for use by those who do not have Perl installed on a Windows system.

Figure 1.10 illustrates an excerpt of the output returned from ndis.exe.

Figure 1.10 Excerpt from the Output of Ndis.exe on Windows XP

```
Dell Wireless WLAN 1350 WLAN Mini
          NDIS_PACKET_TYPE_MULTICAST
          NDIS_PACKET_TYPE_DIRECTED
--> NDIS_PACKET_TYPE_PROMISCUOUS <--
          NDIS_PACKET_TYPE_BROADCAST

VMware Virtual Ethernet Adapter for VMnet8
          NDIS_PACKET_TYPE_MULTICAST
          NDIS_PACKET_TYPE_DIRECTED
          NDIS_PACKET_TYPE_BROADCAST

Broadcom 440x 10/100 Integrated Controller
          NDIS_PACKET_TYPE_MULTICAST
          NDIS_PACKET_TYPE_DIRECTED
          NDIS_PACKET_TYPE_BROADCAST
```

Continued

> The output displayed in Figure 1.10 was generated by launching the WireShark[38.] (formerly known as Ethereal) "sniffer" application on the wireless NIC and then running ndis.exe. The highlighted portion of the output clearly shows that the wireless NIC is in promiscuous mode.
>
> Both the Perl script and the associated executable file are only intended to be run on the local system. However, minor modifications to the code will allow the script (or the executable, after the script is modified and recompiled) to be run against remote systems, in the same manner as promqry.exe.

Another very important use for tools like this is to determine what the active network interfaces might be on a live system. My old Toshiba Tecra 8100 systems require a PCIMCIA card to be able to connect to a wireless network, whereas many of the "newer" systems I've dealt with come with wireless networking capability built right into the system. You never see anything sticking out of the laptop case itself, nor do you see any blinking lights, as you do with the RJ-45 Ethernet connection. It's just there. So when Dave comes into a meeting and sits down behind his laptop, is he just taking notes, or is he also surfing the Web and sending e-mail? Wireless access is becoming more and more ubiquitous, not only because so many locations now have it available but also because it's being built right into our laptops.

This wireless access may be an entryway into your organization or even a route that someone uses to get information out of your infrastructure. I once dealt with an issue in which a public relations person in our company decided that she needed to take her personal laptop into meetings so that she could have access to the Internet. But she decided this without contacting anyone from IT, or even me (I was the security administrator). When she fired up her laptop, she found our wireless access points, which had WEP keys and MAC address filtering enabled. Since she hadn't contacted us and she was in a meeting and needed the access 10 minutes ago, she decided to connect to an open wireless access point that her system detected—one used by a company next door to us, one that was wide open with no security measures in place. Once she made that connection, she created an entry point into our infrastructure that bypassed all the protection mechanisms we had in place, including firewalls and antivirus software. At that point, it was hard to tell which situation was more damaging—her connection being used as a conduit to infect our infrastructure or the legal ramifications should the other company's infrastructure suffer a security breach and any logging mechanisms show her connection during that time.

During an investigation, it is generally a good idea to collect information about the active network interfaces on the system you are examining. This adds context not only to the volatile data you are collecting but also to a post-mortem analysis, which we will discuss later in this book.

Clipboard Contents

The clipboard is simply an area of memory where data can be stored for later use. Most Windows applications provide this functionality through the Edit option on the menu bar. Clicking **Edit** reveals a drop-down menu with choices like Cut, Copy, and Paste. MS Word 2003 includes an Office Clipboard option.

The clipboard is most often used to facilitate moving data in some fashion— between documents or between application windows on the desktop. The user selects text or other data, chooses **Copy**, and then chooses **Paste** to insert that data somewhere else. The Cut functionality removes the data from the document the user is working on, and that data goes into the clipboard.

What many folks don't realize is that they could turn their computer on some Monday morning, work on a file, and copy some information to their clipboard. Let's say that they're editing a document containing sensitive information, and per- sonal information about a customer needs to be added to that document. The user locates, highlights, and copies the information to the clipboard, then pastes it into the document. As long as the computer is left on, the user doesn't log out, and nothing is added to the clipboard to replace what was put there, the data remains on the clipboard.

Try it sometime. Walk up to your computer, open a Notepad or Word docu- ment, and simply use the **Control + V** key combination to paste whatever is cur- rently in the clipboard into a document. Try this on other computers. You might be surprised by what you see. How often do you find URLs, bits of IM conversations, passwords, or entire sections of text from documents still available on the clipboard? The clipboard isn't something that's visible on the system, but it's there, and it has been an issue—so much so that there's a Microsoft KnowledgeBase article entitled *How to Prevent Web Sites from Obtaining Access to Your Windows Clipboard*.[39]

Data found in the clipboard can be useful in a variety of cases, such as informa- tion or intellectual property theft, fraud, or harassment. Sometimes such information can provide you with clues; at other times you might find images or entire sections of documents on the clipboard.

Pclip.exe[40] is a CLI utility that can be used to retrieve the contents of the clip- board. CLI utilities such as pclip.exe make it easy to automate information collection through batch files and scripts.

Service/Driver Information

Services and drivers are started automatically when the system starts, based on entries in the Registry. Most users don't even see these services running as processes on the system because there are really no obvious indications, as there are with processes (for example, you can see processes running in the Task Manager). Yet these services are running nonetheless. Not all services are necessarily installed by the user or even the system administrator. Some malware installs itself as a service or even as a system driver.

Continued

Both the Perl script and the executable will display the following information about services:

- Name of the service
- DisplayName for the service
- StartName (the context used to launch the service)
- The description string for the service
- The process ID (PID) for the service (*Note:* This can be used to map the service to the process information)
- The path to the executable image for the service
- The start mode for the service
- The current state of the service
- Service status
- The type of the service (kernel driver, share process, etc.)
- The tag ID, a unique value used to order service startup within a load order group

Figure 1.11 illustrates an example of the information displayed by this utility.

Figure 1.11 Excerpt from the Output of Svc.exe on Windows XP

```
Name    : UMWdf
Display : Windows User Mode Driver Framework
Start   : NT AUTHORITY\LocalService
Desc    : Enables Windows user mode drivers.
PID     : 1660
Path    : C:\WINDOWS\system32\wdfmgr.exe
Mode    : Auto
State   : Running
Status  : OK
Type    : Own Process
TagID   : 0
```

Both the Perl script and the executable can be modified to output this information in various formats, including comma-separated values (CSVs) to make parsing the information easier or to ease analysis by making the output suitable for opening in a spreadsheet.

Command History

Let's say that you approach a system during an investigation and see one or more command prompts open on the screen. Depending on the situation, valuable clues could hidden in the commands typed by the user, such as *ftp* or *ping*. To see these previously typed commands, you can run the scroll bar for the command prompt up, but that only goes so far. If the user typed the *cls* command to clear the screen, you won't be able to use the scroll bar to see any of the commands that had been entered. Instead, you need to use the *doskey /history* command, which will show the history of the commands typed into that prompt, as illustrated in the following:

```
D:\tools>doskey /history
move proc.exe d:\awl2\ch2\code
perl2exe -small d:\awl2\ch2\code\proc.pl
move proc.exe d:\awl2\ch2\code
y
cd \awl2\ch2\code
proc
cd \perl2exe
perl2exe -small d:\awl2\ch2\code\procmon.pl
procmon
move procmon.exe d:\awl2\ch2\code
cd d:\awl2\ch2\code
procmon
cd \tools
openports -fport
openports -netstat
cls
doskey /history
cd \tools
dir prom*
promqry
dir prom*
promqry
```

I'll give you an example of when I've used this command. I was teaching an incident-response course on the West Coast, and during a lunch break, I "compromised" the student's systems. One step I specifically took on several of the computers was to open a command prompt and type several commands, then type *cls* to clear the screen. When the students returned, I noticed one particular individual in the back of the room who immediately closed (not minimized, but closed) the command prompt that he found open on his screen. As intended, the "clues" I left behind in the command prompt provided context to the rest of the "compromise," as students who hadn't closed their command prompts discovered. However, I'll admit that I've never had the opportunity to use this command outside a training environment. In all instances when I've been confronted with a live system, the user hasn't used a command prompt. However, this doesn't mean that it won't happen to you.

Mapped Drives

During the course of an investigation, you might want to know what drives or shares the system you are examining has mapped to. These mappings could have been created by the user, and they might be an indication of malicious intent (this could be the case if the user has guessed an Administrator password and is accessing systems across the enterprise). Further, there might be no persistent information within the file system or Registry for these connections to mapped shares on other systems, though the volatile information regarding drive mappings can be correlated to network connection information that you've already retrieved.

 Figure 1.12 illustrates the output of the program di.exe (*di* stands for *drive info*), which can be found on the accompanying DVD.

Figure 1.12 Output of Di.exe

```
D:\awl2\ch2\code>di
Drive     Type        File System  Path                    Free Space
-----     -----       -----------  -----                   ----------
C:\       Fixed       NTFS                                 1.15   GB
D:\       Fixed       NTFS                                 8.18   GB
E:\       Fixed       NTFS                                 5.19   GB
F:\       CD-ROM                                           0.00
G:\       Removable   FAT32                                974.45 MB
Z:\       Network     NTFS         \\192.168.1.71\c$       2.96   GB
```

The output of di.exe displayed in Figure 1.12 is the result of the program being run on a Windows XP Home system with one drive mapped to a small Windows 2003 server, specifically to the C$ share on that server.

Notice that the output of di.exe also shows a removable drive assigned the drive letter G:\. This is a USB-connected thumb drive, the artifacts of which will be discussed in Chapter 4, "Registry Analysis."

Shares

Besides resources used by the system you are investigating, you will also want to get information regarding those resources that the system is making available. Information for shares available on a system is maintained in the HKEY_LOCAL_MACHINE\System\CurrentControlSet\Services\lanmanserver\S hares key but can also be retrieved from a live system using CLI tools such as share.exe, which is available on the accompanying DVD. (The Perl source code for the program is also available.)

An excerpt of the output of share.exe appears as follows:

```
Name      -> SharedDocs
Type      -> Disk Drive
Path      -> C:\DOCUMENTS AND SETTINGS\ALL USERS\DOCUMENTS
Status    -> OK
```

Nonvolatile Information

During live response, you might not want to restrict yourself to collecting only volatile information. The situation could dictate that the investigator needs to collect information that would normally be considered persistent even if the system were rebooted, such as the contents of Registry keys or files. The investigator could decide that information needs to be extracted from the Registry or that information about (or from) files needs to be collected, either for additional analysis or because an attacker could be actively logged into the system. In such cases, the investigator may decide that to track the attacker (or botnet), she wants to leave the system live and online, but she also wants to preserve certain information from being modified or deleted.

Once a system has been started, there could have been modifications, such as drives mapped to or from the system, services started, or applications installed. These modifications might not be persistent across a reboot and therefore might need to be recorded and documented by the investigator.

Registry Settings

Several Registry values and settings could impact your follow-on forensic analysis and investigation. Although these settings are nonvolatile themselves, they could have an effect on how you choose to proceed in the conduct of your investigation or even whether you continue with your investigation at all.

There are several tools for collecting information from the Registry. My personal favorite is to write a Perl script that provides the various functionality for retrieving specific values or all values and subkeys of a particular key. Reg.exe is a command-line tool for accessing and managing the Registry that is part of the Windows 2000 Support Tools and is native to Windows XP and 2003.

ClearPageFileAtShutdown

This particular Registry value tells the operating system to clear the page file when the system is shut down. Because Windows uses a virtual memory architecture, some memory used by processes will be paged out to the page file. When the system is shut down, the information within the page file remains on the hard drive and can contain information such as decrypted passwords, portions of IM conversations, and other strings and bits of information that might provide you with important leads in your investigation. However, if this file is cleared during shutdown, this potentially valuable information will be more difficult to obtain.

Microsoft has KnowledgeBase articles for this Registry value that apply to both Windows 2000[42] and XP.[43]

DisableLastAccess

Windows has the ability to disable updating of the last access times on files. This was meant as a performance enhancement,[44] particularly on high-volume file servers. On normal workstations and the sort of desktops and laptops most folks are using, this setting doesn't provide any noticeable improvement in performance. On Windows 2003, you would set the following value to 1:

```
HKEY_LOCAL_MACHINE\System\CurrentControlSet\Control\FileSystem\
Disablelastacess
```

According to the performance-tuning guidelines document[45] from Microsoft for Windows 2003, this value does not exist by default and must be created.

On Windows XP and 2003 systems, this setting can be queried or enabled via the *fsutil* command. For example, to query the setting, use this command:

```
C:\>fsutil behavior query disablelastaccess
```

If this Registry value has been set, particularly sometime prior to you conducting your examination of the system, it is likely that you won't find anything useful with regard to file last-access times.

WARNING

The *DisableLastAccess* functionality is enabled by default on Vista. Keep this in mind when you're performing incident-response and computer forensics investigations. As of this writing, information is still being developed for forensic investigators with regard to this issue.

AutoRuns

There are several areas of the Registry (and the file system) that are referred to as *autostart locations* because they provide a facility to automatically start applications, usually without any direct interaction from the user. Some of these locations will automatically start applications when the system boots, others when a user logs in, and still others when the user takes a specific action. In instances where an application is started when the user performs a certain action, the user will be unaware that what he or she is doing is launching another application.

Okay, I know this stuff is in the Registry, and that fact in itself might make this seem like a daunting, impossible task, but the good news is that there is a finite number of locations that serve this purpose. The number might be large, but it is finite. Rather than listing them here, I'm going to leave a more in-depth of Registry analysis for later in the book. However, if you decide that you need to collect this information as part of your first-response activities, there are two ways to go about it. The first is to use a tool such as reg.exe (mentioned previously) to collect data from specific keys and values. The other is to use a tool such as AutoRuns[46.] to do it for you. The authors (Mark Russinovich and Bryce Cogswell, now Microsoft employees) do a great job of maintaining the list of areas checked by the tool. In some cases, I've found new additions to the tool before I've seen those autostart locations in widespread use in malware. AutoRuns comes in GUI and CLI versions, both with the same functionality. For example, you can use the *-m* switch in the CLI version to hide signed Microsoft entries (entries for executable files that have been signed by the vendor) or the *-v* to verify digital signatures.

AutoRuns also does a great job of checking areas within the file system, such as Scheduled Tasks. Sometimes administrators will use Scheduled Tasks to provide themselves with elevated (i.e., SYSTEM level) privileges to perform such tasks as view portions of the Registry that are normally off limits even to Administrators. An attacker who gains Administrator-level access to the system could do something similar to further extend his presence on the system.

Another area of the Registry that can provide valuable information in an investigation is the Protected Storage area (see the "Protected Storage" sidebar). The information held in Protected Storage is maintained in an encrypted format in the Registry. If you acquire an image of the system, tools such as AccessData's Forensic ToolKit will decrypt and recover the information. However, sometimes it is simpler to collect this information as part of live-response activities, particularly if time is of the essence and the information is pertinent to the case.

Notes from the Underground...

Protected Storage

Protected Storage is an area of memory where sensitive information for the user is maintained. When the system is turned off, this information is stored in encrypted format in the Registry, and when the user logs in, the information is placed into memory. Windows places information such as passwords and AutoComplete data for Web forms in Protected Storage for later use.

The contents of Protected Storage can be viewed on a live system by using tools such as pstoreview.exe[47.] or the Protected Storage Explorer.[48.]

Information within Protected Storage can be useful in cases involving access to Web sites and the use of passwords for services such as HotMail and MSN.

Information in Protected Storage is also useful to bad guys. I've seen systems infected with IRCbots (malicious software that, once installed, connects to an IRC channel awaiting commands; the channel operator can issue one command that is then executed by thousands of bots) that will send information from Protected Storage to the bad guy, on command. On February 19, 2006, Brian Krebs published an article[49.] in the *Washington Post Magazine* about a hacker who wrote bot software and controlled thousands of systems. In that article, Brian wrote that the hacker could type a single command (*pstore*) and retrieve the Protected Storage information from all the infected systems, which contained username and password combinations for PayPal,

Continued

eBay, Bank of America, and Citibank accounts, as well as for military and federal government e-mail accounts.

The information held by the Protected Storage Service is available through the AutoComplete functionality built into the Internet Explorer Web browser.[50] The AutoComplete Settings, shown in Figure 1.13, are available by clicking **Tools** in the Internet Explorer menu bar and then choosing **Internet Options | Content**, and then clicking the **AutoComplete** button.

With AutoComplete enabled, the users of these infected systems have used Internet Explorer to access their online shopping and banking accounts, making it available to an attacker such as the hacker in Brian's article.

Figure 1.13 AutoComplete Settings Dialog Box on Internet Explorer 6.0

Tools such as PassView[51] and the Protected Storage Explorer[52] allow you to view the Protected Storage information in a nice GUI format, and pstoreview.exe[53] is a CLI tool that will provide the same information to STDOUT. You might need to collect this information in the course of an investigation, particularly if the issue you're dealing with involves users accessing Web sites that require passwords.

Event Logs

Event Logs are essentially files within the file system, but they can change. In fact, depending on how they're configured and what events are being audited, they can change quite rapidly.

Depending on how the audit policies are configured on the "victim" system and how you're accessing it as the first responder, entries can be generated within the Event Logs. For example, if you decide to run commands against the system from a remote location (i.e., the system is in another building or another city, and you cannot get to it quickly but you want to preserve some modicum of data), then, if the proper audit configuration is in place, the Security Event Log will contain entries for each time you log in. If enough of these entries are generated, you could end up losing valuable information that pertains to your investigation. Tools such as psloglist.exe[54.] and dumpevt.exe[55.] can be used to retrieve the event records, or the .evt files themselves may be copied off the system (this depends on the level of access and permissions of the account being used). (A detailed discussion of the analysis of these files will be provided in Chapter 5, "File Analysis.")

The question that might be on your mind at this point is, "Okay, given all these tools and utilities, I have an incident on my hands. What data do I need to collect to resolve the issue?" The stock answer is, "It depends." I know that's probably not the answer you wanted to hear, but let me see if, in explaining that response, we can build an understanding of why that *is* the response.

The volatile data that is the most useful to your investigation depends on the type of incident you're faced with. For example, an incident involving a remote intrusion or a Trojan backdoor will generally mean that the process, network connection, and process-to-port-mapping information (and perhaps even the contents of certain Registry keys) will be the most valuable to you. However, if an employee in a corporate environment is suspected of having stolen company-proprietary data or violating the corporate acceptable use policy (AUP), then information about storage devices connected to his system, Web browsing history, contents of the clipboard, and so on could be more valuable to your investigation.

The key to all this is to know what information is available to your investigation, how you can retrieve that information, and how you can use it. As you start to consider different types of incidents and the information you need to resolve them, you will start to see an overlap between the various tools you use and the data you're interested in for your investigation. Although you might not develop a "one size fits all" batch file that runs all the commands you will want to use for every investigation, you could decide that having several smaller batch files (or configuration files for the Forensic Server Project or WFT) is a better approach. That way, you can collect only the information you need for each situation.

Devices and Other Information

You could choose to collect other types of information from a system that might not be volatile in nature, but you want to record it for documentation purposes. For example, perhaps you want to know something about the hard drive installed in the system. Di.pl is a Perl script that implements WMI to list the various disk drives attached to the system as well as partition information. Ldi.pl implements WMI to collect information about logical drives (C:\, D:\, etc.), including local fixed drives, removable storage devices, and remote shares. Sr.pl lists information about System Restore points (more information about System Restore points can be found in Chapter 4, "Registry Analysis," and Chapter 5, "File Analysis") on Windows XP systems.

DevCon,[56.] available from Microsoft, can be used to document devices that are attached to a Windows system. DevCon, a CLI replacement for the Device Manager, can show available device classes as well as the status of connected devices.

A Word about Picking Your Tools...

In this chapter as well as other chapters throughout this book, we mention various tools that can be used to perform certain tasks. This book is not intended as a be-all and end-all list of tools; that's simply not possible. Instead, what I'm trying to do is make you aware of *where* you need to look and show you ways in which you can go about collecting the data you need for your investigations. Sometimes it's simply a matter of knowing that the information is there.

When we're collecting data from live systems, we will most often have to interact with the operating system itself, using the available API. Different tools can use different API calls to collect the same information.

It's always a good idea to know how your tools collect the information they do. What API calls does the executable use? What DLLs does it access? How is the data displayed, and how does that data compare to other tools of a similar nature?

Test your tools to determine the effects they have on a live system. Do they leave any artifacts on the system? If so, what are they? Be sure to document these artifacts because this documentation allows you to identify (and document) steps that you take to mitigate the effects of using, and justify the use of, these tools. For example, Windows XP performs application prefetching, meaning that when you run an application, some information about that application (code pages, for example) is stored in a .pf file located in the %WINDIR%\Prefetch directory. This directory has a limit of 128 .pf files. If you're performing incident-response activities and there are less than 128 .pf files in this directory, one of the effects of the tools you run on the system will be that .pf files for those tools will be added to the Prefetch directory. Under most circumstances, this might not be an issue. However, let's say that your methodology includes using nc.exe (*netcat*). If someone had already used nc.exe on the system, your use of any file by that name would have the effect of overwriting the existing .pf file for nc.exe, potentially destroying evidence (for example, modifying MAC times or data in the file, such as the path to the executable image).

Performing your own tool testing and validation might seem like an arduous task. After all, who wants to run through a tool testing process for every single tool? Well, you might have to, since there are few sites that provide this sort of information for their tools; most weren't originally written to be used for incident response or computer forensics. However, once you have a your framework (tools, process, and so on) in place, it's really not all that hard, and there are some simple things you can do to document and test the tools you use. Documenting and testing your tools is very similar to how you'd go about testing or analyzing a suspected malware program, a topic that is covered in detail in Chapter X.

The basic steps of documenting your tools consist of static and dynamic testing. Static testing includes documenting unique identifying information about the tool, such as:

- Where you got it (URL)
- The file size
- Cryptographic hashes for the file, using known algorithms
- Retrieving information from the file, such as PE headers, file version information, import/export tables, etc.

This information is easily retrievable using command-line tools and scripting languages such as Perl, and the entire collection process (as well as archiving the information in a database, spreadsheet, or flat file) can be easily automated.

Dynamic testing involves running the tools while using monitoring programs to document the changes that take place on the system. Snapshot comparison tools such as InControl5 are extremely useful for this job, as are monitoring tools such as RegMon[57] and FileMon.[58] RegMon and FileMon let you see not only which Registry keys and files are accessed by the process but also those that are created or modified as well. You might also consider using such tools as Wireshark[59] to monitor inbound and outbound traffic from the test system while you're testing your tools, particularly if your static analysis of a tool reveals that it imports networking functions from other DLLs.

Live-Response Methodologies

When you're performing live response, the actual methodology or procedure you use to retrieve the data from the systems can vary, depending on a number of factors. As a consultant and an emergency responder, I've found that it's best to have a complete understanding of what's available and what can go into your toolkit (considering issues regarding purchasing software, licensing, and other fees and restrictions) and then decide what works based on the situation.

There are two basic methodologies for performing live response on a Windows system: local and remote.

Local Response Methodology

Performing live response locally means that you are sitting at the console of the system, entering commands at the keyboard, and saving information locally, either directly to the hard drive or to a removable (thumb drive, USB-connected external drive) or network resource (network share) that appears as a local resource. This is done very often in situations where the responder has immediate physical access to the system and her tools on a CD or thumb drive. Collecting information locally from several systems can often be much quicker than locating a network connection or accessing a wireless network. With the appropriate amount of external storage and the right level of access, the first responder can quickly and efficiently collect the necessary information. To further optimize her activities, the first responder might have all her tools written to a CD and managed via a batch file or some sort of script that allows for a limited range of flexibility (for example, the USB-connected storage device is mapped to different drive letters, the Windows installation is on a D:\ drive, and so on).

The simplest way to implement the local methodology is with a batch file. I tend to like batch files and Perl scripts because instead of typing the same commands over and over (and making mistakes over and over), I can write it once and then have those commands run automatically. An example of a simple batch file that can be used during live response looks like this:

```
tlist.exe -c > %1\tlist-c.log
tlist.exe -t > %1\tlist-t.log
tlist.exe -s > %1\tlist-s.log
openports.exe -fport > %1\openports-fport.log
netstat.exe -ano > %1\netstat-ano.log
```

There you go. Three utilities and five simple commands. Save this file as **local.bat** and include it on the CD, right along with copies of the associated tools.

Also be sure to add to the CD trusted copies of the command processor (cmd.exe) for each operating system. Before you launch the batch file, take a look at the system and see what network drives are available, or insert a USB thumb drive into to the system and see what drive letter it receives (let's say F:\), then run the batch file like so (the D:\ drive is the CD-ROM drive):

```
D:\>local.bat F:
```

Once the batch file completes, you'll have five files on your thumb drive. Of course, you can add a variety of commands to the batch file, depending on the breadth of data you want to retrieve from a system.

There are several freely available examples of the toolkits that were designed to be used in a local response fashion, to include the Incident Response Collection Report (IRCR) version 2,[60.] and the Windows Forensic Toolkit[61.] (WFT), created by Monty McDougal. Although they differ in their implementation and output, the base functionality of both toolkits is substantially the same: run external executable files controlled by a Windows batch file, and save the output locally. WFT does a great job of saving the raw data and allowing the responder to send the output of the commands to HTML reports.

Another approach to developing a local response methodology is to encapsulate as much as possible into a single application using the Windows API, which is what tools such as Nigilant32[62.] from Agile Risk Management LLC attempt to achieve. Nigilant32 uses the same Windows API calls used by external utilities to collect volatile information from a system (see Figure 1.14) and has the added capabilities of performing file system checks and dumping the contents of physical memory (RAM).

Figure 1.14 The Nigilant GUI

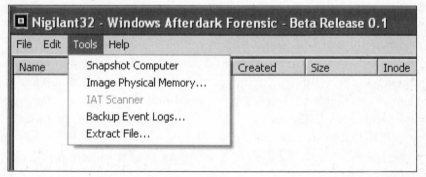

The interesting thing about the batch file-style toolkits is that a lot of folks have them. When I'm at a customer location or a conference, many times I'll talk to folks who are interested in comparing their approach to others'. Some have a copy of my first book and have included tools listed in Chapter 5 of *Windows Forensics and Incident Recovery*, or they've read about other tools and incorporated them into their toolkit. Oddly enough, when it really comes down to it, there is a great deal of overlap between these toolkits. The batch file-style toolkits employ executables that use the same (or similar) Windows API calls as other tools such as Nigilant32.

Remote Response Methodology

The remote response methodology generally consists of a series of commands executed against a system from across the network. This methodology is very useful in situations with many systems, since the process of logging into the system and running commands can be easily automated. In security circles, we call this being *scalable*. Some tools run extremely well when used in combination with psexec.exe from SysInternals.com, and additional information can be easily collected via the use of Window Management Instrumentation (WMI). Regardless of the approach you take, keep in mind that (a) you're going to need login credentials for each system, and (b) each time you log in to run a command and collect the output, you're going to add an entry to the Security Event Log (provided the appropriate level of auditing has been enabled). Keeping that in mind, we see that the order of volatility has shifted somewhat, so I would recommend that the first command you use is to collect the contents of the Security Event Log.

A Windows batch file can be use as the basis of implementing this methodology. Taking three arguments at the command line (the name or IP of the system and the username/password login credentials), you can easily script a series of commands to collect the necessary information. Some commands will need to executed using psexec.exe, which will copy the executable to the remote system, run it, and allow you to collect the output from standard output (STDOUT), or redirect the output to a file, just as though you were running the same command locally. Other commands will take a UNC path (the name of the system prefaced with \\) and the login credentials as arguments, so psexec.exe will not need to be used. Finally, WMI can be implemented via VBScript or Perl to collect data. Microsoft provides a script repository[63] with numerous examples of WMI code implemented in various languages to include Perl,[64] making designing a custom toolkit something of a cut-and-paste procedure.

Implementing our local methodology batch file for the remote methodology is fairly trivial:

```
psexec.exe \\%1 -u %2 -p %3 -c tlist.exe -c > tlist-c.log
psexec.exe \\%1 -u %2 -p %3 -c tlist.exe -t > tlist-t.log
psexec.exe \\%1 -u %2 -p %3 -c tlist.exe -s > tlist-s.log
psexec.exe \\%1 -u %2 -p %3 -c openports.exe -fport > openports-fport.log
psexec.exe \\%1 -u %2 -p %3 c:\windows\system32\netstat.exe -ano >
%1\netstat-ano.log
```

This batch file (remote.bat) sits on the responder's system and is launched as follows:

```
C:\forensics\case007>remote.bat 192.168.0.7 Administrator password
```

Once the batch file has completed, the responder has the output of the commands in five files, ready for analysis, on her system.

If you're interested in using WMI to collect information remotely but you aren't a big VB Script programmer, you might want to take a look at wmic.exe,[65] the CLI for WMI. Ed Skoudis wrote an excellent beginning tutorial[66] on the use of wmic.exe for the SANS Internet Storm Center, which included examples such as collecting a list of installed patches from remote systems. Pretty much anything available to you as a Win32 class[67] via WMI can be queried with wmic.exe. For example, to display the processes running locally on your system, you can use the following command:

```
C:\>wmic PROCESS GET ProcessId,Name,ExecutablePath
```

This is a pretty simple and straightforward command, and when it's executed, we can see the output right there in the console. We can also redirect the output to a file, and we can even choose from among various formats, such as CSVs (for opening in Excel or parsing with Perl) or even an HTML table. Using additional switches such as /Node:, /User:, and /Password:, we can include several wmic.exe commands in a batch file and collect an even wider range of data from remote systems. Further, administrators can use these commands to compile hardware and software inventory lists, determine systems that need to be updated with patches, and more. WMI is a powerful interface into managed Windows systems in and of itself, and wmic.exe provides easy access for automating commands.

With the right error handling and recovery as well as activity logging in the code, this can be a highly effective and scalable way to quickly collect information from a number of systems, all managed from and stored in a central location. ProDiscover Incident Response (IR)[68] from Technology Pathways is a commercial tool that implements this methodology. The responder can install an agent from a central location, query the agent for available information, and then delete the agent. Thanks to ProDiscover's ProScript API, the responder can use Perl to automate the entire process. This approach minimizes the number of logins that will appear in the Security Event Log as well as the amount of software that needs to be installed on the remote system. ProDiscover IR has the added capabilities of retrieving the contents of physical memory as well as performing a live acquisition.

The limitation of the remote response methodology is that the responder must be able to log into the systems via the network. If the Windows-style login (via NetBIOS) has been restricted in some way (NetBIOS not installed, firewalls/routers blocking the protocols, or similar), this methodology will not work.

The Hybrid Approach

I know I said that there are two basic approaches to response methodologies, and that's true. There is, however, a third approach that is really just a hybrid of the local and remote methodologies, so for the sake of simplicity, we'll just call it the *hybrid methodology* (the truth is that I couldn't think of a fancy name for it). This methodology is most often used in situations where the responder cannot log into the systems remotely but wants to collect all information from a number of systems and store that data in a central location. The responder (or an assistant) will go to the system with a CD or thumb drive (ideally, one with a write-protect switch that is enabled), access the system, and run the tools to collect information. As the tools are executed, each one will send its output over the network to the central "forensics server." In this way, no remote logins are executed, trusted tools are run from a non-modifiable source, and very little is written[69] to the hard drive of the "victim" system. With the right approach and planning, the responder can minimize his interaction with the system, reducing the number of choices he needs to make with regard to input commands and arguments as well as reducing the chance for mistakes.

Perhaps the simplest way to implement the hybrid methodology is with a batch file. We've already seen various tools and utilities that we have at our disposal for collecting a variety of information. In most of the cases we've looked at, as with the local methodology, we've used CLI tools and redirected their output to a file. So how do we get the information we've collected off the system? One way to do that is to use *netcat*,[70] described as the "TCP/IP Swiss army knife" because of the vast array of things you can do with it. For our purposes, we won't go into an exhaustive description of netcat; we'll use it to transmit information from one system to another. First, we need to set up a "listener" on our forensics server, and we do that with the following command line:

```
D:\forensics>nc -L -p 80 > case007.txt
```

This command line tells *netcat* (nc.exe) to listen (really hard … keep the listener open after the connection has been closed) on port 80, and anything that comes in on that port gets sent (redirected, actually) to the file named case007.txt. With this setup, we can easily modify our batch file so that instead of writing the output of our commands to files, we send it through netcat to the "listener" on the forensics server:

```
tlist.exe -c | nc %1 %2
tlist.exe -t | nc %1 %2
tlist.exe -s | nc %1 %2
openports.exe -fport | nc %1 %2
netstat.exe -ano | nc %1 %2
```

Save this file as hybrid.bat, and then launch it from the command line, like so (D:\ is still the CD-ROM drive):

```
D:\>remote.bat 192.168.1.10 80
```

Once we run this batch file, we'll have all our data safely off the victim system and on our forensic server for safekeeping and analysis.

Several freeware tools implement this hybrid methodology. One is the Forensic Server Project (FSP), released in my first book in July 2004 and improved on quite a bit since then. The FSP is open source, written in Perl and freely available. The idea for the FSP arose from the use of netcat, where the responder would run a tool from a CD loaded in the CD drive of the "victim" system and then pipe the output of the command through *netcat*. Instead of displaying the output of the command on the screen (*STDOUT*), *netcat* would be responsible for sending the information to a waiting listener on the server, where the output of the command would be stored (and not written to the "victim" system's hard drive). This worked well in some situations, but as the number of commands grew and the commands began having a range of argument options, this methodology became a bit cumbersome. As more commands had to be typed, there was a greater chance for mistakes, and sometimes even a batch file to automate everything just wasn't the answer. So I decided to create the Forensic Server Project, a framework for automating (as much as possible) the collection, storage, and management of live-response data.

The FSP consists of two components: a server and a client. The server component is known as the FSP (really, I couldn't come up with anything witty or smart to call it, and "Back Orifice" was already taken). You copy the files for the FSP to your forensic workstation (I use a laptop when I'm on site), and when they're run, the FSP will sit and listen for connections. The FSP handles simple case management tasks, logging, storage, and the like for the case (or cases) that you're working on.

When a connection is received from the client component, the FSP will react accordingly to the various "verbs" or commands that are passed to it.

The current iteration of the client component is called the First Responder Utility, or FRU. The FRU is very client specific, since this is what is run on the "victim" system, either from a CD or a USB thumb drive. The FRU is really a very simple framework in itself in that it uses third-party utilities, such as the tools we've discussed in this chapter, to collect information from the "victim" system. When one of these commands is run, the FRU captures the output of the command (which you're normally see at the console, in a command prompt window) and sends it out to the FSP, which will store the information sent to it and log the activity. The FRU is also capable of collecting specific Registry values or all values in a specific Registry key. Once all the commands have been run and all data collected, the FRU will "tell" the FSP that it can close the log file, which the FSP will do.

The FRU is controlled by an initialization (i.e., .ini) file, which is a similar format to the old Windows 3.1 INI files and consists of four sections. The first section, [Configuration], has some default settings for the FRU to connect to the FSP—specifically, the server and port to connect to. This is useful in smaller environments or in larger environments where the incident response data collection will be delegated to regional offices. However, these settings can be overridden at the command line.

The next section is the [Commands] section, which lists the external third-party tools to be executed to collect information. Actually, these can be any Windows portable executable (PE) file that sends its output to STDOUT (that is, the console). I have written a number of small tools, in Perl, and then "compiled" them into stand-alone executables so that they can be run on systems that do not have Perl installed. Many of them are useful in collecting valuable information from systems and can be launched via the FRU's INI files. The format of this section is different from the other sections and very important. The format of each line looks like the following:

```
<index>=<command line>::<filename>
```

The index is the order that you want the command run in; for example, you might want to run one command before any others, so the index allows you to order the commands. The command line is the name of the tool you're going to run plus all the command-line options you'd want to include, just as though you were running the command from the command prompt on the system itself. These first two sections are separated by an equals sign (=) and followed by a double colon (::). In most cases, the final sections of one of these lines would be separated by semi-colons, but several tools (psloglist.exe from SysInternals.com) have options that include the possibility of using a semicolon, so I had to choose something that likely would not be used in the command line as a separator. Finally, the last element is the name of the file to be generated, most often the name of the tool, with the .dat extension. When the output is sent to the FSP server, it will be written to a file within the designated directory, with the filename prepended with the name of the system being investigated. This way, data can be collected from multiple systems using the same running instance of the FSP.

One important comment about tools used with the FRU: Due to the fact that the system you, as the investigator, are interacting with is live and running, you should change the name of the third-party tools you are using. One good idea is to prepend the filenames with something unique, such as *f_* or *fru_*. This is in part due to the fact that your interaction with the system will be recorded in some way (more on this in Chapter 4, "Registry Analysis") and due to Windows XP's prefetch capability (more about that in Chapter 5, "File Analysis"). Remember Locard's Exchange Principle? Well, it's a good idea to make sure that the artifacts you leave behind on a system are distinguishable from all the other artifacts.

An example taken from an FRU INI file looks like the following:

```
6=openports.exe -fport::openports.dat
```

There is another client available for copying files off the victim system, if the investigator decides that this is something he or she wants to do. Figure 1.15 illustrates the GUI for the file copy client, or FCLI.

Figure 1.15 File Copy Client GUI

To use the file copy client (FCLI), the investigator simply launches it and selects **File**, then **Config** to enter the IP address and port of the FSP server. Then she selects **File | Open** and chooses the files she wants to copy. Once she's selected all the files she wants to copy, the investigator simply clicks the **OK** button. The FCLI will first collect the MAC times of the file and other metadata, then compute the MD5 and SHA-1 hashes for the file. This information is sent to the FSP. Then the FCLI copies the binary contents of the file to the server. Once the file has completed the copy operation, the FSP server will compute hashes for the copied file and verify those against the hashes received from the FCLI prior to the copy operation. All the actions occur automatically, without any interaction from the investigator, and they're all logged by the FSP.

The accompanying DVD includes several movie files that illustrate how to set up and use the Forensic Server Project, along with instructions on where to get the necessary player.

Summary

In this chapter, we've taken a look at live response, specifically collecting volatile (and some nonvolatile) information from systems. As we've discussed, there is quite a bit of useful data on live systems that can be used to enhance our understanding of an incident; we just need to collect that data before we remove power from the system so that we can acquire an image of the hard drive. We've also discussed how changes to the computing landscape are presenting us, more and more, with situations where our only viable option is to collect volatile data.

All Perl scripts mentioned and described in this chapter are available on the accompanying DVD, along with a stand-alone executable "compiled" with Perl2Exe. ProScripts for Technology Pathways' ProDiscover product are also available on the accompanying DVD but are provided as Perl scripts only.

Notes

1. For more information on netcat, go to www.vulnwatch.org/netcat/.
2. For more information on pmdump, go to www.ntsecurity.nu/toolbox/pmdump/.
3. For more information on strings.exe, go to www.microsoft.com/technet/sysinternals/Miscellaneous/Strings.mspx.
4. For more information go to http://info.sen.ca.gov/pub/01-02/bill/sen/sb_1351-1400/sb_1386_bill_20020926_chaptered.html.

5. For more information go to
http://msdn.microsoft.com/library/default.asp?url=/library/en-
us/sysinfo/base/file_times.asp.

6. For more information on psloggedon, go to www.microsoft.com/technet/sysin-
ternals/SystemInformation/PsLoggedOn.mspx.

7. For more information on loggedonsessions.exe, go to
www.microsoft.com/technet/sysinternals/Security/LogonSessions.mspx.

8. For more information on SubSeven, visit
www.symantec.com/avcenter/venc/data/backdoor.subseven.html.

9. For more information on psfile.exe, go to www.microsoft.com/technet/sysinter-
nals/utilities/psfile.mspx.

10. For more information go to on openfiles.exe, go to
www.microsoft.com/resources/documentation/windows/xp/all/proddocs/en-
us/openfiles.mspx.

11. For a definition of NetBIOS, go to http://en.wikipedia.org/wiki/NetBIOS.

12. For more information go to http://support.microsoft.com/kb/q163409/.

13. For more information go to http://support.microsoft.com/kb/119495/EN-US/.

14. For more information go to http://support.microsoft.com/?id=837243.

15. For more information go to http://support.microsoft.com/kb/137984/.

16. For more information go to http://vil.nai.com/vil/content/v_100559.htm.

17. For more information go to
http://support.microsoft.com/default.aspx?scid=kb;en-us;236995.

18. For more information go to http://support.microsoft.com/kb/222193/EN-US/.

19. For more information go to
www.microsoft.com/whdc/devtools/debugging/default.mspx.

20. For more information go to www.diamondcs.com.au/index.php?page=console-
cmdline.

21. For more information go to www.microsoft.com/resources/documentation/win-
dows/xp/all/proddocs/en-us/tasklist.mspx.

22. For more information go to www.sysinternals.com/Utilities/PsList.html.

23. For more information go to www.sysinternals.com/Utilities/ListDlls.html.

24. For more information go to www.sysinternals.com/Utilities/Handle.html.

25. For more information go to
http://msdn.microsoft.com/library/default.asp?url=/library/en-
us/wmisdk/wmi/win32_process.asp.

26. For more information go to
http://support.microsoft.com/default.aspx?scid=kb;en-us;314056.

27. For more information go to
http://support.microsoft.com/default.aspx?scid=kb;en-us;250320.

28. For more information go to
http://securityresponse.symantec.com/avcenter/venc/data/backdoor.xts.html.
29. For more information go to
http://securityresponse.symantec.com/avcenter/venc/data/backdoor.litmus.203.b.ht
ml.
30. For more information go to http://support.microsoft.com/kb/927229.
31. For more information go to
www.microsoft.com/technet/sysinternals/Networking/TcpView.mspx.
32. For more information go to www.foundstone.com/.
33. For more information go to www.diamondcs.com.au/openports/.
34. For more information go to www.insecure.org/nmap/index.html.
35. For more information go to http://support.microsoft.com/kb/314850.
36. For more information go to www.ntsecurity.nu/toolbox/promiscdetect/.
37. For more information go to http://support.microsoft.com/?kbid=892853.
38. For more information go to www.wireshark.org.
39. For more information go to
http://support.microsoft.com/default.aspx?scid=KB;EN-US;Q224993&.
40. For more information go to http://unxutils.sourceforge.net/.
41. For more information go to
http://msdn.microsoft.com/library/default.asp?url=/library/en-
us/wmisdk/wmi/win32_service.asp.
42. For more information go to http://support.microsoft.com/kb/182086/EN-US/.
43. For more information go to http://support.microsoft.com/kb/314834/EN-US/.
44. For more information go to
http://support.microsoft.com/default.aspx?scid=kb;en-us;555041.
45. For more information go to www.download.microsoft.com/down-
load/2/8/0/2800a518-7ac6-4aac-bd85-74d2c52e1ec6/tuning.doc.
46. For more information go to www.sysinternals.com/Utilities/Autoruns.html.
47. For more information go to www.ntsecurity.nu/toolbox/pstoreview/.
48. For more information go to www.codeproject.com/tools/PSExplorer.asp.
49. For more information go to www.washingtonpost.com/wp-
dyn/content/article/2006/02/14/AR2006021401342.html.
50. For more information go to www.microsoft.com/windows/ie/using/howto/cus-
tomizing/autocomplete.mspx.
51. For more information go to www.nirsoft.net/utils/pspv.html.
52. For more information go to www.forensicideas.com/tools.html.
53. For more information go to www.ntsecurity.nu/toolbox/pstoreview/.
54. For more information go to www.sysinternals.com/Utilities/PsLogList.html.
55. For more information go to www.somarsoft.com/.

56. For more information go to http://support.microsoft.com/?kbid=311272.

57. For more information go to www.microsoft.com/technet/sysinternals/SystemInformation/Regmon.mspx.

58. For more information go to www.microsoft.com/technet/sysinternals/SystemInformation/Filemon.mspx.

59. For more information go to www.wireshark.org/.

60. For more information go to http://tools.phantombyte.com/.

61. For more information go to www.foolmoon.net/security/wft/index.html.

62. For more information go to www.agilerm.net/publications_4.html.

63. For more information go to www.microsoft.com/technet/scriptcenter/default.mspx.

64. For more information go to http://isc.sans.org/diary.php?storyid=1622.

65. For more information go to http://msdn.microsoft.com/library/default.asp?url=/library/en-us/wmisdk/wmi/wmic.asp.

66. For more information go to http://isc.sans.org/diary.php?storyid=1622.

67. For more information go to http://msdn.microsoft.com/library/default.asp?url=/library/en-us/wmisdk/wmi/win32_classes.asp.

68. For more information go to www.techpathways.com/ProDiscoverIR.htm.

69. As we know from Locard's Exchange Principle, there will be an exchange of "material." References to the commands run will appear in the Registry, and on XP systems files will be added to the Prefetch directory. It is not possible to perform live response without leaving some artifacts; the key is knowing how to minimize and document those artifacts.

70. For a definition of netcat, go to http://en.wikipedia.org/wiki/Netcat.

Solutions Fast Track

Live Response

☑ Locard's Exchange Principle states that when two objects come into contact, material is exchanged between them. This rule pertains in the digital realm as well.

☑ Anything an investigator does on a live system, even nothing, will have an effect on the system and leave an artifact. Artifacts occur on the system as it runs with no interaction from a user.

☑ The absence of an artifact where one is expected is itself an artifact.

☑ The order of volatility illustrates to us that some data has a much shorter "lifespan" or "shelf life" than other data.

☑ When we're performing incident response, the most volatile data should be collected first.

☑ The need to perform live response should be thoroughly understood and documented.

☑ Corporate security policies may state that live response is the first step in an investigation.

What Data to Collect

☑ A great deal of data that can give an investigator insight into her case is available on the system while it is powered up and running, and some of that data is available for only a limited time.

☑ Many times, the volatile data you collect from a system will depend on the type of investigation or incident you're presented with.

☑ When collecting volatile data, you need to keep both the order of volatility from RFC 3227 and Locard's Exchange Principle in mind.

☑ The key to collecting volatile data and using that data to support an investigation is thorough documentation.

Nonvolatile Information

☑ Nonvolatile information (such as system settings) can affect your investigation, so you might need to collect that data as part of your live response.

☑ Some of the nonvolatile data you collect could affect your decision to proceed further in live response, just as it could affect your decision to perform a follow-on, post-mortem investigation.

☑ The nonvolatile information you choose to collect during live response depends on factors such as your network infrastructure, security and incident response policies, or system configurations.

Live-Response Methodologies

☑ There are three basic live-response methodologies; local, remote, and a hybrid of the two. Knowing the options you have available and having implementations of those options will increase your flexibility for collecting information.

☑ The methodology you use will depend on factors such as the network infrastructure, your deployment options, and perhaps even the political structure of your organization. However, you do have multiple options available.

☑ When choosing your response methodology, be aware of the fact that your actions will leave artifacts on the system. Your actions will be a direct stimulus on the system that will cause changes to occur in the state of the system, since Registry keys may be added (see Chapter 4, "Registry Analysis," regarding USB-connected removable storage devices), files may be added or modified, and executable images will be loaded into memory. However, these changes are, to a degree, quantifiable, and you should thoroughly document your methodology and actions.

Frequently Asked Questions

The following Frequently Asked Questions, answered by the authors of this book, are designed to both measure your understanding of the concepts presented in this chapter and to assist you with real-life implementation of these concepts. To have your questions about this chapter answered by the author, browse to **www.syngress.com/solutions** and click on the **"Ask the Author"** form.

Q: When should I perform live response?

A: There are no hard and fast rules stating when you should perform live response. However, as more and more regulatory bodies (consider SEC rules, HIPAA, FISMA, Visa PCI, and others) specify security measures and mechanisms that are to be used as well as the questions that need to be addressed and answered (was personal sensitive information accessed?), live response becomes even more important.

Q: I was involved with a case in which, after all was said and done, the "Trojan defense" was used. How would live response have helped or prepared us to address this issue?

A: By collecting information about processes running on the system, network connections, and other areas where you would have found Trojan or backdoor artifacts, you would have been able to rule out whether or not such things were running while the system was live. Your post-mortem investigation would include an examination of the file system, including scheduled tasks and the like, to determine the likelihood that a Trojan was installed, but collecting volatile data from a live system would provide you with the necessary information to determine whether a Trojan was running at the time you were in front of the system.

Q: I'm not doing live response now. Why should I start?

A: Often an organization will opt for the "wipe-and-reload" mentality, in which the administrator will wipe the hard drive of a system thought to be compromised, then reload the operating system from clean media, reinstall the applications, and load the data back onto the system from backups. This is thought to be the least expensive approach. However, this approach does nothing to determine *how* the incident occurred in the first place. Some might say, "I reinstalled the operating system and updated all patches," and that's great, but not all incidents occur for want of a patch or hotfix. Sometimes it's as simple as a weak or nonexistent password on a user account or application (such as the *sa* password on SQL Server) or a poorly configured service. No amount of patching will fix these sorts of issues. If you don't determine how an incident occurred and address the issue, the incident is likely to occur again, in fairly short order after the bright, new, clean system is reconnected to the network. In addition, as we've shown throughout this chapter, a great deal of valuable information is available when the system is still running—information such as physical memory, running processes, network connections, and the contents of the clipboard—that could have a significant impact on your investigation.

Chapter 2

Live Response: Data Analysis

Solutions in this chapter:

- Data Analysis

☑ Summary

☑ Solutions Fast Track

☑ Frequently Asked Questions

Introduction

Now that we've collected volatile data from a system, how do we "hear" what it has to say or how do we figure out what the data is telling us? Once we've collected a process listing, how do we determine which one of the processes, if any, is malware? How do we tell if someone has compromised the system and is currently accessing it? Finally, how can we use the volatile data we've collected to build a better picture of activity on the system, particularly as we acquire an image and perform post-mortem analysis?

The purpose of this chapter is to address these sorts of questions. What you're looking for, what artifacts you will be digging for in the volatile data you've collected depends heavily on the issue you are attempting to address. How do we dig through reams of data to find what we're looking for? In this chapter, I do not think for a moment that I will be able to answer all your questions; rather, my hope is to provide enough data and examples so that when something occurs that is not covered, you will have a process by which you can determine the answer on your own. Perhaps by the time we reach the end of this chapter, you will have a better understanding of why we collect volatile data, and what it can tell us.

Data Analysis

There are a number of sources of information that tell us what data we should collect from a live system in order to troubleshoot an errant application or assess an incident. Look at Web sites such as the e-Evidence Info site,[1] which is updated monthly with new links to conference presentations, papers, and articles that discuss a wide range of topics, to include volatile data collection. Although many of these resources refer to data *collection*, few actually address the issue of data correlation and *analysis*. We will be addressing these issues in this chapter.

To begin, we need to look at the output of the tools, at the data we've collected, to see what the sort of snapshot of data we have available to us. When we use tools such as those discussed in Chapter 1, we are getting a snapshot of the state of a system at a point in time. Many times, we can quickly locate an indicator of the issue within the output from a single tool. For example, we may see something unusual in the Task Manager GUI or the output of tlist.exe (such as an unusual executable image file path or command line). For an investigator who is familiar with Windows systems and what default or "normal" processes look like from this perspective, these indicators may be fairly obvious and jump out immediately.

TIP

Microsoft provides some information regarding default processes on Windows 2000 systems in Knowledge Base article Q263201.[2]

However, many investigators and even system administrators are not familiar enough with Windows systems to recognize default, or normal, processes at a glance. This is especially true when you consider that the Windows version (i.e., Windows 2000, XP, 2003, or Vista) has a great deal to do with what is normal. For example, default processes on Windows 2000 are different from those on Windows XP, and that is just for a clean, default installation, with no additional applications added. Also consider that different hardware configurations often require additional drivers and applications. The list of variations can go on, but the important point to keep in mind is that what constitutes a normal or legitimate process can depend on a lot of different factors, so we need to have a process for examining our available data and determining the source of the issue we're investigating. This is important, as having a process means we have steps that we follow, and if something needs to be added or modified, we can do so easily. Without a process, how do we determine what went wrong, and what we can do to improve it? If we don't know what we did, how do we fix it?

Perhaps the best way to get started is to dive right in. When correlating and analyzing volatile data, it helps to have an idea of what you're looking for. One of the biggest issues that some IT administrators and responders face when an incident occurs is tracking down the source of the incident based on the information that they have available. One example is when an alert appears in the network-based intrusion detection system (NIDS) or an odd entry appears in the firewall logs. Many times, this may be the result of malware (i.e., worm) infection. Usually, the alert or log entry will contain information such as the source IP address and port, as well as the destination IP address and port. The source IP address identifies the system from which the traffic originated, and as we saw in Chapter 1, if we have the source port of the network traffic, we can then use that information to determine the application that sent the traffic, and identify the malware.

WARNING

Keep in mind that for traffic to appear on the network, some process, somewhere, has to have generated it. However, some processes are short-lived, and attempting to locate a process based on traffic seen in firewall logs four hours ago (and not once since then) can be frustrating. If the traffic appears on a regular basis, be sure to check all possibilities.

Another important point is that malware authors often will attempt to hide the presence of their applications on a system by using a familiar name, or a name similar to a legitimate file, something that an administrator may recognize, or if the investigator searches the Web for the name, the search will return information indicating that the file is innocuous or a legitimate file used by the operating system.

WARNING

While responding to a worm outbreak on a corporate network, I determined that part of the infection was installed on the system as a Windows service that ran from an executable image file named alg.exe. Searching for information on this filename, the administrators had determined that this was a legitimate application called the Application Layer Gateway Service.[3] This service appears in the Registry under the CurrentControlSet\Services key, in the ALG subkey, and points to %SystemRoot%\system32\alg.exe as its executable image file. However, the service that I'd found was located within the Application Layer Gateway Service subkey (first hint: the subkey name is incorrect) and pointed to %SystemRoot%\alg.exe. Be very careful when searching for filenames, as even the best of us can be tripped up by the information that is returned via such a search. I've seen seasoned malware analysts make the mistake of determining the nature of a file using nothing more than the file name.

To make this all a little more clear, let's take a look at some examples.

Example Case 1

A scenario that is seen time and time again is one in which the administrator or helpdesk is informed of unusual or suspicious activity on a system. It may be unusual activity reported by a user, or a server administrator finding some unusual files on a web server and when she attempts to delete them, she's informed that they cannot be deleted as they are in use by another process.

In such incidents, the first responder will be faced with a system that cannot be taken down for a detailed post-mortem investigation (due to time and/or business constraints), and a quick (albeit thorough) response is required. Very often, this can be accomplished through live response, in which information about the current state of the system is collected and analyzed quickly, with an understanding that enough information must be collected in order to provide as complete a picture of the system state as possible. When information is collected from a live system, though the process of collecting that information can be replicated, the information itself generally cannot be duplicated, since a live system is always in a state of change.

Whenever something happens on a system, it is the result of some process that is running on that system. Although this statement may appear to be "intuitively obvious to the most casual observer" (a statement one of my graduate school professors used to offer up several times during a class, most often in the presence of a sixth-order differential equation), often this fact is missed during the stress and pressure of responding to an incident. However the simple truth is that for something to happen on a system there must be a process or thread of execution involved in some way.

TIP

In his paper, "Exploiting the Rootkit Paradox with Windows Memory Analysis," Jesse Kornblum[4.] points out that rootkits, like most malware, need to run or execute. Understanding this is the key to live response.

So how does a responder go about locating a suspicious process on a system? The answer is through live response data collection and analysis. And believe me, yes, I have been in the position where a client presents me with a hard drive from a system (or an acquired image of a hard drive) and asks me to tell him what processes were running on the system. The fact of the matter is that in order to show what was happening on a live system, you *must* have information collected from that system while it was running. Using tools discussed in Chapter 1, we can collect information about the state of the system at a point in time, capturing a snapshot of that state. As the information that we're collecting exists in volatile memory, once we shut the system down, that information no longer exists.

In this scenario, we have a Windows 2000 system that has been behaving oddly. The system is an intranet Web server running the Internet Information Server (IIS) version 5.0, and users who have attempted to access pages on the server have reported that they are unable to retrieve any information at all, and are seeing only blank pages in their browser. This is odd, as one would expect to see an error message, perhaps. So, I started up an instance of the Forensic Server (i.e., fspc.exe from Chapter 1) on my forensic workstation (IP address 192.168.1.6) using the following command line:

```
C:\fsp>fspc -c cases -n testcase1 -i "H. Carvey" -v
```

 I then picked up my First Responder CD, which contains my tools (again, from Chapter 1) and a copy of the First Responder Utility (i.e., fruc.exe), and went in search of the affected system. My initial approach in such incidents is one of a minimalist…I like to minimize my impact on the system (remember Locard's Exchange Principle) and optimize my efforts and response time. To that end, over time, I have developed a minimal set of state information that I would need to extract from a live system in order to get a comprehensive enough view to locate potentially suspicious activity. I have also identified a set of tools that I can use to extract that information (the fruc.ini file used with the First Responder Utility in this scenario is included in the ch2\samples directory on the DVD that accompanies this book). The [Commands] section of the fruc.ini file contains the following entries:

```
1=psloggedon.exe::psloggedon.dat
2=netusers.exe -l -h::netusers-lh.dat
3=tlist.exe -c::tlist-c.dat
4=tlist.exe -s::tlist-s.dat
5=tlist.exe -t::tlist-t.dat
6=handle.exe -a -u::handle-au.dat
7=listdlls.exe::listdlls.dat
8=openports.exe -fport::openports-fport.dat
9=openports.exe -netstat::openports-netstat.dat
10=autorunsc.exe -l -d -s -t -w::autorunsc-ldstw.dat
11=svc.exe::svc.dat
12=auditpol.exe::auditpol.dat
```

Each command is run in order, and from this list, we can see commands for collecting information about logged on users (both local and remote) as well as logon history, autostart locations, processes, network connections and open ports, services, and the audit policy on the system. This set of commands will not only provide a comprehensive view of the state of the system at a snapshot in time, but it also collects data that may help direct analysis and follow-on investigative efforts.

TIP

As we saw in Chapter 1, the FRUC can be run against multiple configuration (i.e., INI) files. In issues involving a potential violation of corporate acceptable use policies (employees misusing IT systems), you may want to have additional INI files that collect the contents of the clipboard, perhaps Protected Storage information and the like.

Approaching the affected Windows 2000 system, I placed the FRUC CD into the CD-ROM drive, launched a command prompt, and typed the following command:

```
E:\>fruc -s 192.168.1.6 -p 7070 -f fruc.ini -v
```

Within seconds, all the volatile data that I wanted to collect from the system was extracted and safely stored on my forensic workstation for analysis.

TIP

The data collected during this scenario can be found in the ch2\samples directory on the accompanying DVD, in the archive named testcase1.zip.

Once back at the forensic workstation, I see that as expected, the testcase1 directory contains 16 files. One of the benefits of the Forensic Server Project (FSP) is that it is self-documenting; the fruc.ini file contains the list of tools and command lines used to launch those tools when collecting volatile data. As this file and the tools themselves are on a CD, they cannot be modified, so as long as we maintain that CD, we will have immutable information about what tools (the version of each tool, etc.) we ran on the system, and the options used to run those tools. One of the files in the testcase1 directory is the case.log file, which maintains a list of the data sent to the server by the First Responder Utility (FRU) and the MD5 and SHA-1 hashes for the files to which the data was saved. Also, we see the case.hash file, which contains the MD5 and SHA-1 hashes of the case.log file after it was closed.

The information that we're interested in is contained in the other 14 files within the case directory. One of the first things I generally do to start my analysis is to see if there are any unusual processes that just jump out at me. To do that, I will most often start with the output of the `tlist -c` command, as this will show the command line used to launch each active (and visible) process on the system. For example, one of the processes that are immediately visible is the FRUC process itself:

```
1000 FRUC.EXE
     Command Line: fruc -s 192.168.1.6 -p 7070 -f fruc.ini -v
```

Scrolling through the rest of the file, I see a lot of normal processes; that is, processes that I am used to seeing running on a Windows system. I then run across the process for the IIS Web server that I know to be running on this system:

```
736 inetinfo.exe
     Command Line: C:\WINNT\system32\inetsrv\inetinfo.exe
```

Scrolling further, I run across a process that immediately jumps out at me as unusual and suspicious:

```
816 inetinfo.exe
     Command Line: inetinfo.exe  -L -d -p 80 -e c:\winnt\system32\cmd.exe
```

Most IIS web servers have only one instance of inetinfo.exe running, and this system has two. Not only that, the normal version of inetinfo.exe runs from the system32\inetsrv directory by default, just as we see with the instance of inetinfo.exe with PID 736. However, the instance of inetinfo.exe with PID 816 appears to be running from the system32 directory; not only that, the command line used to launch this process looks suspiciously like the command line used to launch netcat!

Needing more information on this, and noting that the command line for PID 816 appears to have bound the process to port 80 (which would account for the unusual behavior reported by users), I then opened the file containing the output of the ninth command run from the fruc.ini file (i.e., openports.exe –fport) to see:

```
736    inetinfo      -> 443    TCP    C:\WINNT\system32\inetsrv\inetinfo.exe
736    inetinfo      -> 21     TCP    C:\WINNT\system32\inetsrv\inetinfo.exe
736    inetinfo      -> 25     TCP    C:\WINNT\system32\inetsrv\inetinfo.exe
736    inetinfo      -> 1026   TCP    C:\WINNT\system32\inetsrv\inetinfo.exe
816    inetinfo      -> 80     TCP    C:\WINNT\system32\inetinfo.exe
```

Normally, we would expect to see PID 736 bound to port 80, but in this instance, PID 816 is bound to that port instead. The output of the openports.exe –netstat command verifies that the process is indeed listening on that port:

```
TCP    0.0.0.0:80            0.0.0.0:0            LISTENING    816
```

As you can see, we've identified PID 816 as a suspicious process, and it appears that this process would account for the unusual activity that was reported. Checking the output of the other commands, we don't see any unusual services running, or any references to the process in autostart locations. The output of the handle.exe utility shows that the process is running under the Administrator account, but there do not appear to be any files open. Also, the output of the openports.exe –netstat command shows that there are no current connections to port 80 on that system. At this point, we've identified the issue, and now need to determine how this bit of software got on the system and how it ended up running as a process.

Example Case 2

Another popular scenario seen in network environments is unusual traffic that originates from a system appearing in IDS or firewall logs. Most times, an administrator sees something unusual or suspicious, such as traffic leaving the network that is not what is normally seen. Examples of this often include IRCbot and worm infections. Generally, an IRCbot will infect a system, perhaps as the result of the user surfing to a web page that contains some code that exploits a vulnerability in the Web browser. The first thing that generally happens is that an initial downloader application is deposited on the system, which then reaches out to another Web site to download and install the actual IRCbot code itself. From there, the IRCbot accesses a channel on an IRC server and awaits commands from the botmaster.

WARNING

IRCbots have been a huge issue for quite a while, as entire armies of bots, or "botnets" have been found to be involved in a number of cybercrimes. In the 19 February 2006[5] issue of the *Washington Post Magazine*, Brian Krebs presented the story of botmaster "0x80" to the world. His story clearly showed the ease with which botnets are developed and how they can be used. Just a few months later, Robert Lemos's SecurityFocus article[6] warned us that IRCbots seem to be moving from a client-server to a peer-to-peer framework, making them much harder to shut down.

In the case of worm infections, once a worm infects a system, it will try to reach out and infect other systems. Worms generally do this by scanning IP addresses, looking for the same vulnerability (many worms today attempt to use several different vulnerabilities to infect systems) that they used to infect the current host. Some worms are pretty virulent in their scanning; the SQL Slammer[7] worm ran amok on the Internet in January 2003, generating so much traffic that servers and even ATM cash machines across the Internet were subject to massive denial of service (DoS) attacks.

The mention of DoS attacks brings another important aspect of this scenario to mind. Sometimes, IT administrators are informed by an external party that they may have infected systems. In such cases, it is usually the owner of a system that is being scanned by a worm or is under a DoS attack that will see the originating IP address of the traffic in captures of the traffic, do some research regarding the owner of that IP address (usually it's a range and not single IP address that is assigned to someone), and then attempt to contact them. That's right…even in the year 2007 it isn't at all unusual for someone to knock on your door to tell you that you have infected systems.

Regardless of how the administrator is notified, the issue of response remains the same. One of the difficulties of such issues is that armed with an IP address and a port number (both of which were taken from the headers of captured network traffic), the administrator must then determine that nature of the incident. Generally, the steps to do that are to determine the physical location of the system, and then collect and analyze information from that system.

This scenario started and progressed in much the same manner as the previous scenario, in that I launched the FSP on my forensic workstation, went to the target system with my FRUC CD, and collected volatile data from the system.

TIP

The data collected during this scenario can be found in the ch2\samples directory on the accompanying DVD, in the archive named testcase2.zip.

Once back at the forensic workstation, I opened the output of the tlist.exe –t command (which prints the Task Tree showing each process listed indented beneath its parent process); PID 980 stood out as odd to me:

```
System Process (0)
System (8)
  SMSS.EXE (140)
    CSRSS.EXE (164)
    WINLOGON.EXE (160) NetDDE Agent
      SERVICES.EXE (212)
        svchost.exe (404)
        spoolsv.exe (428)
        svchost.exe (480)
        regsvc.exe (532)
        mstask.exe (556) SYSTEM AGENT COM WINDOW
        snmp.exe (628)
        VMwareService.e (684)
        WinMgmt.exe (600)
        svchost.exe (720)
          wuauclt.exe (1080)
        inetinfo.exe (736)
        svchost.exe (1192)
      LSASS.EXE (224)
explorer.exe (520) Program Manager
  VMwareTray.exe (1232)
  VMwareUser.exe (1256)
  WZQKPICK.EXE (1268) About WinZip Quick Pick
  CMD.EXE (812) Command Prompt - svchost 192.168.1.28 80
    svchost.exe (980)
```

In order to see why this process appears odd, it is important to understand that on a default installation of Windows 2000, there are usually only two copies of svchost.exe running.

TIP

MS KB article Q250320[8.] provides a description of svchost.exe on Windows 2000 (KB Q314056[9.] provides a description of svchost.exe on Windows XP). The example output of the tlist –s command not only shows two copies of svchost.exe running, but also references the Registry key that lists the groupings illustrated in the article. Also see MS KB article Q263201[10.] for a list of default processes found on Windows 2000 systems.

The output of the tlist –t command shows an additional copy of svchost.exe, and one that appears to be running from a command prompt window, rather than from services.exe, as with the other instances of svchost.exe.

Checking the output of the tlist –c command to view the command line options used to launch PID 980, we see:

```
980 svchost.exe
    Command Line: svchost 192.168.1.28 80
```

The output of the openports.exe –fport command shows us that PID 980 is using a client port:

```
980    svchost        -> 1103  TCP  C:\WINNT\system\svchost.exe
```

The output of the openports.exe –netstat command shows us that PID 980 has an active network connection to a remote system on port 80:

```
TCP    192.168.1.22:1103    192.168.1.28:80    ESTABLISHED  980
```

At this point, based on the information we have, we may want to install a network sniffer (such as WireShark[11]) to begin capturing network traffic to see what data is being transmitted between the two systems. From the other volatile data that was collected, PID 980 does not appear to have any files open (per the output of the handle.exe tool), and there do not seem to be any additional, unusual processes.

When looking at processes on a system, it helps to know a little bit about how processes are created in relation to each other. For example, as illustrated in the output of the tlist –t command earlier (taken from a Windows 2000 system), most system processes originate from the process named System (PID 8 on Windows 2000, PID 4 on XP), and most user processes originate from Explorer.exe, which is the shell, or as listed by tlist.exe, the Program Manager. Generally (and I use this word carefully, as there may be exceptions) speaking, we see that the System process is the parent process for the Services.exe process, which in turn is the parent process for, well, many services. Services.exe is the parent process for the svchost.exe processes, for instance. On the user side, a command prompt (cmd.exe) will appear as a child process to the Explorer.exe process, and any command run from within the command prompt, such as tlist –t, will appear as a child process to cmd.exe.

So how is this important to live response? Take a look at the output from the tlist –t command again. You'll see an instance of svchost.exe (PID 980) running as a child process to cmd.exe, which is itself a child process to Explorer.exe... not at all where we would expect to see svchost.exe!

Now, let's take this a step further... what if the running svchost.exe (PID 980) had been installed as a service? Although we would not have noticed this in the output of tlist –t, we would have seen something odd in the output of tlist –c, which shows us the command line used to launch each process. The rogue svchost.exe most likely would have had to originate from within a directory other than the system32 directory, thanks to Windows File Protection (WFP). WFP is a mechanism used, starting with Windows 2000, in which certain system (and other very important) files are protected, in that attempts to modify the files will cause WFP to "wake up" and automatically replace the modified file with a fresh copy from its cache (leaving evidence of this activity in the Event Log). Windows 2000 had some issues in which WFP could easily be subverted, but those have been fixed. So, assuming that WFP hasn't been subverted in some manner, we would expect to see the rogue svchost.exe running from another directory, perhaps Windows\System or Temp, alerting us to the culprit.

Agile Analysis

One of the perhaps most often stated reasons for not performing live response at all is an inability to locate the source of the issue in the plethora of data that has been collected. Many of the tools available for collecting volatile (and nonvolatile) data during live response collect a great deal of data, so much so that it may appear to be overwhelming to the investigator. In the example cases that we've looked at, we haven't had to collect a great deal of data in order to pin down the source of the issue. The data collection tools we used in the example cases take two simple facts into account; that malware needs to run to have any effect on a system, and that malware needs to be persistent in order to have any continuing effect on a system (i.e., malware authors ideally want their software to survive reboots and users logging in). We also use these basic precepts in our analysis in order to cull through the available data and locate the source of the issues. In order to perform rapid, agile analysis, we need to look to automation and data reduction techniques.

Although the example cases have been simple and straightforward, they do serve to illustrate a point. The methodology used to locate the suspicious process in each case is not too different from the methodology used to investigate the russiantopz[12.] bot in 2002. In fact, it's akin to differential analysis (i.e., looking for the differences between two states). However, a big caveat to keep in mind, particularly if you're performing live response as a law enforcement officer or a consultant, is that in most cases, an original baseline of the system from prior to the incident will not be available, and the investigator must rely on an understanding of the workings of the underlying operating system and applications for the baseline. For example, in the first example case, had there been only one instance of inetinfo.exe in the process information, and had the investigator not known whether the infected system was running a web server, she could have correlated what she knew (i.e., inetinfo.exe process running) to the output of the svc.exe tool, which in this instance, appears as follows:

```
736,W3SVC,World Wide Web Publishing Service
,C:\WINNT\system32\inetsrv\inetinfo.exe,Running,Auto,Share Process,#
```

This correlation could be automated through the use of scripting tools, and if a legitimate service (such as shown earlier) is found to correlate to a legitimate process (inetinfo.exe with PID 736), then we've just performed data reduction.

NOTE

The svc.exe tool used in the example cases collects information about services on the system, and displays the results in comma-separated value (.csv) format, so that the results can be easily parsed, or opened in Excel for analysis. The column headers are PID, service name, service display name, the path to the executable image, the service state, the service start mode, the service type, and whether (#) or not (*) the service has a description string. Many times malware authors will fail to provide a description string for their service; a lack of this string would be cause to investigate the service further.

A rule of thumb that a knowledgeable investigator should keep in mind while analyzing volatile data is that the existence of an inetinfo.exe process without the corresponding presence of a running W3SVC World Wide Web Publishing service may indicate the presence of malware, or at least of a process that merits additional attention.

However, the investigator must keep in mind that the inetinfo.exe process also supports the MS FTP service and the SMTP e-mail server, as illustrated in the output of the tlist –s command:

```
736 inetinfo.exe    Svcs:  IISADMIN,MSFTPSVC,SMTPSVC,W3SVC
```

Simply put, a running inetinfo.exe process without the corresponding services also running could point to an issue. Again, this check can also be automated. For example, if the output of the FRUC tools were parsed and entered into a database, then SQL statements could be used to extract and correlate information.

TIP

During his presentation at the BlackHat DC 2007 conference, Kevin Mandia stated that a good number of the incidents that his company had responded to over the previous year had illustrated a move by malware authors to maintain persistence in their software by having it install itself as a Windows service. My own experience has shown this to be the case as well.

What this shows is that with some knowledge and work, issues can be addressed in a quick and thorough manner, through the use of automation and data reduction. Automation is important, as incidents are generally characterized by stress and pressure, which just happen to be the conditions under which we're most likely to make mistakes. Automation allows us to codify a process and be able to follow that same process over and over again. If we understand the artifacts and bits of volatile data that will provide use with a fairly complete picture of the state of the system, we can quickly collect and correlate the information, and determine the nature and scope of the incident. This leads to a more agile response, moving quickly, albeit in a thorough manner using a documented process. From here, additional volatile data can be collected, if necessary. Using this minimalist approach up front reduces the amount of data that needs to parsed and correlated, and leads to an overall better response.

With respect to analysis and automation, the rules of thumb used by an investigator to locate suspicious processes within the collected volatile data are based largely on experience and an understanding of the underlying operating system and applications.

TIP

Several years ago, a friend of mine would send me volatile data that he'd collected during various incidents. He used a series of tools and a batch file to collect his volatile data, and long after the case had been completed would send me the raw data files, asking to find out what was wrong. With no access to the state and nature of the original system, I had to look for clues in the data he sent me. This is a great way to develop skills and even some of the necessary correlation tools.

Some of these rules can be codified into procedures and even scripts in order to make the analysis and data reduction process more efficient. One example of this is the svchost.exe process. Some malware authors make use of the fact that there are usually several copies of svchost.exe running on Windows systems (my experience shows two copies running on Windows 2000, five on Windows XP SP2, and seven on Windows 2003) and use that name for their malware (see Symantec's description of the Ranky[13.] backdoor as an example). We know that the legitimate svchost.exe process follows a couple of simple rules, one of which is that the process always originates from an executable image located in the system32 directory. Therefore, we can write a Perl script that will run through the output of the tlist −c command and immediately flag on any copies of an svchost.exe process that is *not* running from the system32 directory.

This is a variation on the *artificial ignorance* (a term coined by Marcus Ranum[14.]) method of analysis in which you perform data reduction by removing everything you know to be good, and what's left is most likely the stuff you need to look at. I've used this approach quite effectively in a corporate environment, not only during incident response activities, but also while performing scans of the network for spyware and other issues. What I did was create a Perl script that would reach out to the primary domain controller and get a list of all the workstations that it "saw" on the network. Then, I'd connect to each one of the workstations using domain administrator credentials, extract the contents of the Run key (see Chapter 4 for more information on this Registry key) from each system, and save that information in a file on my system. The first time I ran this script, I had quite a few pages of data to sort through. So I began investigating some of the things I found, and found out that many of them were legitimate applications and drivers. So I created a list of "known good" entries and then when I scanned systems, I would check the information I retrieved against this list, and write the information to my log file only if it *wasn't* on the list. In fairly short order, I reduced my log file to about half a page.

This is one approach you can use in order quickly analyze the volatile data you've collected. However, the key to agile analysis and a rapid response is to reduce the amount of data that you actually need to investigate. This may mean putting the data that you have collected into a more manageable form, or it may mean weeding out those artifacts that you know to be "good," thereby reducing the amount of data that you need to actually investigate.

Expanding the Scope

What happens when things get a little more complicated than the scenarios we've already looked at? We see security experts in the media all the time, saying that cybercrime is becoming more sophisticated all the time (and it is). So how do we deal with more complicated incidents? After all, not all processes involved in an incident may be as long-lived as the ones illustrated in our example scenarios. For example, a downloader may be on a system through a Web browser vulnerability, and once it has downloaded its designated target software, it has completed its purpose and is no longer active. So information about that process, to include network connections used by the process, will no longer be available.

Not too long ago, I dealt with an incident involving an encrypted executable that was not identified by over two dozen antivirus scanning engines. We also had considerable trouble addressing the issue, as there was no running process with the same name as the mysterious file on any of the affected systems that we looked at. Dynamic analysis (see Chapter 6 for information on dynamic analysis) of the malware showed that the malware injected itself into the Internet Explorer process space and terminated. This bit of information accounted for the fact that we were not able to find a running process using the same name as the mysterious file, and that all of our investigative efforts were leading us back to the Internet Explorer (iexplore.exe) as the culprit. We confirmed our findings by including the fact that on all the systems we'd collected volatile data from, not one had Internet Explorer running on the desktop. So here was the iexplore.exe process, live and running, spewing traffic out onto the network and to the Internet, but there was no browser window open on the desktop.

The interesting thing about this particular engagement wasn't so much the code injection technique used, or the fact that the mysterious executable file we'd found appeared to be unidentifiable by multiple antivirus engines. Rather, I thought that the most interesting aspect of all this was that the issue was surprisingly close to a proof of concept worm called Setiri that was presented by a couple of SensePost[15.] researchers at the BlackHat conference in Las Vegas in 2002. Setiri operated by accessing Internet Explorer as a COM server, and generating traffic through IE. Interestingly enough, Dave Roth wrote a Perl script[16.] called IEEvents.pl that, with some minor modifications, will launch IE invisibly (i.e., no visible window on the desktop) and retrieve Web pages, and so on.

What's the point of all this? Well, I just wanted to point out how sophisticated some incidents can be. Getting a backdoor on a system through a downloader, which itself is first dropped on a system via Web browser vulnerability, isn't particularly sophisticated (although it is just as effective) in the face of having code injected into a process's memory space. Another technique used by malware authors to get their code running (and to keep it running) can be found in spyware circles, such as browser helper objects (more information on BHOs can be found in Chapter 4). For example two BHOs found on a system are the Adobe PDF Reader Link Helper and the DriveLetterAccess helper objects. These can be found in the Internet Explorer process space by using listdlls.exe:

```
C:\Program Files\Adobe\Acrobat 7.0\Activ eX\AcroIEHelper.dll
C:\WINDOWS\System32\DLA\DLASHX_W.DLL
```

If someone compromises a Windows system from the network, you may expect to find artifacts of a login (in the Security Event Log, or in an update of the last login time for that user), open files on the system, and even processes that have been launched by that user. If the attacker is not using the Microsoft login mechanisms (Remote Desktop, "net use" command, etc.), and is instead accessing the system via a backdoor, you can expect to see the running process, open handles, network connections, and the like.

With some understanding of the nature of the incident, live response activities can effectively be targeted to addressing the issue, not only from a data collection perspective, but also from a data correlation and analysis perspective.

Reaction

Many times, the question that comes up immediately following the confirmation of an incident is, what do we do now? I hate to say it, but that really depends on your infrastructure. For example, in our example cases, we saw incidents in which the offending process was running under the Administrator account. Now, this was a result of the set up for the case, but it is not unusual when responding to an incident to find a process running within the Administrator or even the System user context. Much of the prevailing wisdom in cases such as this is that you can no longer trust anything that the system is telling you (i.e., you cannot trust that the output of the tools you're using to collect information are giving you an accurate view of the system) and that the only acceptable reaction is to wipe the system clean and start over, reinstalling the operating system from clean media (i.e., the original installation media) and reloading all data from backups.

To me, this seems like an awful lot of trouble to go through, particularly when it's likely that you're going to have to do it all over again fairly soon. You're probably thinking to yourself, what?? Well, let's say that you locate a suspicious process and using tools such as pslist.exe, you see that process hasn't been running for very long in relation to the overall uptime of the system itself. This tells us that the process started sometime after that system was booted. For example, as I'm sitting here right now, writing this chapter, my system has been running for over eight hours. I can see this in the Elapsed Time column, on the far right in the output of pslist.exe, as illustrated here:

| smss | 1024 | 11 | 3 | 21 | 168 | 0:00:00.062 | 8:28:38.109 |
| csrss | 1072 | 13 | 13 | 555 | 1776 | 0:00:26.203 | 8:28:36.546 |

However, I have other processes that were started well after the system was booted:

| uedit32 | 940 | 8 | 1 | 88 | 4888 | 0:00:03.703 | 4:07:25.296 |
| cmd | 3232 | 8 | 1 | 32 | 2008 | 0:00:00.046 | 3:26:46.640 |

Although the MAC times on files written to the hard drive can be modified to mislead an investigator, the amount of time that a process has been running is harder to fake. With this information, the investigator can develop a timeline of when the incident may have occurred, and determine the overall extent of the incident (similar to the approach used in the earlier example cases). The goal is to determine the root cause of the incident, so that whatever issue led to the compromise can be rectified, and subsequently corrected on other systems as well. If this is not done, then putting a cleanly loaded system back on the network will very likely result in the system being compromised all over again. If systems need to be patched, then patches can be rolled out. However, if the root cause of the incident is really a weak Administrator password, then no amount of patching will correct that issue. The same is true with application configuration vulnerabilities, such as those exploited by network worms.

Now, let's consider another case, in which the suspicious process is found to be a service, and the output of pslist.exe shows us that the process has been running for about the same about of time as the system itself. Well, as there do not appear to be any Windows APIs that allow an attacker to modify the LastWrite times on Registry keys (MAC times on files can easily be modified through the use of publicly documented APIs), an investigator can extract that information from a live system and determine when the service was installed on the system. A knowledgeable investigator knows that to install a Windows service, the user context must be that of an Administrator, so checking user logins and user activity on the system may lead to the root cause of the incident.

Again, it is important to determine the root cause of an incident so that situation can be fixed, not only on the compromised system, but on other systems as well.

WARNING

MS KB article Q328691,[17.] *MIRC Trojan-related Attack Detection and Repair*, contains this statement in the Attack Vectors section: "Analysis to date indicates that the attackers appear to have gained entry to the systems by using weak or blank administrator passwords.

> Microsoft has no evidence to suggest that any heretofore unknown security vulnerabilities have been used in the attacks." Simply reinstalling the operating system, applications, and data on affected systems would lead to their compromise all over again, as long as the same configuration settings were used. In corporate environments, communal Administrator accounts with easy-to-remember (i.e., weak) passwords are used, and a reinstalled system would most likely use the same account name and password as it did prior to the incident.

Determining that root cause may seem like an impossible task, but with the right knowledge and right skill sets, and a copy of this book in your hand, that job should be much easier!

Prevention

One thing that IT departments can do to make the job of responding to incidents easier (keeping in mind that first responders are usually members of the IT staff) is to go beyond simply installing the operating system and applications, and make use of system hardening guides and configuration management procedures. For example, by limiting the running services and processes on a server to only those that are necessary for the operation of the system itself, you limit the attack surface of the system. Then, for those services that you do run, configure them as securely as possible. If you have an IIS Web server running, that system may be a Web server, but is it also an FTP server? If you don't need the FTP server running, disable it, remove it, or don't even install it in the first place. Then, configure your Web server to use only the necessary script mappings[18.] (IIS Web servers with the .ida script mapping removed were not susceptible to the Code Red[19.] worm in 2001), and you may even want to install the URLScan tool.[20.]

This same sort of minimalist approach applies to setting up users on a system as well. Only the necessary users should have the appropriate level of access to a system. If a user does not need access to a system, either to log in from the console or to access the system remotely from the network, then they should not have an account on that system. I have responded to several instances in which old user accounts with weak passwords were left on systems and intruders were able to gain access to the system through those accounts. In another instance, a compromised system showed logins via a user's account during times that it was known that the person who was assigned that account was on an airplane 33,000 feet over the midwestern United States. However, that user rarely used his account to access the systems in question, and the account was left unattended.

By reducing the attack surface of a system, you can make it difficult (maybe even *really* difficult) for someone to gain access to that system, to either compromise data on the system, or use that system as a stepping stone from which to launch further attacks. The attacker may then either generate a great deal of noise on a system, in the form of log entries and error messages, making the attempts more visible to administrators, or simply give up because compromising the system wasn't an easy win. Either way, I'd personally rather deal with a couple of MB of log files showing failed attempts (as when the Nimda[21] worm was prevalent) than a system that was compromised repeatedly due to a lack of any sort of hardening or monitoring. At least if some steps have been taken to limit the attack surface and level to which the system can be compromised, then an investigator will have more data to work with, in log files and such.

Summary

Once you've collected volatile data during live response, the next step is to analyze that data and provide an effective and timely response. Many times, investigators may be overwhelmed with the sheer volume of volatile data that they need to go through, and this can be more overwhelming if they're unsure what it is they're looking for. Starting with some idea of the nature of the incident, the investigator can then begin to reduce the amount of data by looking for and parsing out "known good" processes, network connections, active users, and so on. She can also automate some of the data correlation, further reducing the overall amount of data, and reducing the number of mistakes that may be made.

All these things will lead to timely, accurate, and effective response to incidents.

Notes

1. For more information go to www.e-evidence.info.
2. For more information go to http://support.microsoft.com/?kbid=263201.
3. For more information go to www.microsoft.com/technet/prodtechnol/windowsserver2003/technologies/management/svrxpser_7.mspx#E5C.
4. For more information go to http://en.wikipedia.org/wiki/Jesse_Kornblum.
5. For more information go to www.washingtonpost.com/wp-dyn/content/article/2006/02/14/AR2006021401342.html.
6. For more information go to www.securityfocus.com/news/11390.
7. For more information go to www.cert.org/advisories/CA-2003-04.html.
8. For more information go to support.microsoft.com/?kbid=250320.
9. For more information go to http://support.microsoft.com/kb/314056/EN-US/.
10. For more information go to http://support.microsoft.com/?kbid=263201.
11. For more information go to http://www.wireshark.org/.
12. For more information go to www.securityfocus.com/infocus/1618.
13. For more information go to www.symantec.com/security_response/writeup.jsp?docid=2006-081415-2212-99&tabid=2.
14. For more information go to www.ranum.com/.
15. For more information go to www.sensepost.com/research_conferences.html.
16. For more information go to www.roth.net/perl/scripts/.
17. For more information go to http://support.microsoft.com/default.aspx?scid=kb;en-us;328691.
18. For more information go to www.microsoft.com/technet/prodtechnol/acs/proddocs/accrsc_iisscr.mspx?mfr=true.

19. For more information go to www.cert.org/advisories/CA-2001-19.html.
20. For more information go to
www.microsoft.com/technet/security/tools/urlscan.mspx.
21. For more information go to www.cert.org/advisories/CA-2001-26.html.

Solutions Fast Track

Data Analysis

☑ Live response generally is characterized by stress, pressure, and confusion. Data reduction and automation techniques can be used by the investigator to provide effective response.

☑ Once data has been collected and analyzed, the final response to the incident can be based upon nontechnical factors, such as the business or political infrastructure of the environment, and so on.

☑ Performing a root cause analysis when faced with an incident can go a long way toward saving both time and money further down the road.

☑ Taking a minimalist approach to system configuration often can serve to hamper or even inhibit an incident altogether. At the very least, making a system more difficult to compromise will serve to generate noise and possibly even alerts during the attempts.

Frequently Asked Questions

The following Frequently Asked Questions, answered by the authors of this book, are designed to both measure your understanding of the concepts presented in this chapter and to assist you with real-life implementation of these concepts. To have your questions about this chapter answered by the author, browse to www.syngress.com/solutions and click on the "Ask the Author" form.

Q: What is the difference between a process and a service?

A: From the perspective of live response, there isn't a great deal of difference between the two, except in how each is started or launched, and the user context under which each runs. Windows services are actually processes, and can be started automatically when the system starts. When a process is started as a service, it most often runs with System-level privileges, whereas processes started automatically via a user's Registry hive will run in that user's context.

Q: I'm seeing some intermittent and unusual traffic in my firewall logs. The traffic seems to be originating from a system on my network and going out to an unusual system. When I see the traffic, I go to the system and collect volatile data, but I don't see any active network connections, or any active processes using the source port I found in the traffic. I see the traffic again six hours later. What can I do?

A: In the fruc.ini file used in the example cases in this chapter, we used autorunsc.exe from MS/SysInternals to collection information about autostart locations. Be sure to check for scheduled tasks, as well as any unusual processes that may be launching a child process to generate the traffic.

Q: I have an incident that I'm trying to investigate, but I can't seem to find any indication of the incident on the system.

A: Many times, what appears to be unusual or suspicious behavior on a Windows system is borne from a lack of familiarity with the system rather than an actual incident. I have seen responders question the existence of certain files and directories (Prefetch, etc.) for no other reason than the fact that they aren't familiar with the system. In fact, I remember one case where an administrator deleted all the files with .pf extensions that he found in the C:\Windows\Prefetch directory (see Chapter 5). A couple of days later, many of those files had mysteriously returned, and he felt that the system had been compromised by a Trojan or backdoor.

Chapter 3

Windows Memory Analysis

Solutions in this chapter:

- **Dumping Physical Memory**
- **Analyzing a Physical Memory Dump**
- **Collecting Process Memory**

☑ **Summary**

☑ **Solutions Fast Track**

☑ **Frequently Asked Questions**

Introduction

In Chapter 1, "Live Response: Collecting Volatile Data," we discussed collecting volatile data from a live, running Windows system. From the Order of Volatility listed in RFC 3227, we saw that the first item of volatile data that should be collected during live-response activities is the contents of physical memory, commonly referred to as RAM. Although the specifics of collecting particular parts of volatile memory, such as network connections or running processes, has been known for some time and discussed pretty extensively, the issue of collecting, parsing, and analyzing the entire contents of physical memory is a relatively new endeavor. This field of research has really opened up in the past year or two, beginning in the summer of 2005, at least from a public perspective.

The most important question that needs to be answered at this point is, "Why?" Why would you want to collect the contents of RAM? How is doing this useful, how is it important, and what would you miss if you didn't? Until now, some investigators have collected the contents of RAM in hope of finding something that they wouldn't find on the hard drive during a post-mortem analysis—specifically, passwords. Programs will prompt the user for a password, and if the dialog box has disappeared from view, the most likely place to find that password is in memory. Malware analysts will look to memory in dealing with encrypted or obfuscated malware, because when the malware is launched, it will be decrypted in memory. More and more, malware is obfuscated in such a way that static, offline analysis is extremely difficult at best. However, if the malware were allowed to execute, it would exist in memory in a decrypted state, making it easier to analyze what the malware does. Finally, rootkits will hide processes, files, Registry keys, and even network connections from view by the tools we usually use to enumerate these items, but by analyzing the contents of RAM we can find what's been hidden. We can also find information about processes that have since exited.

As this area of analysis grows and more investigators pursue RAM as a viable source of valuable information and evidence, it will become easier to extract information from RAM and correlate that to what is found during the post-mortem forensic analysis.

A Brief History

In the past, the "analysis" of physical memory dumps has consisted of running strings or *grep* against the "image" file, looking for passwords, IP addresses, e-mail addresses, or other strings that could give the analyst an investigative lead. The drawback method of "analysis" is that it is difficult to tie the information you find to a distinct process. Was the IP address that was discovered part of the case, or was it actually used by some other process? How about that word that looks like a password? Is it the password that an attacker uses to access a Trojan on the system, or is it part of an instant messaging (IM) conversation?

Being able to perform some kind of analysis of a dump of physical memory has been high on the wish lists of many within the forensic community for some time. Others (such as myself) have recognized the need for easily accessible tools and frameworks for retrieving physical memory dumps and analyzing their contents.

In the summer of 2005, the Digital Forensic Research Workshop (DFRWS)[1] issued a "memory analysis challenge" "to motivate discourse, research, and tool development" in this area. Anyone was invited to download the two files containing dumps of physical memory (the dumps were obtained using a modified copy of dd.exe available on the Helix[2] 1.6 distribution) and answer questions based on the scenario provided at the Web site. Chris Betz and the duo of George M. Garner, Jr., and Robert-Jan Mora were selected as the joint winners of the challenge, providing excellent write-ups illustrating their methodologies and displaying the results of the tools they developed. Unfortunately, these tools were not made publicly available.

In the year following the challenge, others continued this research or conducted their own, following their own avenues. Andreas Schuster[3] began releasing portions of his research on the English version of his blog, together with the format of the EPROCESS and ETHREAD structures from various versions of Windows, including Windows 2000 and XP. Joe Stewart posted a Perl script called pmodump.pl as part of the TRUMAN Project,[4] which allows you to extract the memory used by a process from a dump of memory (important for malware analysis). Mariusz Burdach has released information regarding memory analysis (initially for Linux systems but then later specifically for Windows systems) to include a presentation at the BlackHat Federal 2006 conference.[5] Jesse Kornblum has offered several insights in the area of memory analysis to include determining the original operating system from the contents of the memory dump. During the summer of 2006, Tim Vidas,[6] a Senior Research Fellow at Nebraska University, released procloc.pl, a Perl script to locate processes in RAM dumps as well as crash dumps.

Dumping Physical Memory

So, how do you go about collecting the contents of physical memory? Several ways have been identified, each with its own strengths and weaknesses. The goal of this chapter is to provide an understanding of the various options available as well as the technical aspects associated with each option. This way, as a first responder or investigator, you'll make educated choices regarding which option is most suitable, taking the business needs of the client (or victim) into account along with infrastructure concerns.

Hardware Devices

In February 2004, the *Digital Investigation Journal* published a paper by Brian Carrier and Joe Grand, of Grand Idea Studio, Inc.,[7] titled, "A Hardware-Based Memory Acquisition Procedure for Digital Investigations." In the paper, Brian and Joe presented the concept for a hardware expansion card dubbed Tribble (possibly a reference to that memorable *Star Trek* episode) that could be used to retrieve the contents of physical memory to an external storage device. This would allow an investigator to retrieve the volatile memory from the system without introducing any new code nor relying on potentially untrusted code to perform the extraction. In the paper, the authors stated that they had built a proof-of-concept Tribble device, designed as a PCI expansion card that could be plugged into a PC bus. Other hardware devices are available that allow you to capture the contents of physical memory and are largely intended for debugging hardware systems. These devices may also be used for forensics.

As illustrated in the DFRWS 2005 Memory Challenge, one of the limitations of a software-based approach to retrieving volatile memory is that the program the investigator is using has to be loaded into memory. Subsequently, particularly on Windows systems, the program may (depending on its design) rely on untrusted code or libraries (DLLs) that have been subverted by the attacker. Let's examine the pros and cons of such a device:

- **Pros** Hardware devices such as the Tribble are unobtrusive and easily accessible. Dumping the contents of physical memory in this manner introduces no new or additional software to the system, minimizing the chances of data being obscured in some manner.

- **Cons** The primary limitation of using the hardware-based approach is that the hardware needs to be installed prior to the incident. At this point the Tribble devices are not widely available. Other hardware devices *are* available and intended for hardware debugging, but they must still be installed prior to an incident to be of use.

FireWire

Due to technical specifics of FireWire devices and protocols, there is a possibility that with the right software, an investigator can collect the contents of physical memory from a system. FireWire devices use direct memory access (DMA), meaning that they can access system memory without having to go through the CPU. These devices can read from and/or write to memory at much faster rates than systems that do not use DMA. The investigator would need a controller device that contains the appropriate software and is capable of writing a command into a specific area of the FireWire device's memory space. Memory mapping is performed in hardware without going through the host operating system, allowing for high-speed, low-latency data transfers.

Adam Boileau[8.] came up with a way to extract physical memory from a system using Linux and Python.[9.] The software used for this collection method runs on Linux and relies on support for the /dev/raw1394 device as well as Adam's pythonraw1394 library, the libraw1394 library, and Swig (software that makes C/C++ header files accessible to other languages by generating wrapper code). In his demonstrations, Adam even included the use of a tool that will collect the contents of RAM from a Windows system with the screen locked, then parse out the password, after which Adam logs into the system.

Jon Evans, an officer with the Gwent police department in the United Kingdom, has installed Adam's tools and successfully collected the contents of physical memory from Windows systems as well as from various versions of Linux. As part of his master's thesis, Jon wrote an overview on how to install, set up, and use Adam's tools on several different Linux platforms, including Knoppix v.5.01, Gentoo Linux 2.6.17, and BackTrack, from remote-exploit.org. Once all the necessary packages (including Adam's tools) have been downloaded and installed, Jon then walks through the process of identifying FireWire ports and then tricking the target Windows system into "thinking" that the Linux system is an iPod by using the Linux *romtool* command to load a data file containing the Control Status Register (CSR) for an iPod (the CSR file is provided with Adam's tools). Here are the pros and cons of this approach:

- **Pros** Many systems available today have FireWire /IEEE 1394 interfaces built right into the motherboards. Also, code has been released for directly accessing physical memory on Linux and Mac OS systems.

- **Cons** Arne Vidstrom has pointed out some technical issues[10.] regarding the way dumping the contents of physical memory over FireWire can result in a hang or in parts of memory being missed. George M. Garner, Jr., noted in an e-mail exchange on a mailing list in October 2006 that in limited testing, there were notable differences in important offsets between a RAM dump collected using the FireWire technique and one collected using George's own software. This difference could only be explained as an error in the collection method. Furthermore, this method has caused Blue Screens of Death (BSoDs, discussed further in a moment) on some target Windows systems, possibly due to the nature of the FireWire hardware on the system.

Crash Dumps

At one point, we've all seen crash dumps; in most cases they manifest themselves as an infamous Blue Screen of Death[11.] (BSoD). In most cases they're an annoyance, if not indicative of a much larger issue. However, if you want to obtain a pristine, untainted copy of the content of RAM from a Windows system, perhaps the only way to do that is to generate a full crash dump. The reason for this is that when a crash dump occurs, the system state is frozen and the contents of RAM (along with about 4Kb of header information) are written to the disk. This preserves the state of the system and ensures that no alterations are made to the system, beginning at the time the crash dump was initiated.

This information can be extremely valuable to an investigator. First of all, the contents of the crash dump are a snapshot of the system, frozen in time. I have been involved in several investigations during which crash dumps have been found and used to determine root causes, such as avenues of infection or compromise. Second, Microsoft provides tools for analyzing crash dumps—not only in the debugging tools[12.] but also the Kernel Memory Space Analyzer[13.] tools, which are based on the debugging tools.

Sounds like a good deal, doesn't it? After all, other than having a 1GB file written to the hard drive, possibly overwriting evidence (and not really minimizing the impact of our investigation on the system), it is a good deal, right? Under some circumstances, it could be … or you might be willing to accept that condition, depending on the circumstances. However, there are still a couple of stumbling blocks. First, not all systems generate full crash dumps by default. Second, by default, Windows systems do not generate crash dumps on command.

The first issue is relatively simple to deal with, according to MS KnowledgeBase (KB) article Q254649.[14.] This KB article lists the three types of crash dump: small (64KB), kernel, and complete crash dumps. What we're looking for is the complete crash dump because it contains the complete contents of RAM. The KB article also states that Windows 2000 Pro and Windows XP (both Pro and Home) will generate small crash dumps, and Windows 2003 (all versions) will generate full crash dumps. My experience with Windows Vista RC1 is that it will generate small crash dumps, by default.

Along the same lines, MS KB article Q274598[15.] states that complete crash dumps are not available on systems with more than 2GB of RAM. According to the article, this is largely due to the space requirements (i.e., for systems with complete crash dumps enabled, the page file must be as large as the contents of RAM + 1MB) as well as the time it will take to complete the crash dump process.

MS KB article Q307973[16.] describes how to set the full range of system failure and recovery options. These settings are more for system administrators and IT managers who are setting up and configuring systems before an incident occurs, but the Registry key settings can provide some significant clues for an investigator. For example, if the system was configured (by default or otherwise) to generate a complete crash dump and the administrator reported seeing the BSoD, the investigator should expect to see a complete crash dump file on the system.

NOTE

Investigators must be extremely careful when working with crash dump files, particularly from systems that process but do not necessarily store sensitive data. In some cases crash dumps have occurred on systems that processed information such as credit card number, individual's Social Security number, or the like, and the crash dumps have been found to contain that information. Even though the programmers specifically wrote the application so that no sensitive personal information was saved locally on the system, a crash dump wrote the contents of memory to the hard drive.

So, let's say that our system failure and recovery configuration options are set ahead of time (as part of the configuration policies for the systems) to perform a full crash dump. How does the investigator "encourage" a system to perform a crash dump on command, when it's needed? It turns out that there's a Registry key (see KB article Q244139[17.]) that can be set to cause a crash dump when the right Ctrl key is held down and the Scroll Lock key is pressed *twice*. However, once this key is set, the system must be rebooted for the setting to take effect. Let's look at the pros and cons of this technique:

- **Pros** Dumping memory via a crash dump is perhaps the only technically accurate method for creating an image of the contents of RAM. This is due to the fact that when the *KeBugCheck* API function is called, the entire system is halted and the contents of RAM are written to the page file, after which they are written to a file on the system hard drive. Further, Microsoft provides debugging tools as well as the Kernel Memory Space Analyzer[18.] (which consists of an engine, plugins, and UI) for analyzing crash dump files.

- **Cons** Some Windows systems do not generate full crash dumps by default (Vista RC1, for example; I had an issue with a driver when I first installed Vista RC1 and I would get BSoDs whenever I attempted to shut down the machine, which resulted in minidump files). In addition, modifying a system to accept the keystroke sequence to create a crash dump requires a reboot and must be done ahead of time to be used effectively for incident response. Even if this configuration change has been made, the crash dump process will still create a file equal in size to physical memory on the hard drive. To do so, as stated in KB article Q274598, the page file must be configured to be equal to at least the size of physical memory plus 1 MB. This is an additional step that must be corrected to use this method of capturing the contents of physical memory; it's one that is not often followed.

TIP

A support article[19.] located at the Citrix Web site provides a methodology for using LiveKD.exe[20.] and the Microsoft Debugging Tools to generate a full kernel dump of physical memory. Once LiveKD.exe is launched, the command *.dump /f <filepath>* is used to generate the dump file. The support article does include the caveat that RAM dumps generated in this manner can be inconsistent due to the fact that the dump can take a considerable amount of time and that the system is live and continues to run during the memory dump.

Virtualization

VMware is a popular virtualization product (VMware Workstation 5.5.2 was used extensively in this book) that, for one thing, allows the creation of pseudo-networks utilizing the hardware of a single system. This capability has many benefits. For example, you can set up a guest operating system and create a snapshot of that system once you have it configured to your needs. From there, you can perform all manner of testing, including installing and monitoring malware, and you will always be able to revert to the snapshot, beginning anew. I have even seen active production systems run from VMware sessions.

When you're running a VMware session, you can suspend that session, freezing it temporarily. Figure 3.1 illustrates the menu items for suspending a VMware session.

Figure 3.1 Menu Items for Suspending a Session in VMware Workstation 5.5.2

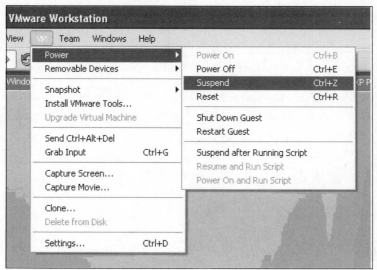

When a VMware session is suspended, the contents of "physical memory" are contained in a file with the .vmem extension. The format of this file is very similar to that of a memory dump using dd.exe, another tool we'll talk about shortly.

VMware isn't the only virtualization product available. Others include VirtualPC from Microsoft as well as the freeware Bochs.[21] These virtualization products are also mentioned in Chapter 6, "Executable File Analysis." However, none of these virtualization products has been tested to see whether it can generate dumps of physical memory. Let's look at the pros and cons:

- **Pros** If this is an option available to you, suspending a VMware session is quick, easy, and minimizes the investigator's interaction with and impact on the system.

- **Cons** VMware or other virtualization technologies do not seem to be widely used in systems that require the attention of a first responder.

Hibernation File

When a Windows (Windows 2000 or later) system "hibernates," the Power Manager saves the compressed contents of physical memory to a file called Hiberfil.sys in the root directory of the system volume. This file is large enough to hold the uncompressed contents of physical memory, but compression is used to minimize disk I/O and to improve resume-from-hibernation performance. During the boot process, if a valid Hiberfil.sys file is located, the NTLDR will load the file's contents into physical memory and transfer control to code within the kernel that handles resuming system operation after a hibernation (loading drivers and so on). This functionality is most often found on laptop systems. Here are the pros and cons:

- **Pros** Analyzing the contents of a hibernation file could give you a clue as to what was happening on the system at some point in the past.
- **Cons** The hibernation file is compressed and in most cases will not contain the current contents of memory. (The hibernation file might be significantly out of date.)

DD

DD is the short name given to the "data dumper" tool from UNIX, which has a variety of uses, not the least of which is to copy files or even entire hard drives. DD has long been considered a standard for producing forensic images, and most major forensic imaging/acquisition tools as well as analysis tools support the dd format. GMG Systems Inc. produced a modified version of dd that runs on Windows systems and can be used to dump the contents of physical memory from Windows 2000 and XP systems. This version of dd is part of the Forensic Acquisition Utilities,[22.] which are available for free download. This utility is able to collect the contents of physical memory by accessing the \Device\PhysicalMemory object from user mode. The following command line can be used to capture the contents of RAM in the file ram.img on the local system:

```
D:\tools>dd if=\\.\PhysicalMemory of=ram.img bs=4096 conv=noerror
```

Of course, you can write the output file to a thumb drive or to a shared folder that is already available on the system. This version of dd.exe also allows compression and the generation of cryptographic hashes for the content. Because of the volatile nature of RAM, however, it is not advisable to hash it until it is written from the disk. If the user images memory twice, even with little delay, the contents of RAM and thus the subsequent hashes will be different. In this case it is only worthwhile to worry about the integrity of the image after it has been collected.

Other tools use a process similar to dd.exe to capture the contents of RAM. ProDiscover IR (version 4.8 was used in writing this book) allows the investigator to collect the contents of physical memory (as well as system BIOS) via a remote server applet that can be distributed to a system via removable storage media (CD, thumb drive, etc.) or via the network. The UI for this capability is illustrated in Figure 3.2.

Figure 3.2 Excerpt of Capture Image Dialog Box from ProDiscover IR

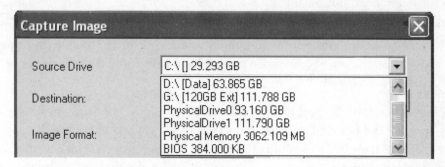

One of the problems with this technique, however, is that as of Windows 2003 SP1, access to the \Device\PhysicalMemory object has been restricted from user mode. That is, only kernel drivers are allowed to use this object. To address this issue, GMG Systems produced a new utility called KntDD, which is part of the KnTTools set of utilities. According to the licensing for KnTTools, the utilities are available for private sale to law enforcement personnel and bona fide security professionals. KntDD includes the following capabilities:

- Able to acquire the contents of physical memory using multiple methods, including via the \Device\PhysicalMemory object.

- Runs on Microsoft operating systems from Windows 2000 through Vista, to include AMD64 versions of the operating systems

- Able to convert raw memory "image" to Microsoft crash dump format so that the resulting data can be analyzed using the Microsoft Debugging Tools

- Able to acquire to a local removable (USB, FireWire) storage device as well as via the network using TCP/IP

- Designed specifically for forensic use, with audit logging and cryptographic integrity checks

The KntTools Enterprise Edition includes the following capabilities:

- Bulk encryption of output using X.509 certifications, AES–256 (default), and downgrading to 3DES on Windows 2000

- Memory acquisition using a KnTDDSvc service

- A remote deployment module that is able to deploy the KnTDDSvc service by either "pushing" it to a remote admin share or "pulling" it from a Web server over SSL, with cryptographic verification of the binaries before they are executed

One of the aspects of using dd.exe, and tools like it, that the investigator needs to keep in mind is Locard's Exchange Principle. To use dd.exe to collect the contents of RAM, dd.exe must be loaded into RAM as a running process. This means that memory space is used and other processes might have pages that are written out to the page file.

Another aspect of these tools to keep in mind is that they do not freeze the state of the system, as occurs when a crash dump is generated. This means that while the tool is reading though the contents of RAM, as the thirtieth "page" is being read, the eleventh page could change as the process using that page continues to run. The amount of time it ultimately takes to complete the dump depends on factors such as processor speed and rates of bus and disk I/O. The question then becomes, are these changes that occur in the limited amount of time enough to affect the results of your analysis?

Let's look at the pros and cons of this technique:

- **Pros** Under most incident response conditions, dd.exe might be the best method for retrieving the contents of physical memory. This tool does not require that the system be taken down, nor does it restrict how and to where the contents of physical memory are written (i.e., using *netcat*, you can write the contents of RAM out over a socket to another system rather than to the local hard drive). Further, tools have been developed and made freely available to parse the contents of these RAM dumps to extract information about processes, network connections, and the like. Further, development of the KnTTools allows for continued support of this methodology beyond Windows 2003 SP1.

- **Cons** The primary issue with using a methodology such as the Forensic Acquisition Utilities or KnTTools is that the system is still running when the contents of physical memory are retrieved. This means that not only are memory pages consumed simply by using the utilities (i.e., executable images are read and loaded into memory), but as the tool enumerates through memory, pages that have already been read can change. That is to say that the state of the system and its memory are not frozen in time, as would be the case with acquiring a forensic image of a hard drive via the traditional means.

Be that as it may, acquiring the contents of physical memory using the Forensic Acquisition Utilities is perhaps the most frequently used methodology to date.

Analyzing a Physical Memory Dump

Now that we have the contents of RAM from a system, what can we do with them? For the most part, prior to the summer of 2005, the standard operating procedure for most folks who had bothered to collect a RAM dump (usually via the Forensic Acquisition Utilities dd.exe) was to run strings.exe against it, run *grep* searches (for e-mail addresses, IP addresses, and so on), or both. Although this would result in investigative leads (finding what appeared to be a password "close" to a username would give investigators a clue) that would often lead to something definitive, what it does not provide is overall context to the information that is found. For example, is that string that was located part of a word processing or text document, or was it copied to the system clipboard? What process was using the memory where that string or IP address was located?

With the DFRWS 2005 Memory Challenge as a catalyst, steps have been taken in an attempt to add context to the information found in RAM. By locating specific processes (or other objects in maintained in memory) and the memory pages used by those processes, investigators can gain greater insight into the information they discover as well as perform significant data reduction by filtering out "known good" processes and data and focusing on the data that appears "unusual." Several individuals have written tools that can be used to parse through RAM dumps and retrieve detailed information about processes and other structures.

Throughout the rest of this chapter, we will be using the memory dumps from the DFRWS 2005 Memory Challenge as exemplars, for examples and demonstrations of tools and techniques for parsing memory dumps. You're probably asking yourself, why even bother with that? Windows 2000 is new MS-DOS, right? Well, that's probably not far from the truth, but the dumps do provide an excellent basis for examples because they have already been examined in great detail. Also, they're freely available for download and examination.

Process Basics

Throughout this chapter, we will focus primarily on parsing information regarding processes from a RAM dump. This is due, in part, to the fact that the majority of the publicly available research and tools focus on processes as a source of forensic information. That is not to say that other objects within memory should be excluded but rather that most researchers seem to be focusing on processes. We will discuss another means of retrieving information from a RAM dump later in the chapter, but for now, we will focus our efforts on processes.

EProcess Structure

Each process on a Windows system is represented as an executive process, or EProcess, block. This EProcess block is a data structure in which various attributes of the process, as well as pointers to a number of other attributes and data structures (threads, the process environment block) relating to the process, are maintained. Because the data structure is a sequence of bytes, each sequence with a specific meaning and purpose, these structures can be read and analyzed by an investigator. However, the one thing to keep in mind is that the only thing consistent between versions of the Windows operating system regarding these structures is that they aren't consistent. You heard right: The size and even the values of the structures change not only between operating system versions (for example, Windows 2000 to XP) but also between service packs of the same version of the operating system (Windows XP to XP SP 2).

Andreas Schuster has done a great job of documenting the EProcess block structures in his blog.[23] However, it is relatively easy to view the contents of the EProcess structure (or any other structure available on Windows). First, download and install the Microsoft Debugging Tools[24] and the correct symbols for your operating system and Service Pack. Then download LiveKD.exe from SysInternals.com (when you type **sysinternals.com** into the address bar of your browser, you will be automatically redirected to the Microsoft site, since Mark Russinovich is now employed by Microsoft) and for convenience, copy it into the same directory as the debugging tools. Once you've done this, open a command prompt, change to the directory where you installed the debugging tools, and type the following command:

```
D:\debug>livekd -w
```

This command will open WinDbg, the GUI interface to the debugger tools. To see what the entire contents of an EProcess block "look like" (with all the substructures that make up the EProcess structure broken out), type **dt -a -b -v _EPRO-CESS** into the command window and press **Enter**. The *–a* flag shows each array element on a new line, with its index, and the *–b* switch displays blocks recursively. The *-v* flag creates more verbose output, telling you the overall size of each structure, for example. In some cases it can be helpful to include the *-r* flag for recursive output. The following illustrates a short excerpt from the results of this command, run on a Windows 2000 system:

```
kd> dt -a -b -v _EPROCESS
struct _EPROCESS, 94 elements, 0x290 bytes
   +0x000 Pcb                 : struct _KPROCESS, 26 elements, 0x6c bytes
      +0x000 Header           : struct _DISPATCHER_HEADER, 6 elements, 0x10
bytes
         +0x000 Type          : UChar
         +0x001 Absolute      : UChar
         +0x002 Size          : UChar
         +0x003 Inserted      : UChar
         +0x004 SignalState   : Int4B
         +0x008 WaitListHead  : struct _LIST_ENTRY, 2 elements, 0x8 bytes
            +0x000 Flink      : Ptr32 to
            +0x004 Blink      : Ptr32 to
      +0x010 ProfileListHead  : struct _LIST_ENTRY, 2 elements, 0x8 bytes
         +0x000 Flink         : Ptr32 to
         +0x004 Blink         : Ptr32 to
      +0x018 DirectoryTableBase : (2 elements)  Uint4B
```

The entire output is much longer (according to the header, the entire structure is 0x290 bytes long), but don't worry, we will address important (from a forensics/investigative aspect) elements of the structure as we progress through this chapter.

An important element of a process that is pointed to by the EProcess structure is the *process environment block,* or PEB. This structure contains a great deal of information, but the elements that are important to us, as forensic investigators, are:

- A pointer to the loader data (referred to as *PPEB_LDR_DATA*) structure that includes pointers or references to modules (DLLs) used by the process

- A pointer to the image base address, where we can expect to find the beginning of the executable image file

- A pointer to the process parameters structure, which itself maintains the DLL path, the path to the executable image, and the command line used to launch the process

Parsing this information from a dump file can prove to be extremely useful to an investigator, as we will see throughout the rest of this chapter.

Process Creation Mechanism

Now that we know a little bit about the various structures involved with processes, it would be helpful to know something about how those structures are used by the operating system, particularly when it comes to creating an actual process.

There are a number of steps that are followed when a process is created. These steps can be broken down into six stages:[25.]

1. The image (.exe) file to be executed is opened. During this stage, the appropriate subsystem (Posix, MS-DOS, Win 16, etc.) is identified. Also, the Image File Execution Options Registry key (see Chapter 4, "Registry Analysis") is checked to see if there is a Debugger value, and if there is, the process starts over.

2. The EProcess object is created. The kernel process block (KProcess), the process environment block, and the initial address space are also set up.

3. The initial thread is created.

4. The Windows subsystem is notified of the creation of the new process and thread, along with the ID of the process's creator and a flag to identify whether the process belongs to a Windows process.

5. Execution of the initial thread starts. At this point, the process environment has been set up and resources have been allocated for the process's thread(s) to use.

6. The initialization of the address space is completed, in the context of the new process and thread.

At this point, the process now consumes space in memory in accordance with EProcess structure (which includes the KProcess structure) and the PEB structure. The process has at least one thread and may begin consuming additional memory resources as the process itself executes. At this point, if the process or memory as a whole is halted and dumped, there will at the very least be something to analyze.

Parsing Memory Contents

The tools described in the DFRWS 2005 Memory Challenge used a methodology for parsing memory contents of locating and enumerating the active process list, using specific values/offsets (derived from system files) to identify the beginning of the list and then walking through the doubly linked list until all the active processes had been identified. The location of the offset for the beginning of the active process list was derived from one of the important system files, ntoskrnl.exe.

Andreas Schuster took a different approach in his Perl script called ptfinder.pl. His idea was to take a "brute-force" approach to the problem—identifying specific characteristics of processes in memory and then enumerating the EProcess blocks as well as other information about the processes based on those characteristics. Andreas began his approach by enumerating the structure of the *DISPATCHER_HEADER*, which is located at offset 0 for each EProcess block (actually, it's within the structure known as the KProcess block). Using LiveKD, we see that the enumerated structure from a Windows 2000 system has the following elements:

```
+0x000 Header      : struct _DISPATCHER_HEADER, 6 elements, 0x10 bytes
   +0x000 Type             : UChar
   +0x001 Absolute         : UChar
   +0x002 Size             : UChar
   +0x003 Inserted         : UChar
   +0x004 SignalState      : Int4B
```

In a nutshell, Andreas found that some of the elements for the *DIS-PATCHER_HEADER* were consistent in all processes on the system. He examined the *DISPATCHER_HEADER* elements for processes (and threads) on systems ranging from Windows 2000 up through early betas of Vista and found that the *Type* value remained consistent across each version of the operating system. He also found that the *Size* value remained consistent within various versions of the operating system (for example, all processes on Windows 2000 or XP had the same *Size* value) but changed between those versions (for instance, for Windows 2000, the *Size* value is 0x1b, but for early versions of Vista, it was 0x20).

Using this information as well as the total size of the structure and the way the structure itself could be broken down, Andreas wrote his ptfinder.pl Perl script, which would enumerate processes and threads located in a memory dump. At the DFRWS 2006 conference he also presented a paper, *Searching for Processes and Threads in Microsoft Windows Memory Dumps,*[26.] which addressed not only the data structures that make up processes and threads but also various rules to determine whether what was found was a legitimate structure or just a bunch of bytes in a file.

> **NOTE**
>
> In fall 2006, Richard McQuown of ForensicZone.com put together a GUI front end for Andreas Schuster's PTFinder tools. The PTFinder tools are Perl scripts and require that the Perl interpreter be installed on a system to run them. (Perl is installed by default on many Linux distributions and is freely available for Windows platforms from ActiveState.com.)
>
> Not only can Richard's tool detect the operating system of the RAM dump (rather than have the user enter it manually) using code I'll discuss later in this chapter; it can also provide a graphical representation of the output. PTFinderFE has some interesting applications, particularly with regard to visualization.

In spring 2006, I wrote some of my own tools to assist in parsing through Windows RAM dump files. Since the currently available exemplars at the time were the dumps for Windows 2000 systems available from the DFRWS 2005 Memory Challenge, I focused my initial efforts on producing code that worked for that platform. This allowed me to address various issues in code development without getting too wrapped up in the myriad differences between the various versions of the Windows operating system. The result was four separate Perl scripts, each run from the command line. These scripts are all provided on the accompanying DVD, and we'll go through each one separately.

Lsproc.pl

 LSproc, short for *list processes*, is similar to Andreas's PTFinder.pl; however, lsproc.pl locates processes but not threads. Lsproc.pl takes a single argument, the path and name to a RAM dump file:

```
c:\perl\memory>lsproc.pl d:\dumps\drfws1-mem.dmp
```

The output of lsproc.pl appears at the console (i.e., *STDOUT*) in six columns; the word *Proc* (I was anticipating adding threads at a later date), the parent process ID (*PPID*), the process ID (*PID*), the name of the process, the offset of the process structure within the dump file, and the creation time of the process. An excerpt of the lsproc.pl output appears as follows:

```
Proc  820   324    helix.exe             0x00306020  Sun Jun  5 14:09:27
2005
Proc  0     0      Idle                  0x0046d160
```

Proc	600	668	UMGR32.EXE	0x0095f020	Sun Jun	5 00:55:08
2005						
Proc	324	1112	cmd2k.exe	0x00dcc020	Sun Jun	5 14:14:25
2005						
Proc	668	784	dfrws2005.exe(x)	0x00e1fb60	Sun Jun	5 01:00:53
2005						
Proc	156	176	winlogon.exe	0x01045d60	Sun Jun	5 00:32:44
2005						
Proc	156	176	winlogon.exe	0x01048140	Sat Jun	4 23:36:31
2005						
Proc	144	164	winlogon.exe	0x0104ca00	Fri Jun	3 01:25:54
2005						
Proc	156	180	csrss.exe	0x01286480	Sun Jun	5 00:32:43
2005						
Proc	144	168	csrss.exe	0x01297b40	Fri Jun	3 01:25:53
2005						
Proc	8	156	smss.exe	0x012b62c0	Sun Jun	5 00:32:40
2005						
Proc	0	8	System	0x0141dc60		
Proc	668	784	dfrws2005.exe(x)	0x016a9b60	Sun Jun	5 01:00:53
2005						
Proc	1112	1152	dd.exe(x)	0x019d1980	Sun Jun	5 14:14:38
2005						
Proc	228	592	dfrws2005.exe	0x02138640	Sun Jun	5 01:00:53
2005						
Proc	820	1076	cmd.exe	0x02138c40	Sun Jun	5 00:35:18
2005						
Proc	240	788	metasploit.exe(x)	0x02686cc0	Sun Jun	5 00:38:37
2005						
Proc	820	964	Apoint.exe	0x02b84400	Sun Jun	5 00:33:57
2005						
Proc	820	972	HKserv.exe	0x02bf86e0	Sun Jun	5 00:33:57
2005						
Proc	820	988	DragDrop.exe	0x02c46020	Sun Jun	5 00:33:57
2005						
Proc	820	1008	alogserv.exe	0x02e7ea20	Sun Jun	5 00:33:57
2005						
Proc	820	972	HKserv.exe	0x02f806e0	Sun Jun	5 00:33:57
2005						
Proc	820	1012	tgcmd.exe	0x030826a0	Sun Jun	5 00:33:58
2005						
Proc	176	800	userinit.exe(x)	0x03e35020	Sun Jun	5 00:33:52
2005						

```
Proc  800    820     Explorer.Exe          0x03e35ae0  Sun Jun  5 00:33:53
2005

Proc  820    1048    PcfMgr.exe            0x040b4660  Sun Jun  5 00:34:01
2005
```

The first process listed in the lsproc.pl output is "helix.exe. According to the information provided at the DFRWS 2005 Memory Challenge Web site, utilities on the Helix Live CD[27] were used to acquire the memory dump.

The aforementioned listing shows only an excerpt of the lsproc.pl output. There were a total of 45 processes located in the memory dump file. You'll notice in the output that several of the processes have *(x)* after the process name. This indicates that the processes have exited. In these cases, the contents of physical memory (for example, pages) have been freed for use but have not been overwritten yet, so it would seem that some information is retained in physical memory following a reboot.

NOTE

Looking closely, you'll notice some interesting things about the lsproc.pl output. One is that the csrss.exe process (PID = 168) has a creation date that appears to be a day or two earlier than the other listed processes. Looking even more closely, you'll see something similar for two winlogon.exe processes (PID = 164 and 176). Andreas Schuster noticed these as well, and according to an entry on data persistence in his blog,[28] the system boot time for the dump file was determined to be Sunday, Jan 5, 2005, at approximately 00:32:27. So, where do these processes come from?

As Andreas points out in his blog, without having more definitive information about the state of the test system prior to collecting data for the memory challenge, it is difficult to develop a complete understanding of this issue. However, the specifications of the test system were known and documented, and it was noted that the system suffered a crash dump during data collection.

It is entirely possible that the data survived the reboot. There don't seem to be any specifications that require that when a Windows system shuts down or suffers a crash dump, the contents of physical memory are zeroed out or wiped in some manner. It is possible, then, that contents of physical memory remain in their previous state, and if they are not overwritten when the system is restarted, the data is still available for analysis. Many BIOS versions have a feature to overwrite memory during boot as part of a RAM test, but this feature is usually disabled to speed up the boot process.

This is definitely an area that requires further study. As Andreas states,[29.] this area of study has "a bright future."

Lspd.pl

Lspd.pl is a Perl script that will allow you to list the details of the process. Like the other tools that we will be discussing, lspd.pl is a command-line Perl script that relies on the output of lsproc.pl to obtain its information. Specifically, lspd.pl takes two arguments: the path and name of the dump file and the offset from the lsproc.pl output of the process that you're interested in. Although lsproc.pl took some time to parse through the contents of the dump file, lspd.pl is much quicker, since you're telling it exactly where to go in the file to enumerate its information.

Let's take a look at a specific process. In this case, we'll look at dd.exe, the process with PID 284. The command line to use lspd.pl to get detailed information about this process is:

```
c:\perl\memory>lspd.pl d:\dumps\dfrws1-mem.dmp 0x0414dd60
```

Notice that with lspd.pl, we're using two arguments: the name and path to the dump file and the physical offset in the dump file where we found the process with lsproc.pl. We'll take a look at the output of lspd.pl in sections, starting with some useful information pulled directly from the EProcess structure itself:

```
Process Name : dd.exe
PID          : 284
Parent PID   : 1112
TFLINK       : 0xff2401c4
TBLINK       : 0xff2401c4
FLINK        : 0x8046b980
BLINK        : 0xff1190c0
SubSystem    : 4.0
Exit Status  : 259
Create Time  : Sun Jun  5 14:53:42 2005
Exit Called  : 0
DTB          : 0x01d9e000
ObjTable     : 0xff158708 (0x00eb6708)
PEB          : 0x7ffdf000 (0x02c2d000)
         InheritedAddressSpace        : 0
         ReadImageFileExecutionOptions : 0
```

```
BeingDebugged                        : 0
CSDVersion                           : Service Pack 1
Mutant          = 0xffffffff
Img Base Addr   = 0x00400000 (0x00fee000)
PEB_LDR_DATA    = 0x00131e90 (0x03a1ee90)
Params          = 0x00020000 (0x03a11000)
```

Lspd.pl also follows pointers provided by the EProcess structure to collect other data as well. For example, we can also see the path to the executable image and the command line used to launch the process (bold added for emphasis):

```
Current Directory Path = E:\Shells\
DllPath               =
E:\Acquisition\FAU;.;C:\WINNT\System32;C:\WINNT\system;
C:\WINNT;E:\Acquisition\FAU\;E:\Acquisition\GNU\;E:\Acquisition\CYGWIN\;E:\I
R\bin\;E:\IR\WFT;E:\IR\windbg\;E:\IR\Foundstone\;E:\IR\Cygwin;E:\IR\somarsof
t\;E:\IR\sysinternals\;E:\IR\ntsecurity\;E:\IR\perl\;E:\Static-
Binaries\gnu_utils_win32\;C:\WINNT\system32;C:\WINNT;C:\WINNT\System32\Wbem
ImagePathName         = E:\Acquisition\FAU\dd.exe
Command Line          = ..\Acquisition\FAU\dd.exe if=\\.\PhysicalMemory
of=F:\intrusion2005\physicalmemory.dd conv=noerror --md5sum --verifymd5  --
md5out=F:\intrusion2005\physicalmemory.dd.md5 --
log=F:\intrusion2005\audit.log
Environment Offset    = 0x00000000 (0x00000000)
Window Title          = ..\Acquisition\FAU\dd.exe if=\\.\PhysicalMemory
of=F:\intrusion2005\physicalmemory.dd conv=noerror --md5sum --verifymd5  --
md5out=F:\intrusion2005\physicalmemory.dd.md5 --
log=F:\intrusion2005\audit.log
Desktop Name          = WinSta0\Default
```

Lspd.pl also retrieves a list of the names of various modules (DLLs) used by the process and whatever available handles (file handles and so on) it can find in memory. For example, lspd.pl found that the dd.exe had the following file handle open:

```
Type : File
     Name = \intrusion2005\audit.log
```

As we can see from the preceding command line, the file \intrusion\audit.log is located on the F:\ drive and is the output file for the log of activity generated by dd.exe, which explains why it would be listed as an open file handle in use by the process. Using this information as derived from other processes, you can get an understanding of files you should be concerned with during an investigation. In this particular instance, we can assume that the E:\ drive listed in *ImagePathName* is a

CD-ROM drive, since Helix can be run from a CD. We can confirm this by checking Registry values in an image of the system in question (a system image is not provided as part of the memory challenge, however). We can also use similar information to find out a little bit more about the F:\ drive. This information will be covered in Chapter 4, "Registry Analysis."

Finally, one other thing that lspd.pl will do is go to the location pointed to by the Image Base *Addr* value (once it has been translated from a virtual address to a physical offset within the memory dump file) and check to see if a valid executable image is located at that address. This check is very simple; all it does is read the first 2 bytes starting at the translated address to see if they're *MZ*. These 2 bytes are not a definitive check, but portable executable (PE) files (files with .exe, .dll, .ocs, .sys, and etc. extensions) start with the initials of Mark Zbikowski, one of the early architects of MS-DOS and Windows NT. The format of the PE file and its header is addressed in greater detail in Chapter 6, "Executable File Analysis."

Parsing Process Memory

We discussed the need for context for evidence earlier in this chapter, and this can be achieved, in part, by extracting the memory used by a process. In the past, investigators have used tools such as strings.exe or *grep* searches to parse through the contents of a RAM dump and look for interesting strings (passwords), IP or e-mail addresses, URLs, and the like. However, when we're parsing through a file that is about half a megabyte in size, there isn't a great deal of context to the information we find. Sometimes an investigator will open the dump file in a hex editor and locate the interesting string, and if she saw what appeared to be a username nearby, she might assume that the string is a password. However, investigating a RAM dump file in this manner does not allow the investigator to correlate that string to a particular process. Remember the example of Locard's Exchange Principle from Chapter 1? Had we collected the contents of physical memory during the example, we would have had no way to definitively say that a particular IP address or other data, such as a directory listing, was tied to a specific event or process. However, if we use the information provided in the process structure within memory and locate all the pages the process used that were still in memory when the contents were dumped, we could then run our searches and determine which process was using that information.

The tool lspm.pl allows us to do this automatically. Lspm.pl takes the same arguments as lspd.pl (the name and path of the dump file, and the physical offset within the file of the process structure) and extracts the available pages from the dump file, writing them to a file within the current working directory. To run lspm.pl against the dd.exe process, we use the following command line:

```
c:\perl\memory>lspm.pl d:\dumps\dfrws1-mem.dmp 0x0414dd60
```

The output looks like this:

```
Name : dd.exe -> 0x01d9e000
There are 372 pages (1523712 bytes) to process.
Dumping process memory to dd.dmp...
Done.
```

Now we have a file called dd.dmp that is 1,523,712 bytes in size and contains all the memory pages (372 in total) for that process that were still available when the dump file was created. You can run strings.exe or use BinText (see Figure 3.3) from Foundstone.com to parse through the file looking for Unicode and ASCII strings, or run *grep* searches for IP or e-mail addresses and credit card or Social Security numbers.

Figure 3.3 Contents of Process Memory in BinText

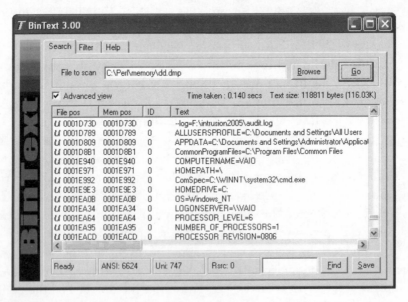

In Figure 3.3, we can see some of the Unicode strings contained in the memory used by the dd.exe process, including the name of the system and the name of the *LogonServer* for the session. All of this information can help further the investigator's understanding of the case; an important aspect of this capability is that now we can correlate what we find to a specific process.

Extracting the Process Image

As we saw earlier in this chapter, when a process is launched, the executable file is read into memory. One of the pieces of information that we can get from the process details (via lspd.pl) is the offset within the dump file to the Image Base Address. As we saw, lspd.pl will do a quick check to see whether an executable image can be found at that location. One of the things we can do to develop this information further is to parse the PE file header (the contents of which will be covered in detail in Chapter 6, "Executable File Analysis") and see whether we can extract the entire contents of the executable image from the dump file. Lspi.pl lets us do this automatically.

Lspi.pl is a Perl script that takes the same arguments as lspd.pl and lspm.pl and locates the beginning of the executable image for that process. If the Image Base Address offset does indeed lead to an executable image file, lspi.pl will parse the values contained in the PE header to locate the pages that make up the rest of the executable image file.

Okay, so we can run lspi.pl against the dd.exe process (with the PID of 284) using the following command line:

```
c:\perl\memory>lspi.pl d:\dumps\dfrws1-mem.dmp 0x0414dd60
```

The output of the command appears as follows:

```
Process Name : dd.exe
PID          : 284
DTB          : 0x01d9e000
PEB          : 0x7ffdf000 (0x02c2d000)
ImgBaseAddr  : 0x00400000 (0x00fee000)
e_lfanew = 0xe8
NT Header = 0x4550
Reading the Image File Header
Sections = 4
Opt Header Size  = 0x000000e0 (224 bytes)
Characteristics:
        IMAGE_FILE_EXECUTABLE_IMAGE
        IMAGE_FILE_LOCAL_SYMS_STRIPPED
        IMAGE_FILE_RELOCS_STRIPPED
        IMAGE_FILE_LINE_NUMS_STRIPPED
        IMAGE_FILE_32BIT_MACHINE
Machine = IMAGE_FILE_MACHINE_I860
Reading the Image Optional Header
```

```
Opt Header Magic = 0x10b
Subsystem       : IMAGE_SUBSYSTEM_WINDOWS_CUI
Entry Pt Addr : 0x00006bda
Image Base     : 0x00400000
File Align     : 0x00001000
Reading the Image Data Directory information
Data Directory        RVA        Size
--------------        ---        ----
ResourceTable         0x0000d000 0x00000430
DebugTable            0x00000000 0x00000000
BaseRelocTable        0x00000000 0x00000000
DelayImportDesc       0x0000af7c 0x000000a0
TLSTable              0x00000000 0x00000000
GlobalPtrReg          0x00000000 0x00000000
ArchSpecific        0x00000000 0x00000000
CLIHeader             0x00000000 0x00000000
LoadConfigTable     0x00000000 0x00000000
ExceptionTable        0x00000000 0x00000000
ImportTable           0x0000b25c 0x000000a0
unused                0x00000000 0x00000000
BoundImportTable      0x00000000 0x00000000
ExportTable           0x00000000 0x00000000
CertificateTable    0x00000000 0x00000000
IAT                   0x00007000 0x00000210
Reading Image Section Header Information
Name     Virt Sz     Virt Addr    rData Ofs    rData Sz    Char
----     -------     ---------    ---------    --------    ----
.text    0x00005ee0  0x00001000   0x00001000   0x00006000  0x60000020
.data    0x000002fc  0x0000c000   0x0000c000   0x00001000  0xc0000040
.rsrc    0x00000430  0x0000d000   0x0000d000   0x00001000  0x40000040
.rdata   0x00004cfa  0x00007000   0x00007000   0x00005000  0x40000040
Reassembling image file into dd.exe.img
Bytes written = 57344
New file size = 57344
```

As you can see, the output of lspi.pl is pretty verbose, and much of the information displayed might not be readily useful to (or understood by) an investigator unless that investigator is interested in malware analysis. Again, this information will be discussed in detail in Chapter 6, "Executable File Analysis." For now, the important elements are the table that follows the words "Reading Image Section Header Information" and the name of the file to which the executable image was reassembled. The section header information provides us with a road map for reassembling the executable image because it lets us know where to find the pages that make up that image file. Lspi.pl uses this road map and attempts to reassemble the executable image into a file. If it's successful, it writes the file out to the file based on the name of the process, with .img appended (to prevent accidental execution of the file). Lspi.pl will not reassemble the file if any of the memory pages have been marked as invalid and are no longer located in memory (for example, they have been paged out to the swap file, pagefile.sys). Instead, lspi.pl will report that it could not reassemble the complete file because some pages (even just one) were not available in memory.

Now, the file that we extract from the memory dump will not be exactly the same as the original executable file. This is due to the fact that some of the file's sections are writeable, and those sections will change as the process is executing. As the process executes, various elements of the executable code (addresses, variables, and so on) will change according to the environment and the stage of execution. However, there are a couple of ways that we can determine the nature of a file and get some information about its purpose. One of those ways is to see whether the file has any file version information compiled into it, as is done with most files created by legitimate software companies. As we saw from the section headers of the image file, there is a section named .rsrc, which is the name often used for a resource section of a PE file. This section can contain a variety of resources, such as dialogs and version strings, and is organized like a file system of sorts. Using BinText, we can look for the Unicode string *VS_VERSION_INFO*[30.] and see whether there is any identifying information available in the executable image file. Figure 3.4 illustrates some of the strings found in the dd.exe.img file using BinText.

Figure 3.4 Version Strings Found in dd.exe.img with BinText

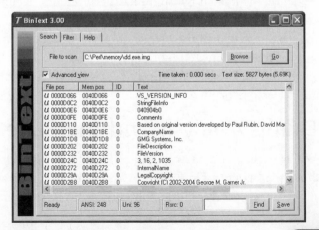

Another method of determining the nature of the file is to use file hashing. You're probably thinking, "Hey, wait a minute! You just said that the file created by lspi.pl isn't exactly the same as the original file, so how can we use hashing?" Well, you're right ... up to a point. We can't use MD5 hashes for comparison, because as we know, altering even a single bit—flipping a 1 to a 0—will cause an entirely different hash to be computed. So what can we do?

In summer 2006, Jesse Kornblum released a tool called sdeep[31] that implements something called *context-triggered piecewise hashing*, or *fuzzy hashing*. For a detailed understanding of what this entails, be sure to read Jesse's DFRWS 2006 paper[32] on the subject. In a nutshell, Jesse implemented an algorithm that will tell you a weighted percentage of the identical sequences of bits the files have in common, based on their hashes, computed by ssdeep. Since we know that in this case, George Garner's version of dd.exe was used to dump the contents of RAM from a Windows 2000 system for the DFRWS 2005 Memory Challenge, we can compare the dd.exe.img file to the original dd.exe file that we just happen to have available.

First, we start by using ssdeep.exe to compute a hash for our image file:

```
D:\tools>ssdeep c:\perl\memory\dd.exe.img > dd.sdp
```

We've now generated the hash and saved the information to the dd.sdp file. Using other switches available for ssdeep.exe, we can quickly compare the .img file to the original executable image:

```
D:\tools>ssdeep -v -m dd.sdp d:\tools\dd\old\dd.exe
d:\tools\dd\old\dd.exe matches c:\perl\memory\dd.exe.img (97)
```

This can also be done in one command line using either the *-d* or *-p* switches:

```
D:\tools\> ssdeep -d c:\perl\memory\dd.exe.img d:\tools\dd\old\dd.exe
C:\perl\memory\dd.exe.img matches d:\tools\dd\old\dd.exe (97)
```

We see that the image file generated by lspi.pl has a 97 percent likelihood of matching the original dd.exe file.

Remember, for a hash comparison to work properly, we need something to which we can compare the files created by lspi.pl. Ssdeep.exe is a relatively new, albeit extremely powerful, tool, and it will likely be a while before hash sets either are generated using ssdeep.exe or incorporate hashes calculated using ssdeep.exe.

Memory Dump Analysis and the Page File

So far, we've looked at parsing and analyzing the contents of a RAM dump in isolation—that is, without the benefit of any additional information. This means that tools such as lspm.pl that rely solely on the contents of the RAM dump will provide an incomplete memory dump, since memory pages that have been swapped out to the page file (pagefile.sys on Windows systems) will not be incorporated in the resulting memory dump. To overcome this deficiency, in the spring of 2006 Nicholas Paul Maclean published his thesis work, *Acquisition and Analysis of Windows Memory* (at the time of this writing, I could not locate an active link to the thesis), which explains the inner workings of the Windows memory management system and provides an open-source tool called *vtop* (written in Python) to reconstruct the virtual address space of a process.

Jesse Kornblum released his "Buffalo" paper (the full title is *Using Every Part of the Buffalo in Windows Memory Analysis*) early in 2007 via his Web site; the paper was also published in the *Digital Investigation Journal*. In this paper, Jesse demonstrates the nuances of page address translation and how the page file can be incorporated into the memory analysis process to establish a more complete (and accurate) view of the information that is available.

Determining the Operating System of a Dump File

Have you ever been handed an image of a system, and when you asked what the operating system is/was, you simply get "Windows" in response? Shakespeare doesn't cut it here, my friends, because a rose by any other name might *not* smell as sweet. When you're working with an image of a system, the version of Windows that you're confronted with *matters*, and depending on the issue you're dealing with, it could matter a lot. The same is true when you're dealing with a RAM dump file; in fact, it could be even more so. As I've already stated, the structures that are used to define threads and processes in memory vary not only between major versions of the operating system but also within the same version with different service packs installed.

So, when someone hands you a RAM dump and says, "Windows," you'd probably want to know how to figure that out, wouldn't you? After all, you don't want to waste a lot of time running the dump file through every known tool until one of them starts producing valid hits on processes, right? Through personal correspondence (that's a fancy term for "e-mail") a while ago, Andreas Schuster suggested to me that the Windows kernel might possibly be loaded into the same location in memory every time Windows boots. Now, that location is likely to, and does, change for every version of Windows, but so far, it seems to be consistent for each version. The easiest way to find this location is to run LiveKD as we did earlier in this chapter, but note the information that's displayed as it starts up, particularly (on a Windows XP SP2 system):

```
Windows XP Kernel Version 2600 (Service Pack 2) MP (2 procs) Free x86
compatible
Product: WinNt, suite: TerminalServer SingleUserTS
Built by: 2600.xpsp.050329-1536
Kernel base = 0x804d7000 PsLoadedModuleList = 0x8055c700
```

We're most interested in the information that I've boldfaced—the address of the kernel base. We subtract 0x80000000 from that address and then go to the resulting physical location within the dump file. If the first 2 bytes located at that address are *MZ*, we could have a full-blown Windows PE file at that location, and we *might* have the kernel. From this point, we can use code similar to what's in lspi.pl to parse apart the PE header and locate the various sections within the PE file. Since the Windows kernel is a legitimate Microsoft application file, we can be sure that there is a resource section within the file that contains a *VS_VERSION_INFO* section. Following information provided by Microsoft regarding the various structures that make up this section, we can then parse through it looking for the file description string.

On the accompanying DVD, you'll find a file called osid.pl that does just that. Osid.pl began life as kern.pl and found its way into Rick McQuown's PTFinderFE utility. Rick asked me via e-mail one day if there was a way to shorten and clarify the output, so I made some modifications to the file (changed the output, added some switches, and so on) and renamed it.

In its simplest form, you can simply run osid.pl from the command line, passing in the path to the image file as the sole argument:

```
C:\Perl\memory>osid.pl d:\hacking\xp-laptop1.img
```

Alternatively, you can designate a specific file using the *-f* switch:

```
C:\Perl\memory>osid.pl -f d:\hacking\xp-laptop1.img
```

Both of these commands will give you the same output; in this case, the RAM dump was collected from a Windows XP SP2 system, so the script returns *XPSP2*. If this isn't quite enough information and you'd like to see more, you can add the *-v* switch (for *verbose*), and the script will return the following for the xp-laptop1.img file:

```
OS      : XPSP2
Product : Microsoft« Windows« Operating System ver 5.1.2600.2622
```

As you can see, the strings within the *VS_VERSION_INFO* structure that refer to the product name and the product version get concatenated to produce the additional output. If we run the script with both the *-v* and the *-f* switches against the first RAM dump file from the DFRWS 2005 Memory Challenge, we get:

```
OS      : 2000
Product : Microsoft(R) Windows (R) 2000 Operating System ver 5.00.2195.1620
```

This script also works equally well against VMware .vmem files. I ran the script against a .vmem file from a Windows 2000 VMware session and received the following output:

```
OS      : 2000
Product : Microsoft(R) Windows (R) 2000 Operating System ver 5.00.2195.7071
```

Pool Allocations

When the Windows memory manager allocates memory, it generally does so in 4K (4096 bytes) pages. However, allocating an entire 4K page for, say, a sentence copied to the clipboard would be a waste of memory. So the memory manager allocates several pages ahead of time, keeping an available *pool* of memory. Andreas Schuster has done extensive research in this area, and even though Microsoft provides a list of pool headers used to designate commonly used pools, documentation for any meaningful analysis of these pools is simply not available. Many of the commonly used pool headers are listed in the pooltag.txt[33.] file provided with the Microsoft Debugging Tools, and Microsoft provides a KnowledgeBase article that describes how to locate pool tags/headers used by third-party applications.[34.] Andreas used a similar method to determine the format of memory pools used to preserve information about network connections in Windows 2000 memory dumps;[35.] he searched for the pool header in the tcpip.sys driver on a Windows 2000 system and was able to determine the format of network connection information within the memory pool.

The downside to searching for memory pool allocations is that although the pool headers do not seem to change between versions of Windows, the format of the data resident within the memory pool changes, and there is no available documentation regarding the format of these memory pools.

Collecting Process Memory

During an investigation, you might be interested in only particular processes rather than a list of all processes, and you'd like more than just the contents of process memory available in a RAM dump file. For example, you might have quickly identified processes of interest that required no additional extensive investigation. There are ways to collect all the memory used by a process—not just what is in physical memory but what is in virtual memory or the page file as well.

To do this, the investigator has available a couple of tools. One is pmdump.exe,[36.] written by Arne Vidstrom and available from NTSecurity.nu. However, as the NTSecurity.nu Web site states, pmdump.exe allows you to dump the contents of process memory *without* stopping the process. As we discussed earlier, this allows the process to continue and the contents of memory to change while being written to a file, thereby creating a "smear" of process memory. Also, pmdump.exe does not create an output file that can be analyzed with the debugging tools.

Tobias Klein has come up with another method for dumping the contents of process memory in the form of a free (albeit not open-source) tool called Process Dumper.[37.] Process Dumper (pd.exe) dumps the entire process space along with additional metadata and the process environment to the console (STDOUT) so that the output can be redirected to a file or a socket (via *netcat* or other tools; see Chapter 1 for a discussion of some of those tools). A review of the documentation that Tobias makes available for pd.exe provides no indication that the process is debugged, halted, or frozen prior to the dumping process. Tobias also provides the Memory Parser GUI utility for parsing the metadata and memory contents collected by the Process Dumper. These tools appear to be an extension of Tobias's work toward extracting RSA private keys and certificates from process memory.[38.]

Another tool that is available and recommended by a number of sources is userdump.exe, available from Microsoft. Userdump.exe will allow you to dump any process on the fly, without attaching a debugger and without terminating the process once the dump has been completed. Also, the dump file generated by userdump.exe can be read by the MS debugging tools. However, userdump.exe requires that a driver be installed for it to work, and depending on the situation, this might not be something you'd want to do.

Based on conversations with Robert Hensing, formerly of the Microsoft PSS Security team, the preferred method of dumping a process is to use the adplus.vbs script that ships with the debugging tools. *Adplus* stands for *Autodumplus* and was originally written by Robert (the documentation for the script states that versions 1 through 5 were written by Robert, and as of version 6, Israel Burman has taken over). The help file (debugger.chm) for the debugging tools contains a great deal of information about the script as well as the debugging tool (cdb.exe) that it uses to dump the processes that you designate. The debugging tools do not require that an additional driver be installed and can be run from a CD. This means that the tools (adplus.vbs and cdb.exe as well as supporting DLLs) can be written to a CD (adplus.vbs uses the Windows scripting host version 5.6, also known as cscript.exe, which comes installed on most systems) and used to dump processes to a shared drive or to a USB-connected storage device. Once the dumps have been completed, you can then use the freely available debugging tools to analyze the dump files. In addition, you can use other tools, such as BinText to extract ASCII, Unicode, and resource strings from the dump file. You can use still other tools to collect additional information about the process. Handle.exe[39] (which requires that you have Administrator rights on the system when running it) will provide you with a list of handles (to files, directories, and so on) that have been opened by the process, and listdlls.exe[40] will show you the full path to and the version numbers of the various modules loaded by a process.

There is extensive help available for using adplus.vbs, not only in the debugging tools help file but also in KB article 286350.[41] Adplus.vbs can be used to hang the process while it is being dumped (in other words, halt it, dump it, and then resume the process) or to crash the process (halt the process, dump it, and then terminate). To run adplus.vbs in hang mode against a process, you would use the following command line:

```
D:\debug>cscript adplus.vbs -quiet -hang -p <PID>
```

This command will create a series of files within the debug directory within a subdirectory prefaced with the name *Hang_mode_* that includes the date and time of the dump. (*Note:* You can change the location where the output is written using the -*o* switch.) What you will see is an adplus.vbs report file, the dump file for the process (multiple processes can be designated using multiple -*p* entries), a process list (generated by default using tlist.exe; you can turn this off using the -*noTList* switch), and a text file showing all the loaded modules (DLLs) used by the process.

Although all the information collected about processes using adplus.vbs can be extremely useful during an investigation, this tool can be used only on processes that are visible via the API. If a process is not visible (say, if it's hidden by a rootkit), you cannot use these tools to collect information about the process.

Summary

By now it should be clear that you have several options for collecting physical or process memory from a system during incident response. In Chapter 1, we examined a number of tools for collecting various portions of volatile memory during live response (processes, network connections, and the like), keeping in mind that there's always the potential for the Windows API (on which the tools rely) being compromised by an attacker. This is true in any case where live response is being performed, and therefore, we might decide to use multiple disparate means of collecting volatile information. A rootkit can hide the existence of a process from most tools that enumerate the list of active processes (tlist.exe, pslist.exe), but dumping the contents of RAM will allow the investigator to list active and exited processes as well as processes hidden using kernel-mode rootkits. (More about rootkits in Chapter 7, "Rootkits and Rootkit Detection.")

Notes

1. For more information go to www.dfrws.org.
2. For more information go to www.e-fense.com/helix/.
3. For more information go to http://computer.forensikblog.de/en/topics/windows/memory_analysis/.
4. For more information go to www.lurhq.com/truman/.
5. For more information go to www.blackhat.com/html/bh-federal-06/bh-fed-06-speakers.html#Burdach.
6. For more information go to http://nucia.unomaha.edu/tvidas/.
7. For more information go to www.grandideastudio.com/.
8. For more information go to www.storm.net.nz/projects/16.
9. For more information go to www.python.org.
10. For more information go to http://ntsecurity.nu/onmymind/2006/2006-09-02.html.
11. For more information go to http://en.wikipedia.org/wiki/Blue_Screen_of_Death.
12. For more information go to www.microsoft.com/whdc/devtools/debugging/default.mspx.
13. For more information go to www.microsoft.com/downloads/details.aspx?FamilyID=E84D3B35-63C3-445B-810D-9FED3FDEB13F&displaylang=en.
14. For more information go to http://support.microsoft.com/kb/254649/.
15. For more information go to http://support.microsoft.com/kb/274598/.

16. For more information go to http://support.microsoft.com/kb/307973/.

17. For more information go to http://support.microsoft.com/kb/ 244139/.

18. For more information go to www.microsoft.com/downloads/details.aspx?FamilyID=E84D3B35-63C3-445B-810D-9FED3FDEB13F&displaylang=en.

19. For more information go to http://support.citrix.com/article/CTX107717&parentCategoryID=617.

20. For more information go to www.microsoft.com/technet/sysinternals/SystemInformation/LiveKd.mspx.

21. For more information go to http://bochs.sourceforge.net/.

22. For more information go to http://users.erols.com/gmgarner/forensics/develop.

23. For more information go to http://computer.forensikblog.de/en/topics/windows/memory_analysis/.

24. For more information go to www.microsoft.com/whdc/devtools/debugging/default.mspx.

25. Mark E. Russinovich and David A. Solomon, *Windows Internals*, fourth edition, Chapter 6 (Redmond, WA: Microsoft Press, 2005).

26. For more information go to www.dfrws.org/2006/proceedings/2-Schuster.pdf.

27. For more information go to www.e-fense.com/helix/.

28. For more information go to http://computer.forensikblog.de/en/2006/04/persistance_through_the_boot_process.html.

29. For more information go to http://computer.forensikblog.de/en/2006/04/data_lifetime.html.

30. For more information go to http://msdn.microsoft.com/library/default.asp?url=/library/en-us/mobilesdk5/html/wce50lrfVSVERSIONINFO.asp.

31. For more information go to http://ssdeep.sourceforge.net/.

32. For more information go to http://dfrws.org/2006/proceedings/12-Kornblum.pdf.

33. For more information go to www.microsoft.com/whdc/driver/tips/PoolMem.mspx.

34. For more information go to http://support.microsoft.com/default.aspx?scid=kb;en-us;298102.

35. For more information go to http://computer.forensikblog.de/en/2006/07/finding_network_socket_activity_in_pools.html.

36. For more information go to www.ntsecurity.nu/toolbox/pmdump/.

37. For more information go to www.trapkit.de/research/forensic/pd/index.html.

38. For more information go to www.trapkit.de/research/sslkeyfinder/index.html.

39. For more information go to
www.microsoft.com/technet/sysinternals/ProcessesAndThreads/Handle.mspx.
40. For more information go to
www.microsoft.com/technet/sysinternals/ProcessesAndThreads/ListDlls.mspx.
41. For more information go to http://support.microsoft.com/kb/286350

Solutions Fast Track

Dumping Physical Memory

- ☑ Several methodologies are available for dumping the contents of physical memory. The investigator should be aware of the available options as well as their pros and cons so that he or she can make an intelligent choice as to which methodology should be used.

- ☑ Dumping the contents of physical memory from a live system can present issues with consistency due to the fact that the system is still live and processing information while the memory dump is being generated.

- ☑ When dumping the contents of physical memory, the investigator must keep Locard's Exchange Principle in mind.

Analyzing a Physical Memory Dump

- ☑ Depending on the means used to collect the contents of physical memory, various tools are available to extract useful information from the memory dump. The use of strings.exe, BinText, and *grep* with various regular expressions has been popular, and research conducted beginning in spring 2005 revealed how to extract specific processes.

- ☑ Dumps of physical memory contain useful information and objects such as processes, the contents of the clipboard, and network connections.

- ☑ Continuing research in this area has demonstrated how the page file can be used in conjunction with a RAM dump to develop a more complete set of information.

Collecting Process Memory

☑ An investigator could be presented with a situation in which it is not necessary to collect the entire contents of physical memory; rather, the contents of memory used by a single process would be sufficient.

☑ Collecting the memory contents of a single process is an option that is available for only those processes that are seen in the active process list by both the operating system and the investigator's utilities. Processes hidden via some means (see Chapter 7, "Rootkits and Rootkit Detection") might not be visible, and the investigator will not be able to provide the process identifier to the tools he or she is using to collect the memory used by the process.

☑ Dumping process memory allows the investigator to collect not only the memory used by the process that can be found in RAM but the memory located in the page file as well.

☑ Once process memory has been collected, additional information about the process, such as open handles and loaded modules, can then be collected.

Frequently Asked Questions

The following Frequently Asked Questions, answered by the authors of this book, are designed to both measure your understanding of the concepts presented in this chapter and to assist you with real-life implementation of these concepts. To have your questions about this chapter answered by the author, browse to **www.syngress.com/solutions** and click on the **"Ask the Author"** form.

Q: Why should I dump the contents of RAM from a live system? What use does this have, and what potentially useful or important information will be available to me?

A: As we discussed in Chapter 1, a significant amount of information available on a live system can be extremely important to an investigation. This volatile information exists in memory, or RAM, while the system is running. We can use various third-party tools (discussed in Chapter 1) to collect this information, but it might be important to collect the entire contents of memory so that we not only have a complete record of information available, we can also "see" those things that might not be "visible" via traditional means (for example, things hidden by a rootkit; see Chapter 7, "Rootkits and Rootkit Detection," for more information regarding rootkits). You might also find information regarding exited processes as well as process remnants left over after the system was rebooted.

Q: Once I've dumped the contents of RAM, what can I then do to analyze them?

A: Investigators have historically used standard file-based search tools to "analyze" RAM dumps. Strings.exe and *grep* searches have been used to locate passwords, e-mail addresses, URLs, and the like within RAM dumps. Tools now exist to parse RAM dumps for processes, process details (command lines, handles) threads, and other objects as well as extract executable images, which is extremely beneficial to malware analysis (see Chapter 6, "Executable File Analysis," for more information on this topic) as well as more traditional computer forensic examinations.

Q: I have an issue in which a person is missing. On examination of a computer system in their home, I found an active instant messaging (IM) application window open on the desktop. When I scrolled back through the window and reviewed the conversation, it is clear that there could be useful information available from that process. What can I do?

A: If the issue you're faced with is primarily one that centers around a single visible process, dumping the entire contents of physical memory might not be necessary. One useful approach would be to dump the contents of process memory, then use other tools to extract specific information about the process, such as loaded modules, command line used to launch the process, or open handles. Once all information is collected, the next step could be saving the contents of the IM conversation. After all pertinent information has been collected, searching the contents of process memory for remnants of a previous conversation or other data might provide you with useful clues.

Chapter 4

Registry Analysis

Solutions in this chapter:

- **Inside the Registry**
- **Registry Analysis**

☑ **Summary**

☑ **Solutions Fast Track**

☑ **Frequently Asked Questions**

Introduction

To most administrators and forensic analysts, the Registry probably looks like the entrance to a dark, forbidding cave on the landscape of the Windows operating system. Others might see the Registry as a dark door at the end of a long hallway, with the words "abandon hope, all ye who enter here" scrawled on it. The truth is that the Registry is a veritable gold mine of information for both the administrator and the forensics investigator. Software used by attackers will, in many cases, create a footprint within the Registry, leaving the investigator clues about the incident. Knowing where to look within the Registry, and how to interpret what you find, will go a long way toward giving you valuable insight into activity that occurred on the system.

The purpose of this chapter is to provide you with a deeper understanding of the Registry and the wealth of information it holds. Besides configuration information, the Windows Registry holds information regarding recently accessed files and considerable information about user activities. All of this can be extremely valuable, depending on the nature of the case you're working on. Most of the Registry analysis that we address in this chapter will be post mortem—in other words, after you've acquired an image of the system. However, in some instances we will discuss analysis from a live system as well as provide examples of what the keys and values look like on a live system. There are a few minor considerations to keep in mind when we're performing live vice post-mortem analysis; those will be pointed out when the subject is being discussed.

Throughout this chapter, we will discuss various Registry keys and values that can be of interest during an investigation. However, this chapter should not be considered a comprehensive listing of all possible Registry values that might be of interest. Although Registry keys associated directly with the operating system could be fairly stagnant once the system has been installed, they can change as Service Packs and patches are installed, as well as across versions of the Windows operating system itself. Also, a great many applications are available, all with their own unique Registry entries that can also change between application versions. Think of this chapter as a guide and a reference listing, but also keep in mind that it is by no means complete. Our goal in this chapter is to describe the format of Registry files, how the Registry can be examined, and some important keys within the Registry and how to analyze them. By the time you reach the end of this chapter, you should have an understanding of what the Registry holds and be adept at retrieving and analyzing information from within the Registry.

Inside the Registry

So, what *is* the Registry? If you remember back to DOS and early versions of Windows (3.1, 3.11, and so on), configuration information (drivers, settings) for the system was largely managed by several files—specifically, autoexec.bat, config.sys, win.ini (on Windows), and system.ini. Various settings within these files determined what programs were loaded and how the system looked and responded to user input.

Later versions of Windows replaced these files with the Registry, a central hierarchal database[1] that maintains configuration settings for applications, hardware devices, and users. This "database" (using the term loosely) replaces the text-based configuration files used by the previous versions of Microsoft operating systems.

For the most part, administrators directly interact with the Registry through some intermediary application, the most common of which are the graphical user interface (GUI) Registry editors that ship with Windows—Regedit.exe or Regedt32.exe. In many cases, the extent of a user or Administrator's interaction with the Registry is through an installation program (software applications, patches), which does not permit the user to directly interact with specific keys and values within the Registry. Windows XP and 2003 distributions include reg.exe, a CLI tool that can be used from the command prompt or in scripts. For more information on the GUI Registry editing utilities, see the "RegEdit and RegEdt32" sidebar.

Tools & Traps...

RegEdit and RegEdt32

Interestingly, the two Registry editing utilities provided with Windows operating systems are not equivalent on all versions of Windows.[2]

For example, on Windows NT and 2000, you would use RegEdit.exe primarily for its search capabilities but not to modify access control lists (ACLs) on Registry keys. RegEdit.exe has an added limitation of not "understanding" the *REG_EXPAND_SZ* (a variable length string) or *REG_MULTI_SZ* (a multiple string) data types. If values with either of these data types are edited, the data is saved as a *REG_SZ* (a fixed-length string) data type and the functionality of the key is lost. RegEdt32.exe, on the other hand, does not allow you to import or export hive (.reg) files.

Continued

> On Windows XP and 2003, RegEdit.exe allows you to do all these things, and RegEdt32.exe is nothing more than a small program that runs RegEdit.exe.

When the administrator opens Regedit.exe, he sees a tree-like structure with five root folders, or "hives," in the navigation area of the GUI, as illustrated in Figure 4.1. This folder-like structure allows the administrator to easily navigate through the Registry, much like a file system.

Figure 4.1 Regedit.exe View Showing Five Root Hives

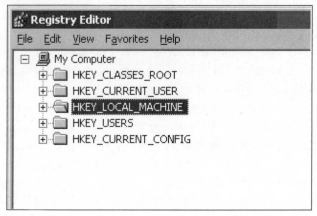

Each of these hives plays an important role in the function of the system. The HKEY_USERS hive contains all the actively loaded user profiles for that system. HKEY_CURRENT_USER is the active, loaded user profile for the currently logged-on user. The HKEY_LOCAL_MACHINE hive contains a vast array of configuration information for the system, including hardware settings and software settings. The HKEY_CURRENT_CONFIG hive contains the hardware profile the system uses at startup. Finally, the HKEY_CLASSES_ROOT hive contains configuration information relating to which application is used to open various files on the system. This hive is subclassed to both HKEY_CURRENT_USER\Software\Classes (user-specific settings) and HKEY_LOCAL_MACHINE\Software\Classes (systemwide settings).

All this is good and fine, but it helps to know where the hives come from and where they exist on the hard drive within the file system. The contents of much of the Registry visible in the Registry Editor can be found in several files, as listed in Table 4.1.

Table 4.1 Registry Paths and Corresponding Files

Registry Path	File Path
HKEY_LOCAL_MACHINE\System	%WINDIR%\system32\config\System
HKEY_LOCAL_MACHINE\SAM	%WINDIR%\system32\config\Sam
HKEY_LOCAL_MACHINE\Security	%WINDIR%\system32\config\Security
HKEY_LOCAL_MACHINE\Software	%WINDIR%\system32\config\Software
HKEY_LOCAL_MACHINE\Hardware	Volatile hive
HKEY_LOCAL_MACHINE\System\Clone	Volatile hive
HKEY_USERS*User SID*	User profile (NTUSER.DAT); "Documents and Settings*User* (changed to "Users*User*" on Vista)
HKEY_USERS\.Default	%WINDIR%\system32\config\default

You'll notice that several of the Registry paths are volatile and do not exist in files on the hard drive. These hives are created during system startup and are not available when the system shuts down. This is important to remember when you're performing post-mortem forensic analysis as well as live response on a running system.

In addition to the different sections or hives, the Registry supports several different data types for the various values that it contains. Table 4.2 lists the various data types and their descriptions.

Table 4.2 Registry Data Types and Descriptions

Data Type	Description
REG_BINARY	Raw binary data
REG_DWORD	Data represented as a 32-bit (4-byte) integer
REG_SZ	A fixed-length text string
REG_EXPAND_SZ	A variable-length data string
REG_MULTI_SZ	Multiple strings, separated by a space, comma, or other delimiter

Continued

Table 4.2 continued Registry Data Types and Descriptions

Data Type	Description
REG_NONE	No data type
REG_QWORD	Data represented by a 64-bit (8-byte) integer
REG_LINK	A Unicode string naming a symbolic link
REG_RESOURCE_LIST	A series of nested arrays designed to store a resource list
REG_RESOURCE_ REQUIREMENTS_LIST	A series of nested arrays designed to store a device driver's list of possible hardware resources
REG_FULL_RESOURCE_ DESCRIPTOR	A series of nested arrays designed to store a resource list used by a physical hardware device

As you can see, a variety of data types are found in the Registry. There don't seem to be any rules or consistency between values found in different keys; values that serve similar purposes may have different data types, allowing their data to be formatted and stored differently. This can become an issue when you're performing text searches for data within the Registry. Where one application might store a list of recently accessed documents as ASCII text strings, another might store a similar list as Unicode strings in a binary data type, in which case an ASCII text search would miss that data. In fact, a KnowledgeBase article[3] specifically states that the Find tool in RegEdit can only be used to find ASCII string data rather than DWORD or binary data.

Registry Structure within a Hive File

Now that you've seen where the Registry hive files are located, let's take a look inside those files and see the structure of the Registry itself, at a much lower level. You're probably wondering at this point why we would want to do this. Well, by understanding the basic components of the Registry, we might be able to glean some extra information through keyword searches of other locations and sources, such as the page file, physical memory, or even unallocated space. If we know what to look for or what we're looking at, we might able to extract an extra bit of information. Also, by knowing more about the information that is available within the Registry, we will know better what is possible and what to look for.

Mark Russinovich wrote an excellent article for *WindowsNT Magazine* called "Inside the Registry,"[4] which describes the different components, or cells, of the Registry. This same information is covered in *Windows Internals*, which was coauthored by Mark with David Solomon.

Each type of cell has a specific structure and contains specific types of information. The various types of cells are:

- **Key cell** This cell contains Registry key information and includes offsets to other cells as well as the *LastWrite* time for the key (signature: *kn*).

- **Value cell** This cell holds a value and its data (signature: *kv*).

- **Subkey list cell** This cell is made up of a series of indexes (or offsets) pointing to key cells; these are all subkeys to the parent key cell.

- **Value list cell** This cell is made up of a series of indexes (or offsets) pointing to values cells; these are all values of a common key cell.

- **Security descriptor cell** This cell contains security descriptor information for a key cell (signature: *ks*).

Figure 4.2 illustrates the various types of cell (with the exception of the security descriptor cell) as they appear in the Registry Editor.

Figure 4.2 Excerpt of Windows Registry Showing Keys, Values, and Data

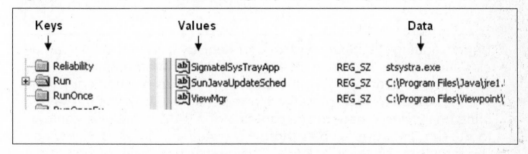

Figure 4.3 illustrates an excerpt of a Registry file opened in a hex editor. The figure shows the signatures for a key cell as well as for a value cell. Note that due to endian issues, the signature for a key cell (i.e., *kn*) appears as *nk* and for a value cell (i.e., *kv*) appears as *vk*.

Figure 4.3 Excerpt of a Raw Registry File Showing Key and Value Cell Signatures

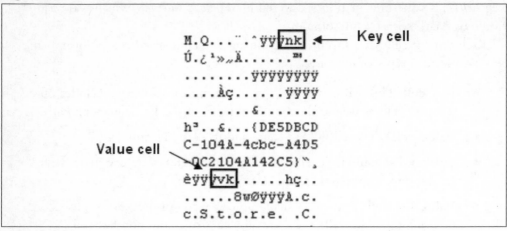

As mentioned earlier, these signatures can provide us with extremely valuable information during an investigation. Using these signatures, we can potentially carve Registry key and value information out of the unallocated clusters of an acquired image or even out of RAM dumps. (See Chapter 3, "Windows Memory Analysis," for more information on RAM dumps.)

TIP

Understanding the binary structure of Registry keys and values can be extremely useful during an investigation. Most investigations that involve some degree of Registry analysis will focus on the Registry files themselves, using tools presented in this chapter. However, in examining unallocated space or the contents of a RAM dump, you could locate the signatures such as those illustrated in Figure 4.3. Knowing the format of the Registry key and value structures allows you to, if necessary, extract and parse the data into something understandable. You might find a Registry key in memory, for example, and be able to extract the *LastWrite* time.

The best reference for the actual programmatic binary structure of the various cells within Registry hive files isn't available from the vendor; oddly enough, it's available from a guy who wrote a Linux utility. Peter Nordahl-Hagen created the

Offline Registry and Password Editor,[5] a utility that allows you to boot a Windows system (assuming that you have physical access to the system) to a Linux diskette and edit the Registry to include changing passwords. Peter provides the source for his utility, and if you choose to download it, you'll be most interested in the file named ntreg.h. This is a C header file that defines the structures for the different types of cells that make up the Registry.

From Peter's source code, we can see that the key cell is 76 bytes long, plus a variable-length name. Therefore, if we locate the signature for a key cell (as illustrated in Figure 4.3) in a RAM dump or in unallocated clusters, we might very well have the contents of a key cell. From there, we can parse the next 74 bytes (the signature is 2 bytes long—in little endian hex format, 0x6B6E) and see such things as the name of the key and its *LastWrite* time.

For example, say that you have some unallocated clusters or a RAM dump from a system and you've located a key cell. Given a variable called *$offset* that is the offset within the file to the key cell you've located, Perl code to parse that key cell and extract data from it looks like this:

```
seek(FH,$offset,0);
read(FH,$data,76);
my %nk;
my (@recs) = unpack("vvV17vv",$record);
$nk{id}             = $recs[0];
$nk{type}           = $recs[1];
$nk{time1}          = $recs[2];
$nk{time2}          = $recs[3];
$nk{time3}          = $recs[4];
$nk{no_subkeys}     = $recs[6];
$nk{ofs_lf}         = $recs[8];
$nk{no_values}      = $recs[10];
$nk{ofs_vallist}    = $recs[11];
$nk{ofs_sk}         = $recs[12];
$nk{ofs_classname}  = $recs[13];
$nk{len_name}       = $recs[19];
$nk{len_classname}  = $recs[20];
# Get the name
seek(FH,$offset + 76,0);
read(FH,$data,$nk{len_name});
```

In this code, *FH* is a Perl file handle to the file containing the data we're examining, and *$data* is a scalar variable meant to hold the contents of what we've just read from the file. This code provides a simple, straightforward method for parsing essential information from a key cell. We can see values that give us the *LastWrite* time as well as the numbers of subkeys and values associated with the key cell. We can also get offsets to additional data structures, such as lists of other key cells (i.e., the subkeys), as well as to the value list (i.e., values for this key).

The value cells are only 18 bytes long with a variable-length name and variable-length data. The data type is stored in a 4-byte (*DWORD*) value located within the value cell itself. Using the same technique as with the key cell, we can parse information about the value cell from whatever source we're looking at and see the actual values. Perl code to parse the value cell looks like this:

```
seek(FH,$offset,0);
my $bytes = read(FH,$data,20);
my (@recs)      = unpack("vvVVVvv",$data);
$vk{id}         = $recs[0];
$vk{len_name} = $recs[1];
$vk{len_data} = $recs[2];
$vk{ofs_data} = $recs[3];
$vk{val_type} = $recs[4];
$vk{flag}       = $recs[5];
if ($vk{len_name} == 0) {
$vk{valname} = "Default";
}
else {
seek(FH,$offset + 20,0);
        read(FH,$data,$vk{len_name});
        $vk{valname}  = $data;
}
```

Although we can parse this data from various sources, there could be insufficient information to add context to what we discover, such as which Registry key the value originally belonged to, when it was created, or how it was used. Extracting information about key and value cells from RAM dumps and unallocated space might be of limited value, depending on the needs of the investigation.

I wrote a Perl script that I call the Offline Registry Parser, or regp.pl for short, based on the structures that Peter provided. It incorporates the Perl code we just saw. The script will allow you to parse a raw Registry file, extracting the key and value cell information and printing the information to the console in ASCII format. The output can be redirected to a file for archiving, searching, or comparing with other files. There are several advantages to using this script and code like it. First, it provides an open-source example for how to parse through the raw Registry files; someone with an understanding of Perl programming can easily extend the capabilities of the script, such as recording the output in a spreadsheet or database for easier processing. Second, the script relies only on basic Perl functionality; it does not use any fancy platform-specific modules, nor does it rely on the MS API. This means that the script can be run on any system that supports Perl, including Linux. If an investigator is using TSK[6] or PyFlag[7] on a Linux system as an analysis platform, then she is not prevented from parsing, viewing, and analyzing the contents of the Registry files. Although this doesn't add any new functionality to any of the available forensic analysis tools, it does provide options for data reduction and faster, more efficient processing.

With careful attention to coding practices, the regp.pl script can be extended to only look for and print out specific keys or to translate specific data into something readable by humans.

The reg.pl Perl script (as well as a stand-alone Windows executable "compiled" from the script using Perl2Exe) is available on the DVD that accompanies this book.

Another interesting file Peter provides in the source code for his utility is sam.h. This file provides some very valuable information regarding structures within the SAM portion of the Registry. We will discuss these structures and how we can use them later in this chapter, in the "Finding Users" section.

The Registry As a Log File

The key cells within the Registry constitute the keys or folders that you see when you open the Registry Editor. This is the only one of the structures that contains a time value, called the *LastWrite* time. The LastWrite time is a 64-bit FILETIME object, which is analogous to the last modification time on a file (see the "Registry Key LastWrite Time" sidebar for more information). Not only does this information provide a timeframe reference for certain user activities on the system, but in several cases, it will also tell us when a specific value was added to a key or modified.

Notes from the Underground…

Registry Key LastWrite Time

Registry keys have several properties associated with them, one of which is the *LastWrite* time, which is similar to the last modification time associated with files and directories. The *LastWrite* time is stored as a FILETIME[8] object (or structure) that represents the number of 100-nanosecond intervals since 1 Jan 1601 (don't ask me why that particular date was chosen as the starting point!). To convert this 64-bit value into something legible, you must translate[9] it to a SYSTEMTIME structure. Translating the FILETIME structure directly to a SYSTEMTIME structure using the *FileTimeToSystemTime()* API will allow you to display the date in UTC format, which is loosely defined as Greenwich Mean Time (GMT). To translate these values into something that accurately represents the current system time, you must first pass the FILETIME structure through the *FileTimeToLocalFileTime()* API. This API takes into account daylight savings time and the time zone information of the local system.

One particular instance where I've found this to be useful is during post-mortem intrusion investigations. I like to open the Registry Viewer in ProDiscover and locate the area where Registry keys specific to Windows services are maintained. From there, I will sort the first level of keys based on their *LastWrite* times, and invariably I've been able to easily locate services that were installed during the intrusion, such as remote access backdoors or even rootkits.

TIP

Rootkits are discussed in greater detail in Chapter 7, "Rootkits and Rootkit Detection." However, the W32/Opanki.worm!MS06-040, as identified by Network Associates, serves as a useful example.[10] The worm installs a rootkit component, creating two Windows services (in addition to a number of other activities). Because most compromises occur sometime after the operating system is installed, sorting the Services keys based on their *LastWrite* times will often quickly reveal the issue.

In addition to the *LastWrite* times, the Registry also maintains timestamp information in some of the data associated with specific values. We will discuss some of these values later in this chapter, but for now, it's enough to know that there are Registry keys whose values contain 8 bytes of data that comprise a FILETIME object.

So why do I refer to the Registry as a log file? It's because log files generally have some sort of action or event associated with a time, and in many cases, this is true for the Registry. Although the Registry can hold literally thousands of entries, not all of them are of interest during an investigation. There are specific keys that we will be interested in during different types of investigations, and if we understand how those keys and values are created, modified, and used by the system, we will begin to see how the Registry actually records the occurrence of different events, along with an associated timestamp.

Monitoring Changes to the Registry

There is really no single, consolidated resource of Registry keys that will be useful in any particular situation. A spreadsheet containing many of the keys that I and others find useful during various types of investigations is included in the "Chapter 5" directory on the accompanying CD. However, this is not a be-all and end-all solution, because there simply isn't one. In some cases, Registry keys that are created during installation or modified during use may change between versions of a particular application. Shortly after this book goes to print, is published, and is ready for purchase, you can be sure that a new application will be available that records configuration and setting information in the Registry.

So how do we go about determining Registry keys and values that are important to us? One way is to snapshot the Registry, perform an atomic action (that is, do just one thing), snapshot the Registry again, and look at the two snapshots for differences. One particular tool that is useful for this task is InControl5.[11.] InControl5 is a great utility for doing all kinds of analysis. I generally tend to run InControl5 in two-phase mode, where I open the application, have it snapshot my system, do whatever it is I'm going to do (install a P2P file sharing application or some bit of malware), then open InControl5 again and have it complete the process. The HTML output is most often enough for my purposes, and I can clearly see the Registry keys (and files) that were added, modified, or deleted during the process.

Another way to discover useful or important keys is to use Regmon[12.] from Microsoft to monitor the Registry in real time. When I was trying to determine where user information was kept within the Registry, I found that by running

Regmon while executing the *net user* command I could determine which keys and values were accessed when retrieving user information, as illustrated in Figure 4.4.

Figure 4.4 Excerpt of Regmon Output

lsass.exe:1052	QueryValue	HKLM\SAM\SAM\C	
lsass.exe:1052	QueryValue	HKLM\SAM\SAM\Domains\Account\V	
lsass.exe:1052	OpenKey	HKLM\SAM\SAM\DOMAINS\Account\Users\Names	
lsass.exe:1052	Enumerate...	HKLM\SAM\SAM\DOMAINS\Account\Users\Names	
lsass.exe:1052	OpenKey	HKLM\SAM\SAM\DOMAINS\Account\Users\Names\Administrator	
lsass.exe:1052	QueryValue	HKLM\SAM\SAM\DOMAINS\Account\Users\Names\Administrator\(Default)	
lsass.exe:1052	CloseKey	HKLM\SAM\SAM\DOMAINS\Account\Users\Names\Administrator	
lsass.exe:1052	Enumerate...	HKLM\SAM\SAM\DOMAINS\Account\Users\Names	
lsass.exe:1052	OpenKey	HKLM\SAM\SAM\DOMAINS\Account\Users\Names\Guest	
lsass.exe:1052	QueryValue	HKLM\SAM\SAM\DOMAINS\Account\Users\Names\Guest\(Default)	
lsass.exe:1052	CloseKey	HKLM\SAM\SAM\DOMAINS\Account\Users\Names\Guest	
lsass.exe:1052	Enumerate...	HKLM\SAM\SAM\DOMAINS\Account\Users\Names	

Figure 4.4 shows an excerpt of the Regmon output used to monitor the *net user* command. I started the capture, ran the command, then halted the capture and searched all the output for *SAM*. That way, I was able to see that although I had used net.exe to request the information, net.exe passed off the request to lsass.exe, which accessed the Registry to obtain the information about usernames on the system.

Test Drive...

Monitoring the Registry

Here's something you can try. Download a copy of Regmon to your system, open it, and then halt the capture (click the magnifying glass icon so that it has a red X over it). Then open a command prompt and type **net accounts**, but do not press Enter. Go back to Regmon and start the capture, and then go back to the command prompt and immediately press **Enter**. As soon as you see the account policies appear in the command prompt, go back to Regmon and stop the capture. To make things easier, filter on lsass.exe and see which Registry keys were accessed to provide the information you see in the command prompt. Now when you're performing a post-mortem investigation you'll know which keys to look in for information pertaining to the account policies.

Throughout the rest of the chapter, you'll see several references to using InControl5 as well as Regmon. It would be a good idea to have copies of them on hand (due to the terms of the licenses for each of the tools, they cannot be distributed on the media accompanying the book), particularly if you want to follow along and try out some of the different techniques mentioned.

Registry Analysis

Now that we know the structure of the Registry, let's take a look at retrieving and analyzing information from within the Registry. Much of this information will be available to us during live response (with the exception of those keys we cannot access due to permissions), and all of it (with the exception of the volatile portions of the Registry) will be available during a post-mortem investigation.

ProDiscover provides a simple interface (actually, an API) for accessing the Registry during post-mortem analysis. When a case is loaded into ProDiscover, the investigator need only right-click the **Windows** directory in the Content View and choose **Add to Registry Viewer**. ProDiscover then locates the necessary files to populate the Registry Viewer, as shown in Figure 4.5.

Figure 4.5 Registry Viewer in ProDiscover IR

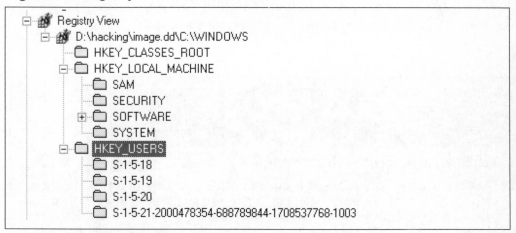

ProDiscover's scripting language, ProScript, is based on Perl and provides an excellent facility for extracting information from the Registry in an automated fashion. The ProScript.pm module facilitates an API for writing Perl scripts that interact almost completely with ProDiscover; just about anything you can do through the ProDiscover user interface can also be done with a ProScript. With respect to the Windows Registry and post-mortem forensic analysis, ProScripts can be used to completely automate a great deal of tedious data collection and formatting. Throughout this chapter, we'll describe ProScripts for performing various tasks such as extracting and analyzing information from within the Registry during post-mortem analysis. Each of these ProScripts can be found in the ch4\code directory on the DVD that accompanies this book.

System Information

When working with an acquired image of a Windows system during post-mortem analysis, there is a great deal of basic information about the system that you might be interested in. Much of this information is relatively easy to obtain during live response; for example, in many cases, you can determine the version of the operating system (such as Windows 2000, XP, 2003, or Vista) by simply looking at the shell. Or you can right-click **My Computer** and choose **Properties** to see a lot of basic information, such as the version of the operating system, the Service Pack level, and the name of the computer. This information is also available in the Registry, where it is easily accessed during post-mortem analysis.

If you remember, the *CurrentControlSet* is a volatile portion of the Registry, and you won't find it in an acquired image. The "Finding the *CurrentControlSet*" sidebar illustrates ways in which you can determine which *ControlSet* was marked as "current" on the live system. Once you determine which *ControlSet* was current, you want to focus your examination on keys within that particular *ControlSet*.

Forensic Feats...

Finding the *CurrentControlSet*

Most times when you access an acquired image, you'll be interested to know which of the two *ControlSets* visible in the Registry Viewer (in ProDiscover) was used as the *CurrentControlSet* by the operating system. To do so, navigate to the HKEY_LOCAL_MACHINE\System\Select key and you'll find several values, as illustrated in Figure 4.6.

Figure 4.6 Locating the *CurrentControlSet* in an Image

☐ 🔤	(Default)	REG_SZ	(value not set)
☐ 🔟	Current	REG_DWORD	0x00000001 (1)
☐ 🔟	Default	REG_DWORD	0x00000001 (1)
☐ 🔟	Failed	REG_DWORD	0x00000000 (0)
☐ 🔟	LastKnownGood	REG_DWORD	0x00000002 (2)

As shown in Figure 4.6, the *ControlSet* that the operating system used as the *CurrentControlSet* while it was active is numbered 1. Within the Registry Viewer are two *ControlSets*: *ControlSet001* and *ControlSet002*. (In some cases, you'll find different numbers, including *ControlSet03* and *ControlSet04*; however, you will generally only see two *ControlSets*.)

The computer's name can be found in the following key, in the *ComputerName* value:

```
SYSTEM\CurrentControlSet\Control\ComputerName\ActiveComputerName
```

The time that the system was last shut down can be found in the following key:

```
SYSTEM\ControlSet00x\Control\Windows
```

The *ShutdownTime* value beneath this key is a FILETIME object and can be correlated with other times on the system, such as Event Log entries (discussed in Chapter 6) and the like to assist in developing a timeline of activity and system use.

The following key could also be of value during an investigation:

```
SOFTWARE\Microsoft\Windows NT\CurrentVersion
```

This key holds several values that provide information about the system. The *ProductName*, *CurrentBuildNumber*, and *CSDVersion* values will tell you which operating system and version (including the Service Pack) you're working with. The *RegisteredOrganization* and *RegisteredOwner* values, although not always filled in, can be used to further identify the system. The *ProductId* and *InstallDate* values can also be of use.

TimeZoneInformation

Information about the time zone settings can be found in the following key:

`SYSTEM\CurrentControlSet\Control\TimeZoneInformation`

This information can be extremely important for establishing a timeline of activity on the system. Throughout the rest of this chapter, we'll discuss various scripts that can be used to retrieve information from the Registry; in other chapters we will discuss files, Event Log entries, and the like. Many of the available tools will extract information regarding times and dates in UTC/GMT time, and you can use the *ActiveTimeBias* (listed in minutes) value from the *TimeZoneInformation* key to translate or normalize the times to other sources from the system, such as entries in log files.

Shares

By default, Windows 2000, XP, 2003, and Vista systems will create hidden administrative shares on a system. There are the IPC$ (interprocess communications) share, ADMIN$, shares that refer to the root of the hard drive(s) on the system (C$, D$, etc.), among others. If a user creates an additional share, such as via the *net share* command, that share will appear in the following key (unless otherwise specified, all Registry keys in this section are located in the HKEY_LOCAL_MACHINE hive):

`SYSTEM\CurrentControlSet\Services\lanmanserver\Shares`

On a sample image that I have, I found the following entry when I was using the Offline Registry Parser to extract information from the SYSTEM hive file:

```
\$$$PROTO.HIV\ControlSet001\Services\lanmanserver\Shares
LastWrite time: Fri Aug 20 15:19:35 2004 (UTC)
       --> Temp;REG_MULTI_SZ;CSCFlags=0 MaxUses=4294967295 Path=C:\Temp
Permissions=0 Remark= Type=0
```

In the case of this particular image, I booted it in VMware using LiveView[13.] and confirmed that the C:\Temp directory was indeed shared out as Temp. The *LastWrite* time of the key gives an idea of when the share was added to the system. If there are multiple shares, however, possibly added over a period of time, the *LastWrite* time might not be as useful to us, since this key does not maintain a most recently used (MRU) list. (MRU lists will be discussed later in the chapter.)

Again, by default, you might not see any shares listed under the Shares key. This simply means that the user hasn't created any new shares. However, if the user or Administrator took steps to disable the hidden administrative shares, you'll want to look beneath the following key:

```
SYSTEM\CurrentControlSet\Services\lanmanserver\parameters
```

If you see a value named *AutoShareServer*[14.] beneath this key and the data is 0, this is an indication that the system has been modified specifically to prevent the creation of the hidden administrative shares.

Audit Policy

The system's audit policy[15.] is maintained in the Security hive, beneath the Policy\PolAdtEv key. The *(Default)* value is a *REG_NONE* data type and contains binary information into which the audit policy is encoded. The audit policy extracted from a sample image using the Offline Registry Parser shows:

```
\SECURITY\Policy\PolAdtEv
LastWrite time: Fri Sep  9 01:11:43 2005
      --> Default;REG_NONE;01 17 f5 77 03 00 00 00 03 00 00 00 00 00 00 00
00 00 00 00 00 00 00 00 03 00 00 00 03 00 00 00 00 00 00 00 03 00 00 00 09
00 00 00
```

The first *DWORD* (4 bytes) of the binary data (actually, the first byte) lets you know whether auditing was enabled. In this case, the value is 01, so auditing was enabled (00 indicates that it was disabled). Windows 2000 and XP systems have nine event types that can be audited, and each of those areas is represented by a *DWORD* value in the sequence of bytes. The final *DWORD* value is not used.

To decipher this information, we need to understand a bit about the format. Map the following template over the data retrieved from the *PolAdtEv* key:

```
0Z XX XX XX AA 00 00 00 BB 00 00 00 CC 00 00 00 DD 00 00 00 EE 00 00 00 FF
00 00 00 GG 00 00 00 HH 00 00 00 II 00 00 00 XX 00 00 00
```

The value for *Z* determines whether or not auditing is enabled (1 for enabled, 0 for disabled). The rest of the values correspond to the following listing (we don't care about the *X* values):

```
AA      Audit System Events
BB      Audit Logon Events
CC      Audit Object Access
DD      Audit Privilege Use
EE      Audit Process Tracking
FF      Audit Policy Change
GG      Audit Account Management
HH      Audit Directory Service Access
II      Audit Account Logon Events
```

For each of the lettered pairs, 00 means that there is no auditing, 01 means that success events are audited, 02 means the failure events are audited, and 03 means that both success and failure events are audited.

We can see that both success and failure auditing was enabled on the sample image for System events, Logon events, Policy Change events, Account Management, and Account Logon events.

This information can be useful during an investigation because it will tell us what sorts of events we should expect to see in the Event Log. (We discuss Event Log analysis in the next chapter.)

Wireless SSIDs

On live systems (most often laptops), Windows XP will maintain a list of service set identifiers (SSIDs) to which it has connected. This list is maintained in the following Registry key:

```
SOFTWARE\Microsoft\WZCSVC\Parameters\Interfaces\{GUID}
```

The *GUID* in this case is the GUID for the wireless interface. Beneath this key, you might see a value *ActiveSettings* and then several other values called *Static#000x*, where *x* is an integer, starting at 0. These values are all binary, and the SSIDs for any wireless access points that have been accessed will be included within the binary data. Within the binary data, at offset 0x10, is a *DWORD* value that contains the length of the SSID. The SSID name immediately follows this *DWORD* value for the number of bytes/characters listed. Figure 4.7 illustrates the binary contents of the *ActiveSettings* value, taken from a live system. Note that the SSID has been highlighted.

Figure 4.7 ActiveSettings Value from a Live System, Showing the SSID

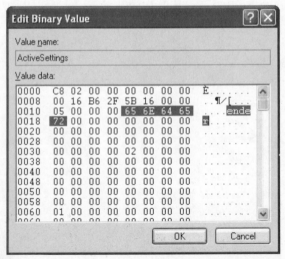

Now and again, a question appears on a public listserv regarding determining SSIDs to which the system has been connected. This can be useful in situations where unauthorized access is an issue or in a case where it's important to trace the IP address that the individual was using.

Autostart Locations

Autostart locations within the Registry are locations that allow applications to be launched without any interaction from the user and very often unbeknownst to the user as they do … *something* on the system. These locations were originally provided for the user's convenience. Some applications, such as touch pad drivers and applications on laptops, as well as antivirus and firewall applications, are most useful when they're started automatically. In other cases, users like to have applications such as instant-messaging clients started automatically when they log into their systems, as a matter of convenience.

In 2004, members of the Microsoft Research Center's CyberSecurity and Systems Management Research group presented a paper, *Gatekeeper: Monitoring Auto-Start Extensibility Points for System Management,* at a Usenix conference. In that paper, the authors refer to the autostart locations as *auto-start extensibility points,* or ASEPs. The paper categorizes the ASEPs in a different manner than I have and provides a graph showing that perhaps the most popular ASEP used by spyware (at the time that the data was compiled) was to install as a browser helper object, or BHO. A BHO is essentially a DLL that is loaded automatically by Internet Explorer when it starts, and from there it can monitor the user's activities. See the "BHOs" case study for an example of how this autostart/ASEP can be used.

Are You Owned?

Case Study: BHOs

I was the security admin at a financial services firm when I ran into an interesting use of browser helper objects. My employer provided credit monitoring and identity theft protection services to its customers, allowing for a variety of levels of monitoring of their credit, from quarterly reports to nearly instant pages and/or e-mails whenever a query appeared. And like most businesses, my employer had competition. At one point, I got a call from folks on the business development side of the house with a potential security issue. Several users had gone to the company Web site, and when they loaded the main Web

Continued

page, each instance of our company's name was highlighted, and clicking it took the user to a competitor's Web site!

It turned out that a BHO had been installed on the user's system (it was happening to several people, and our business development staff had figured out how to get "infected" as well) and would monitor the user's browsing activity. Various companies would subscribe to this adware/BHO provider, and whenever their competitor's names appeared in a Web page, the BHO would automatically turn the name into a hyperlink to their subscriber's Web site. So let's say Consumer Electronics Company A signed up with the adware provider. When the adware had infected a user's system, every time a Web page was loaded that had the names of A's competitors, those names would be made into hyperlinks to A's Web site.

Fortunately, MS is kind enough to provide KB article 298931[16] to tell users how to disable BHOs. The KB article provides links to more detailed information regarding BHOs, which are listed beneath the Registry key HKLM\SOFTWARE\Microsoft\Windows\CurrentVersion\Explorer\Browser Helper Objects.

Note that this key is in the HKEY_LOCAL_MACHINE hive, which means that browser loads the BHOs whenever it is opened, regardless of the user.

The bho.pl Perl script located on the accompanying DVD allows you to view the BHOs that have been installed on a live system.

One school of thought seems to be that most users and administrators aren't all that familiar with autostart locations within the Registry and believe that only a very few keys (in particular, the ubiquitous Run and RunOnce keys) can be used for such purposes. This manner of thinking is supported, in part, by documentation and applications provided by the operating system vendor. For example, on a live Windows XP system, a command called *MSConfig* launches the System Configuration utility.[17] You can run this command by clicking the **Start** button on the Task Bar, choosing **Run**, and typing **msconfig** into the textbox, then pressing **Enter**. Figure 4.8 illustrates the System Configuration utility opened to show the contents of the Startup tab.

Run this command on your XP system and take a closer look at the Location column. You'll see that the Registry keys examined are the Run key from both the HKEY_CURRENT_USER and HKEY_LOCAL_MACHINE hives. Unfortunately, these seem to be the only keys examined. There is a WMI class named Win32_StartupCommand[18] that will allow a programmer to automatically retrieve the contents of these keys, but as with the System Configuration Utility, it checks only a very limited number of startup locations within the Registry.

Figure 4.8 System Configuration Utility Startup Tab

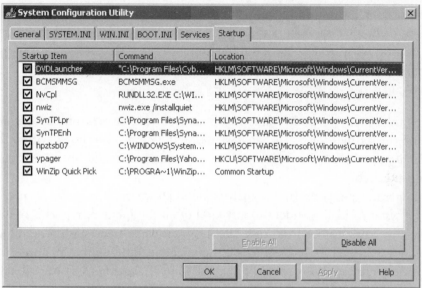

Another school of thought is that the sheer number of autostart locations within the Registry is so large that examining these locations is best left to professionals and/or software created by professionals, such as commercial antivirus and antispyware utilities.

The truth is somewhere in between. Yes, there are a number of autostart locations within the Registry, but for the most part, they are finite and limited. In the following sections we break down these locations into three areas and describe some of the Registry keys that are accessed when the system boots, those accessed when a user logs in, and those accessed when a user performs some activity on the system. Then we'll look at ways to enumerate the entries in these locations. However, the listed keys should not be considered all inclusive or a complete and comprehensive list of all keys. The DVD that accompanies this book includes a spreadsheet named regref.xls that contains several worksheets. Each worksheet includes various Registry keys that fall into that worksheet's category as well as a brief description of the key, and where applicable, a credible reference that describes the functionality of that key. This spreadsheet should be considered a starting point for Registry analysis, but because there are a great many applications out there and new versions being produced all the time, it should not be considered complete.

System Boot

Autostart locations within the Registry that are accessed when the system boots are favorites of malware authors because they allow the malware to be launched with no user interaction whatsoever—not even logging into the system. One location is the Windows services, or more specifically:

```
HKEY_LOCAL_MACHINE\System\CurrentControlSet\Services
```

When the system starts, the value for the current *ControlSet* to be used is determined, and the settings for that *ControlSet* are used. The services listed within that *ControlSet* are scanned, and services that are set to start automatically (*Start* value is 0x02) are launched.

When performing an intrusion analysis, often all we have to go on is an acquired image of a system and an incident report (and often the incident report isn't much more than "we saw this occur on this date"). When we're faced with something like this, an easy way to get started is to open the image in ProDiscover, populate the Registry Viewer, locate the *ControlSet* marked *Current*, and then sort the subkeys beneath the Services key based on their *LastWrite* times. These times should generally line up in accordance with the installation date of the operating system (when most of the services and drivers were installed) and the installation dates of legitimate applications that the Administrator knows about. However, in several cases I've found services and drivers installed by the attacker, including rootkits and a driver called rdriv.sys, which is a rootkit driver file used by Trojans and IRC bots. In some cases I've located these services, and neither the names of the services nor the *LastWrite* times correlated to the incident report I had received. Essentially, I'd found an intrusion separate from the one I was investigating!

You can find other interesting things in this manner. For example, I've located npf.sys, the driver installed with the WinPcap utilities that allow you to perform packet sniffing on your system. This driver is installed by tools such as WireShark and the sniffer tools available with the WinPcap utilities—but they might also be installed by an attacker.

User Login

According to Microsoft documentation, the startup process for a system is not considered complete until a user logs in. When a user logs into a system, certain Registry keys are accessed and parsed so that listed applications can be run. Those keys are (in order):[19]

1. HKLM\ Software \Microsoft\Windows\CurrentVersion\Runonce

2. HKLM\ Software\Microsoft\Windows\CurrentVersion\
    Policies\Explorer\Run

3. HKLM\ Software\Microsoft\Windows\CurrentVersion\Run

4. HKCU\Software\Microsoft\Windows
    NT\CurrentVersion\Windows\Run

5. HKCU\Software\Microsoft\Windows\CurrentVersion\Run

6. HKCU\Software\Microsoft\Windows\CurrentVersion\RunOnce

For the sake of brevity, *HKLMrefers* to the HKEY_LOCAL_MACHINE hive, and *HKCU* refers to the HKEY_CURRENT_USER hive.

Each time a new user logs into the system, keys 1, 3, 5, and 6 are parsed, and the programs listed are run.[20.] By default, these Run keys are ignored if the system is started in Safe Mode. However, on Windows XP and 2003 systems, if you preface the RunOnce values (keys 1 and 6) with an asterisk (*), you can force the associated program to be run even if the system is started in Safe Mode.[21.] Further, on Windows XP, keys 1, 3, 5, and 6 are provided for legacy programs and backward compatibility[22.] so that programs written for earlier versions of Windows (or prior to Windows XP being released) can still be used.

User Activity

Autostart Registry locations that fall under this category are those that are accessed when the user performs an action, such as opening an application like Internet Explorer or Outlook. If you run RegMon on a system and just move the mouse or open an application (or do nothing whatsoever), you'll see that there are quite a number of accesses to the Registry, even when there is apparently nothing going on with regard to the user interacting with the system. As with other autostart locations, malware (virus, Trojan, worm, and so on) authors find these Registry keys extremely useful in maintaining the persistence of their products, ensuring that they're up and running.

One such notable location is:

```
HKEY_LOCAL_MACHINE\Software\Classes\Exefile\Shell\Open\command
```

This Registry key as well as the keys for other classes of files (batfile, comfile, and so on) control what happens when that class of file is opened. For example, in Windows Explorer, right-click any file and a context menu will appear with the word *Open* at the top of the menu in bold. The boldfaced action is, in most cases, what happens when that file is double-clicked. When you double-click a file, Windows will scan the Registry for that file class and then determine what actions to take, based on the Registry settings for the file class. Malware such as the SirCam[23.] and PrettyPark[24.] worms have used this Registry location to maintain persistence on an infected system.

For example, let's say that you want to play Solitaire on your system. You go to the command prompt and type the command:

```
C:\>dir /s sol.exe
```

The output of this command tells you where the executable for Solitaire is located within the file system. (On my Windows XP Home system, sol.exe is located in the C:\Windows\system32 directory.) Just out of curiosity, you wonder what happens when you double-click the file icon for Solitaire, so you type the following command:

```
C:\>ftype exefile
```

The output of the command shows you *exefile="%1" %**. This basically tells the system to launch the file with the first argument (the filename) and any successive arguments. However, additions can be made to the *shell\open\command* Registry entry so that other files are launched whenever a particular class of file is opened. Entries in this key (and others similar to it, as described in a moment) should contain simply *'%1' %** and nothing else, by default. Any other data in this value should be considered suspicious and investigated immediately.

Another entry to check for similar information is:

```
HKEY_CLASSES_ROOT\Exefile\Shell\Open\Command
```

This functionality does not apply to just the Exefile entry beneath HKEY_CLASSES_ROOT. Some malware will modify other entries of the same type to ensure its persistence on the system. For example, some backdoors modify entries to the following key:

```
HKEY_CLASSES_ROOT\Word.Document.x\shell\open\command
```

In this case, *x* is the version number (8, 9, and so on) for Word. This tells the system that whenever the Open command for MS Word documents is run through the shell (Windows Explorer), such as when the user double-clicks a document, the malware will be executed.

Another location that can be used in a similar fashion is the following key:

```
HKEY_LOCAL_MACHINE\Software\Microsoft\Command Processor\AutoRun[25.]
```

This Registry value lists commands that are run whenever the command processor (cmd.exe) is run. For example, it will run an application whenever a command prompt is opened. The value is empty by default. Entries can also be made in the same value within the HKEY_CURRENT_USER hive, and if there is an entry there, it takes precedence over the entry in the HKEY_LOCAL_MACHINE hive.

To illustrate how simple this is, open RegEdit and navigate to the Command Processor key. On my Windows XP Pro SP2 system, that value is visible, but there is no data associated with it. Right-click the value and choose **Modify**, and then press **Enter**. Figure 4.9 illustrates an example of data that can be added to the Registry value.

Figure 4.9 Adding Data to the Command Processor\AutoRun value

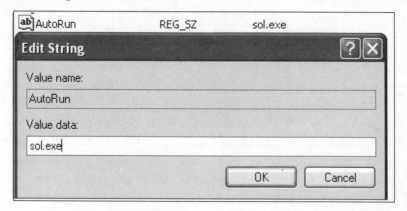

Once you've changed the value, click **OK**. Then click **Start | Run**, type **cmd**, and press **Enter**. The command prompt will open, as will the application that you chose. In Figure 4.9, I chose an application with a nice GUI interface so that when I ran command prompt, it would be obvious that something else was opened as well. A number of other actions can be performed, such as silently installing a user or service or starting a Trojan backdoor that doesn't have a GUI.

Speaking of GUIs, there's a little-known Registry key that can be used to load a DLL into memory whenever a GUI application is started. This key is:

```
HKLM\Software\Microsoft\Windows NT\CurrentVersion\Windows\AppInit_DLLs[26.]
```

In 2000, J. D. Glaser (formerly with FoundStone, now running NTObjectives) gave presentations at BlackHat and Usenix conferences regarding tracking down the compromise of a server and finding an entry in the AppInit_DLLs key.

The AppInit_DLLs key is extremely effective as a hiding place for malware. The CoolWebSearch spyware is known to use this key, for example. Why is this key so effective? When I teach hands-on incident-response training, one of the first exercises I run is a simple "infection" exercise that is meant to look at the attendees' process rather than determine who can find the "infection" first. I've taught the course to new and experienced Windows administrators as well as experienced UNIX and Linux admins who also have responsibilities for Windows systems. Invariably, across the board, 100 percent of the time, the first step that every attendee takes is to open a GUI tool on the desktop. It could be the Event Viewer, it could be the Task Manager, or even Windows Explorer. However, their first instinct is to always reach for a GUI application.

Windows operating systems provide the ability to alert external functions when certain events occur on the system, such as when a user logs on or off or when the screensaver starts. These notifications are handled by the following Registry key:

```
HKLM\Software\Microsoft\Windows NT\CurrentVersion\Winlogon\Notify\[27]
```

Entries beneath this key point to DLLs that receive notifications of certain events. Googling for *Winlogon\Notify* will give you a long list of links to malware that uses this key's functionality. When you're performing forensic analysis of a system, it would be a good idea to sort the subkeys beneath *Notify* based on their *LastWrite* times and pay particular attention to any entries that are near the date of the suspected incident, as well as to any entries that list DLLs in the *DLLName* value that have suspicious file version information or no file version information at all. (Getting file version information from an executable file is covered in Chapter 6.)

Beneath the WinLogon key (listed previously) is a value named *TaskMan* that might be of interest to investigators because it allows the user to choose an application to replace the Task Manager. This value doesn't exist by default but can be added. In fact, installing Process Explorer from SysInternals allows you to choose Process Explorer to replace the usual Task Manager. If the *TaskMan* value exists beneath the WinLogon key, you should consider this "suspicious" under most normal circumstances and investigate the application listed in the data thoroughly.

There is an interesting Registry key that allows a user (usually an application developer or someone debugging applications) to specify a debugger to be launched when an application is run. The Registry key is:

```
HKLM\SOFTWARE\Microsoft\Windows NT\CurrentVersion\Image File Execution
Options
```

Microsoft provides several KnowledgeBase articles that discuss using this key to debug CGI applications[28] as well as to turn off the Windows Update feature under Windows XP.[29] Creating a subkey for the application you want to block, for example, and adding the *Debugger* value with the *ntsd —* (*ntsd* followed by a space and two dashes) data will cause the debugger to attach to the process and then exit immediately. However, Dan Epps[30.] identified a method of using this key as an "attack vector," or perhaps more appropriately, as a method of persistence for malware. To see this in action, first add a subkey to the Image File Execution Options key that is the name of the executable you want to circumvent (for example, notepad.exe). You don't need to provide a path, just the name of the executable. Then add to the key a string value called *Debugger* and point it to the command prompt, as illustrated in Figure 4.10.

Figure 4.10 Adding the Debugger Value to the Image File Execution Options Key

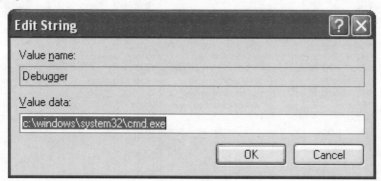

Click **OK** and then choose **Start | Run** and type **notepad**. You'll see the command prompt open instead of Notepad. No reboot is required for the change to take effect.

At this point, I could point out some interesting ways to take advantage of this sort of thing, like pointing the *Debugger* value to a Trojan'ed copy of notepad.exe that not only opens Notepad but launches a backdoor or an IRCbot or a worm of some kind. However, enough examples of malware are currently available that establish a foothold in this Registry key to make it clear that this is definitely a key worth examining. Simply navigate through all the subkeys and examine the executable pointed to by the *Debugger* value (if there is one; not all subkeys will have a *Debugger* value).

Enumerating Autostart Registry Locations

One of the best tools currently available for retrieving information from a great number of autostart locations on a live system is AutoRuns[31.] from SysInternals.com.

This is an updated tool that comes in both GUI and CLI versions. Figure 4.11 shows the GUI version of AutoRuns.

Figure 4.11 AutoRuns (GUI) from SysInternals

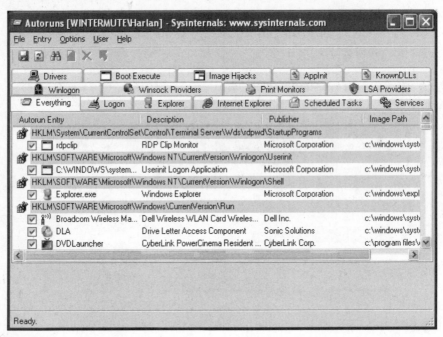

As shown in Figure 4.11, AutoRuns will retrieve entries from a number of Registry keys and display what it finds. AutoRuns will also retrieve the description and publisher from the executable file pointed to by each Registry value and listed in the Image Path column (not shown). This information provides a quick indicator to the investigator as to whether anything that could be suspicious is running in one of these locations and should be investigated.

Other tools exist for enumerating the contents of autostart Registry locations. One in particular is the Visual Basic script called Silent Runners, which can be found at www.silentrunners.org. The Web site includes a complete list of launch points enumerated by the script, which was first made available to users via the NTBugTraq (www.ntbugtraq.com) on May 12, 2004. The script is intended to run on most versions of Windows, including Windows 98, which is outside the scope of this book. Keep this in mind when running the script, since several of the locations enumerated (in the Registry and within the file system) apply only to those versions of Windows. These locations are pointed out in the listing of launch points.

For post-mortem investigations, analysts require tools that allow not only viewing but enumeration of a Registry that has been reconstructed from the component files with a system image. ProDiscover's ProScript capability allows the analyst to use Perl scripts similar to those written for live systems to search the Registry on an image during post-mortem analysis. Tools such as AutoRuns are kept up to date and provide the most comprehensive lists of Registry keys that have some sort of autostart functionality.

USB Removable Storage Devices

One of the more popular topics when I've presented at conferences has been how to track USB removable storage devices across Windows systems. When I first presented on this topic, there was a lot of the "Hey, I didn't know you could do that" kind of interest. Since then, I've answered or witnessed a continual stream of questions regarding this topic.

When a USB removable storage device, such as a thumb drive, is connected to a Windows system, footprints or artifacts are left in the Registry. (Artifacts are left in the setupapi.log file as well.) When the device is plugged in, the Plug and Play (PnP) Manager receives the event and queries the device descriptor in the firmware (this information is *not* located within the memory area of the device) for information about the device, such as manufacturer. The PnP Manager then uses this information to locate the appropriate driver for the device (based on the contents of .inf files) and, if necessary, loads that driver. (This information is recorded in the setupapi.log file.) Once the device has been identified, a Registry key will be created beneath the following key:

```
HKEY_LOCAL_MACHINE\System\CurrentControlSet\Enum\USBSTOR
```

Beneath this key, you will see subkeys that look like:

```
Disk&Ven_###&Prod_###&Rev_###
```

This subkey represents the device class identifier, since it identifies a specific class of device. The fields represented by ### are filled in by the PnP Manager based on information found in the device descriptor. For example, I have a 1GB Geek Squad thumb drive that I purchased from Best Buy; the class ID for the device looks like this:

```
Disk&Ven_Best_Buy&Prod_Geek_Squad_U3&Rev_6.15
```

We can use UVCView[32] to view the contents of the device descriptor. Figure 4.12 illustrates a portion of the device descriptor for the Geek Squad thumb drive mentioned previously.

Figure 4.12 Portion of a Device Descriptor Via UVCView

```
iManufacturer:                               0x01
     English (United States)    "Best Buy"
iProduct:                                    0x02
     English (United States)    "Geek Squad U3"
iSerialNumber:                               0x03
     English (United States)    "0C90195032E36889"
```

As you can see in Figure 4.12, the iManufacturer and iProduct information from the device descriptor is mapped to the device class ID.

Once the device class ID has been created, a unique instance identifier needs to be created for the specific device. Notice that in Figure 4.12 there's a value called *iSerialNumber*. This is a unique instance identifier for the device, similar to the MAC address of a network interface card. This value is used as the unique instance ID for the device so that multiple devices of the same class (two 1GB Geek Squad thumb drives, for instance) can be uniquely identified on the system. From the USB FAQ: Intermediate:[33.]

> If the device has a serial number, Microsoft requires that the
> serial number uniquely identify each instance of the same device.
> For example, if two device descriptors have identical values for
> the *idVendor, idProduct,* and *bcdDevice* fields, the *iSerialNumber*
> field will distinguish one from the other.

Figure 4.13 illustrates a device class ID and subordinate unique instance ID as it appears in RegEdit.

Figure 4.13 Portion of RegEdit Showing Device Class ID and Unique Instance ID

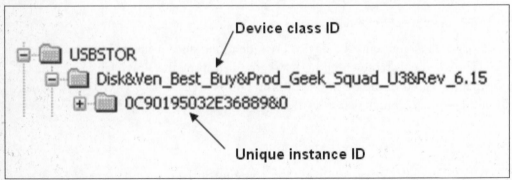

Although a unique serial number is required for devices that manufacturers want to qualify for the Windows Logo[34] program, not all devices include a serial number. For devices that do not have a serial number, the PnP Manager will create a unique instance ID for that device, which will look similar to the following:

```
6&26c97b61&0
```

Notice that the second character is an ampersand (&). If you see a unique instance ID beneath the USBStor key that looks like this, you know that the device that was plugged into the system does not have a serial number in its device descriptor.

So, if the unique instance ID does not have an & as the second character, you might be able to identify the unique device that was connected to the system. In cases involving multiple systems and storage media, investigators should be sure to include the use of UVCView in their methodology so that the devices can later be tied to the system, not only through Registry artifacts in the USBSTOR key but also in the MountedDevices key as well as in Shortcuts and other references to files located on the system.

Once the unique instance identifier key has been created, the key is then populated with several values, including a *FriendlyName*. The value of interest to investigators will be the *ParentIdPrefix* value. Microsoft does not provide any information regarding how this value is created or whether this value is unique across Windows systems. However, the *ParentIdPrefix* value can be used to correlate additional information from within the Registry.

For example, using both the unique instance identifier and the *ParentIdPrefix*, we can determine the last time that the USB device was connected to the Windows system. On a live system, you need to navigate to the following key:

```
HKEY_LOCAL_MACHINE\SYSTEM\CurrentControlSet\Control\DeviceClasses
```

You'll see a number of subkeys beneath this key. The specific device classes that we're interested in are {53f56307-b6bf-11d0-94f2-00a0c91efb8b} and {53f5630d-b6bf-11d0-94f2-00a0c91efb8b}. These two classes are defined in the ntddstor.h header file because they are globally unique identifiers (GUIDs) for the disk and volume device interfaces, respectively. Navigating to the first GUID, we see a number of subkeys with some really long names; referring back to the device illustrated in Figure 4.13, we see a subkey with the following name:

```
USBSTOR#Disk&Ven_Best_Buy&Prod_Geek_Squad_U3&Rev_6.15#0C90195032E36889&0#{53
f56307-b6bf-11d0-94f2-00a0c91efb8b}
```

For the purpose of this example, I've highlighted the unique instance identifier (in this case, the serial number of the device) to illustrate where within the key name the ID is located. The *LastWrite* time of this key corresponds to the last time the disk device was connected to the system. We can also conduct the same correlation with the Volume device interface GUID, using the *ParentIdPrefix* for the device, as follows:

```
##?#STORAGE#RemovableMedia#7&326659cd&0&RM#{53f5630d-b6bf-11d0-94f2-
00a0c91efb8b}
```

Again, I've highlighted the *ParentIdPrefix* within the device subkey to illustrate where it can be found. The *LastWrite* time of this key corresponds to the last time the volume was connected to the system. We will cover more information regarding use of the *ParentIdPrefix* to correlate information from the Registry in the "Mounted Devices" section later in this chapter.

USB Device Issues

USB removable storage devices have long been known (particularly by security professionals) to pose a threat to security, particularly within the corporate infrastructure. Since the days of the floppy disk (even back as far as when these things really were floppy!), the amount of storage capacity has increased as the size of the device (the "form factor") has decreased. As I write this, thumb drives with 2GB and 4GB capacity are available on the shelves of many local stores, all at reasonable prices. Want to steal a file from an organization? How about an entire database? And they call these things "thumb" drives … remove the plastic casing and strip the device down to just the circuit board, and you've got a "thumbnail" drive that is quite literally the size of a thumbnail.

To make matters worse, these devices are ubiquitous. It used to be that anyone who had a 64MB thumb drive was probably some kind of Über-admin. Now just about everyone has these things and uses them for storing pictures, presentations, and more. How about iPods and MP3 players? We see them in the gym, in the office, on the bus; they're everywhere. In fact, we're *used* to seeing them, so seeing one on a desk, plugged into a laptop, isn't unusual at all. Right now, you can purchase an 8GB iPod Nano for around $200. If someone plugs one of these into a laptop that's connected to a corporate LAN, who's to know whether the user is listening to music or downloading financial forecasts, compensation plans, contract bids, and other confidential information to the storage device?

Another issue has to do with AutoPlay functionality. When a CD or DVD is placed in the drive on a Windows system, the new media is detected, and if there is an autorun.inf file located in the root of the drive, it is parsed and the *run=* and *load=* lines are executed. This is all part of the enhanced user experience Windows offers. Be default, autorun functionality is not enabled for removable storage devices such as thumb drives. The autoplay functionality is controlled by the NoDriveTypeAutoRun[35.] Registry key (note that this applies for both the HKEY_USERS and HKEY_LOCAL_MACHINE hives).

The company U3 provides a utility to give users more mobility with their applications. This utility creates a small partition at the beginning of a thumb drive and marks it as a CDFS (CD file system) partition so that Windows systems recognize the partition as a CD rather than a removable storage device. The utilities (browser and the like) are then run from the CDFS partition, and the rest of the device is used for storage. However, this means that even though autorun functionality is disabled (by default) for removable storage devices, it is *enabled* (by default) for the CDFS partition.

When I connected a U3-enabled thumb drive to my Windows XP system, I found that two separate device class ID entries were created for the same device:

`CdRom&Ven_Best_Buy&Prod_Geek_Squad_U3&Rev_6.15`

and

`Disk&Ven_Best_Buy&Prod_Geek_Squad_U3&Rev_6.15`

Both of these device class IDs had the same unique instance ID subkey beneath them. When you're performing post-mortem forensic analysis, this is definitely something to look for because it might identify an infection vector or method of compromise. Where this comes into play is that an attacker can create a custom ISO image to install into the CDFS partition and then remove all indication of the U3 utilities or logo on the device. If someone plugs that device into a system, the autorun functionality for the CDFS partition will kick in, and anything the attacker can conceive of (installing Trojan backdoors, collecting Protected Storage info and other passwords) will be executed automatically.

See the "USBDumper" sidebar for additional information regarding threats posed by removable storage devices. Although not specifically associated with Registry analysis, these threats do pose interesting issues for security professionals.

Tools & Traps...

USBDumper

A utility called USBDumper exposes another security risk associated with USB removable storage devices, but with a different twist.[36] USBDumper is installed on a Windows system, and whenever a USB removable thumb drive is connected to the system, the contents of the device are silently copied off the device. There has also been talk of a utility that silently acquires an image of a thumb drive when it's connected to a system so that not only can all the currently active files be retrieved, but deleted files can be as well. Both of these issues were mentioned in Bruce Schneier's "Schneier on Security" blog on August 25, 2006.

Mounted Devices

The MountedDevices key stores information about the various devices and volumes mounted to the NTFS file system. The complete path to the key is:

```
HKEY_LOCAL_MACHINE\System\MountedDevices
```

For example, when a USB removable storage device is connected to a Windows system, it is assigned a drive letter; that drive letter shows up in the MountedDevices key. If the device is assigned the drive letter F:\, the value in the MountedDevices key will appear as \DosDevices\F:. We can map the entry from the USBSTOR key to the MountedDevices key using the *ParentIdPrefix* value found within the unique instance ID key for the device. The *ParentIdPrefix* value for the USB device discussed in the previous section has the data 7&326659cd&0. Note that this is *not* the unique instance ID and is therefore not the serial number we discussed earlier.

Once we have the data from the *ParentIdPrefix* Registry value, we then locate the drive letter that was assigned to it by locating the *DosDevices* entry within the MountedDevices key that contains the *ParentIdPrefix* within its data. On a live system, we can do this easily by right-clicking each of the Registry values and choosing **Modify**; when the **Edit Binary Value** dialog opens, we can view the contents of the data to see if the *ParentIdPrefix* value is there. The *ParentIdPrefix* value is stored in the Registry as a string, but the *DosDevices* values within the MountedDevices Registry key are stored as binary data types, so some translation is

necessary. Figure 4.14 illustrates the Edit Binary Value dialog box for the
\DosDevices\F: entry.

Figure 4.14 Data for the MountedDevices \DosDevices\F: Value

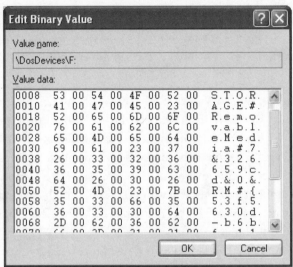

We can clearly see the *ParentIdPrefix* value of *7&326659cd&0* in Figure 4.14.
Using the *ParentIdPrefix* value to map between the USBSTOR and MountedDevices
Registry keys, we can locate the driver letter assigned to the device. As we continue
our post-mortem forensic investigation, we might find references in other locations
in the Registry or in Shortcut files that point to the F:\ drive. We can then correlate
the *LastWrite* times of the unique instance ID key, the MountedDevices key, and the
MAC times on files to develop a timeline.

WARNING

When performing correlation between the USBStor and
MounteDevices keys using a device's *ParentIdPrefix* value, be sure to
keep in mind that several devices might have been connected to the
system and mapped to the same drive letter. I have several different
USB thumb drives from different manufacturers and of different sizes,
and whenever I connect them to my laptop one at a time, they all get
mapped to the F:\ drive. When performing this type of correlation, it
is important to keep this in mind.

Looking at the MountedDevices key, you might notice that there are \DosDevices entries (in particular, \DosDevices\C:) whose data is only 12 bytes (3 *DWORDs*) long. An example of this is illustrated in Figure 4.15.

Figure 4.15 Data for MountedDevices \DosDevices\C: and D: Values

⊞ \DosDevices\C:	REG_…	16 23 ab 41 00 7e 00 00 00 00 00 00
⊞ \DosDevices\D:	REG_…	16 23 ab 41 00 5e c6 52 07 00 00 00

The binary values shown in Figure 4.15 consist of the drive signature (also known as a *volume ID*) for the hard drive (first *DWORD*) and the partition offset (second and third *DWORDs*). A drive's signature is located at offset 0x1b8 (440 in decimal) within the Master Boot Record (MBR) of the hard drive.

For the \DosDevices\C: value shown in Figure 4.15, the second and third *DWORDs* together translate to the hex value 0x7e00, which is 32256 in decimal. Each sector on the hard drive is 512 bytes in size; 32256/512 = 63, so the C:\ partition starts at sector 63.

Looking at the entry for \DosDevices\D: in Figure 4.15, we see that the binary data indicates that the D:\ drive has the same drive signature as the C:\ drive but a different partition offset. This is because the D:\ drive is another partition on the same physical disk as the C:\ drive. Using the information about the partition offsets, we can compute the C:\ partition to be a little more than 29GB in size.

To show how to find this information during a forensic investigation, I opened ProDiscover and then opened a sample case. I located the \DosDevices\C: entry in the MountedDevices key in the Registry Viewer and saw that the drive signature was 5D EC 5D EC in hex. I then clicked the cluster view for the case (which starts at 0). Figure 4.16 illustrates an excerpt from ProDiscover, showing a portion of the MBR.

As shown in Figure 4.16, the drive signature we got from the MountedDevices key is clearly visible at offset 0x1B8.

Figure 4.16 Extract from ProDiscover Cluster View Showing Drive
Signature

```
00000180   00 00 00 00 00 00 00 00    00 00 00 00 00 00 00 00    ................|
00000190   00 00 00 00 00 00 00 00    00 00 00 00 00 00 00 00    ................¦
000001A0   00 00 00 00 00 00 00 00    00 00 00 00 00 00 00 00    ................
000001B0   00 00 00 00 00 2C 44 63    5D EC 5D EC 00 00 80 01    .....,Dc]ì]ì..€.
000001C0   01 00 07 FE BF 4F 3F 00    00 00 11 1E 91 00 00 00    ...þ¿O?.....'...
000001D0   00 00 00 00 00 00 00 00    00 00 00 00 00 00 00 00    ................
000001E0   00 00 00 00 00 00 00 00    00 00 00 00 00 00 00 00    ................
000001F0   00 00 00 00 00 00 00 00    00 00 00 00 00 00 55 AA    ..............Uª
```

Why is this important? After all, if we've acquired an image of the hard drive, we should already have and be able to verify the drive signature from both the Registry and the MBR. However, where this information becomes useful to us is if there are external hard drives associated with the case. In my "day job" as an incident responder and forensic engineer, I use external hard drives for storing things like client data, drive images, and log files. I do this because once the case is complete and the final report has been accepted, I can easily wipe the external drive. If I maintained all this data on my laptop's hard drive, I would have to wipe the drive and reinstall the operating system and all my applications and data, including PGP keys and the like. Also, as I'm writing this book, all the files associated with the book are maintained on a 120GB Western Digital USB-connected hard drive. This device appears in the USBSTOR key with the following device class ID:

```
Disk&Ven_WDC_WD12&Prod_00UE-00KVT0&Rev_0000
```

As one might expect, this device has a serial number (which I can verify with UVCView), as evidenced by the unique instance ID I see in my Registry. However, within the unique instance ID Registry key, there is *no value named ParentIdPrefix*. When the device is plugged into my laptop, it appears as the G:\ drive, and the appropriate information, including the drive signature, is stored in the MountedDevices key. Had this been a case I was investigating, I could then uniquely tie the external hard drive to the system, even though there is no *ParentIdPrefix* value for the external drive.

Volumes listed in the MountedDevices key can be correlated to subkeys found in the MountPoints2 key within the user's hive (i.e., NTUSER.DAT file):

```
Software\Microsoft\Windows\CurrentVersion\Explorer\MountPoints2
```

Subkeys listed beneath this key come in various forms. First, the subkeys that appear as globally unique identifiers (GUIDs) can be mapped to the \??\Volume entries in the MountedDevices key, allowing you to see which user (if there are multiple users of the system) had access to the volume as well as when the volume was originally connected to the system, based on the *LastWrite* time associated with the key. (In this case, the last time the key was modified was when it was created.)

Finding Users

Information about users is maintained in the Registry, in the SAM hive. Under normal circumstances, this hive is not accessible even to Administrators—not without taking special steps to manually edit the access permissions on the hive. There's a good reason for this: Although much of the Registry can be "messed with," there are areas of the Registry where minor changes can leave the system potentially unusable. The SAM file is one of those areas.

Much of the useful information in the SAM hive is encoded in binary format, and fortunately, Peter Nordahl-Hagen's sam.h file is extremely helpful in deciphering the structures and revealing something understandable.

The UserDump.pl ProScript (v.0.31, 20060522 provided on the accompanying DVD) can be used to extract user and group membership information from the Registry Viewer in ProDiscover, once it has been populated. To run the ProScript, click the **Run ProScript** button on the menu bar and select the location of the ProScript from the **Run ProScript** dialog box. (Optionally, you can enter any arguments for a ProScript as well.) Select the UserDump.pl ProScript, and once it has completed, the information parsed from the SAM hive will be visible in the results window, where it can be selected, copied, and pasted into a file or report.

Running the UserDump.pl ProScript against a sample case that I have available, we can view excerpts from the results to see the breadth of information returned by the script. For example, the ProScript parses information about user accounts on the system, including the username, comment, account creation date, number of logins, and user flags (which provide information about the account). The ProScript will also display the last login time, if it is nonzero.

```
Username : Administrator
Comment  : Built-in account for administering the computer/domain
Acct Creation Date : Thu Aug 19 17:17:29 2004
RID             : 500
Logins          : 0
Flags           :
             Password does not expire
```

```
                    Normal user account
Username : Mr. Evil
Acct Creation Date : Thu Aug 19 23:03:54 2004
RID               : 1003
Logins            : 15
Flags             :
                    Password does not expire
                    Normal user account
```

This user information is maintained in the F value located in the following path:

`SAM\SAM\Domains\Account\Users\{RID}`

The {*RID*}, or relative identifier, is the portion of a security identifier (SID) that identifies a user or group in relation to the authority that issued the SID. Besides providing quite a bit of information about how SIDs are created, Microsoft also provides a list of RIDs[37] for well-known users and groups as well as well-known aliases (seen in the SAM\SAM\Domains\Builtin\Aliases key).

The F value within the key is a binary data type and must be parsed appropriately (see the sam.h file, part of the source code for Petter's utility) to extract all the information. There are some important dates available in the contents of the binary data for the F value—specifically, several time/date stamps represented as 64-bit FILETIME objects. Those values and their locations are:

- Bytes 8–15 represent the last login date for the account

- Bytes 24–31 represent the date that the password was last reset (if the password hasn't been reset or changed, this date will correlate to the account creation date)

- Bytes 32–39 represent the account expiration date

- Bytes 40–47 represent the date of the last failed login attempt (since the account name has to be correct for the date to be changed on a specific account, this date can also be referred to as the date of the last incorrect password usage)

Tools such as AccessData's Registry Viewer will decode this information for you automatically, as illustrated in Figure 4.17.

Figure 4.17 Portion of AccessData's Registry Viewer Showing Decode of a User's *F* Value

Key Properties	
Last Written Time	9/26/2005 23:37:51 UTC
SID unique identifier	1003
Logon Name	Harlan
Last Logon Time	9/26/2005 23:37:51 UTC
Last Password Change Time	8/18/2004 0:49:42 UTC
Last Failed Login Time	9/26/2005 23:37:47 UTC

SAM\SAM\Domains\Account\Users\000003EB

AccessData's Registry Viewer is available for download[38.] and will run in demo mode if you do not have an AccessData dongle. To use the Registry Viewer to decode these values, you must first extract the raw Registry file (in this case, the SAM file) from the image, copying it to another location.

The Perl module Parse::Win32Registry[39.] provides a freely available cross-platform method for parsing the contents of raw Registry files that have similarly been extracted from an acquired image (or been made available via some other means). To install the module on Windows systems, simply download the archive and copy the subdirectories containing all the modules to the \site\lib directory in your Perl installation. The Perl script sam_parse.pl (located on the accompanying DVD) uses this module to extract and display much of the same information available from the Registry Viewer, plus some additional information:

```
Name : Harlan
LastWrite = Mon Sep 26 23:37:51 2005 (UTC)
Last Login = Mon Sep 26 23:37:51 2005 (UTC)
Pwd Reset = Wed Aug 18 00:49:42 2004 (UTC)
Pwd Fail = Mon Sep 26 23:37:47 2005 (UTC)
 --> Password does not expire
 --> Normal user account
Number of logins = 35
```

The sam_parse.pl Perl script not only displays the timestamps available from the user information in the SAM file, it also parses the user flags and the number of times the user has logged into the system.

Because the Parse::Win32Registry module does not rely on Windows APIs, Perl scripts that use the module will be platform independent. This means that analysts and investigators are not restricted to a Windows platform when they want to parse the contents of raw Registry files. As long as the files are available (that is, extracted from an image file and so on), code written using the module can be run on Linux, Windows, or even Mac OS X systems that support Perl.

Each of these keys also has a *V* value that is also a binary data type and can be parsed to get the user's account settings, such as full name, comment, path to the login script (if any), and the encrypted password hashes.

The UserDump.pl ProScript also retrieves information about groups on the system, including the group name, comment, and the users assigned to the group.

```
Group     : Administrators
Comment   : Administrators have complete and unrestricted access to the
computer/domain
--> 500 (Administrator)
--> 1003 (Mr. Evil)
```

Information about group membership is maintained in the SAM\SAM\Domains\Builtin\Aliases key. Each of the RID subkeys beneath the Aliases key has a *C* value that is a binary data type and needs to be parsed to determine which users are members of the group. The best road map I found for parsing this binary data is available from Andreas Schuster's blog.[40.] This information was incorporated into the UserDump.pl ProScript.

Information about users and group membership is extremely valuable in understanding the context of a case, specifically which users had access to the system and what level of access they had (via group membership). Much of this information is easily extracted during live response using available tools. With a bit more information about the various structures maintained within the Registry, we are able to extract similar information from a post-mortem image.

Tracking User Activity

A number of Registry keys can be used to track user activity. This is type of Registry key is different from the autostart/user activity Registry keys, which are keys accessed when a user performs a specific action. These Registry keys can be found in the NTUSER.DAT file for the user and are updated (i.e., entries added) when a user performs specific actions. When this happens, the key's *LastWrite* time is updated, which brings us back to the concept of the Registry as a log file. Also, there are keys that track user activity and add or modify timestamp information associated with the Registry values; this timestamp information is maintained in the value data.

The majority of the locations where user activity is recorded in the Registry are in the HKEY_CURRENT_USER hive. Many of these locations are referred to as most recently used, or MRU, lists. This name comes from the fact that, as we'll see, these keys maintain a list of files or commands as well as a value referred to as the MRUlist. Each of the values within the key is designated by an identifier, such as a lowercase letter, and the MRUlist value displays the order in which they were accessed.

The UserAssist keys

Quite a lot has been written about the UserAssist keys, most of which has appeared in the form of questions. The specific keys we're interested in are located beneath the following key path in the user's NTUSER.DAT file:

```
Software\Microsoft\Windows\CurrentVersion\Explorer\UserAssist\{GUID}\Count
```

The *GUID* is a globally unique identifier; in this case, there are two such keys beneath the UserAssist key: 5E6AB780-7743-11CF-A12B-00AA004AE837 and 75048700-EF1F-11D0-9888-006097DEACF9. Within the HKEY_CLASSES_ROOT hive, the GUID 5E6AB780-7743-11CF-A12B-00AA004AE837 points to the Internet Toolbar (such as %SystemRoot%\system32\browseui.dll), and the GUID 75048700-EF1F-11D0-9888-006097DEACF9 points to the ActiveDesktop (such as %SystemRoot%\system32\SHELL32.dll). The importance of this will become apparent after we discover what's in these keys and why it's useful.

Beneath each of the Count keys are several values; in fact, there might be many, many values. When I first began researching these keys (most often referred to as UserAssist keys rather than Count keys), I found sites on the Internet that reported upward of 18,000 or more entries beneath one key and 400 or so beneath the other. That system was a Windows 2000 system that had been running for about five years when the post was made to the Web site. What's so special about these keys? In a nutshell, they log user activity, to a degree. Yes, that's right, you read it correctly. To a degree, these keys actually record user activity like a log file.

However, if you navigate to these keys in RegEdit, you won't see that at all. You'll see something like HRZR_HVGBBYONE, which makes absolutely no sense at all. That's because the value names beneath these two keys are Rot-13 "encrypted." *Rot-13* refers to a Caesarian cipher in which each letter is replaced with the letter 13 spaces further down in the alphabet. Using a simple substitution (in Perl, tr/N-ZA-Mn-za-m/A-Za-z/), we can then see that HRZR_HVGB-BYONE is really UEME_UITOOLBAR. Okay, that's a little more readable, but we're really no closer to an answer at this point, are we?

The value names beneath both keys are Rot-13 encrypted and can be easily decrypted. In fact, the Perl script uAssist.pl (included on the accompanying DVD) illustrates how simple this translation is to accomplish on a live system. The real treasure within these keys is in the data associated with each of the values. In many cases, the decrypted value name points to an application or an executable. In those cases, the data is often 16 bytes (4 *DWORDs*) long and includes not only a run count (the number of many times that application or executable has been run) but also a last run time (an 8-byte FILETIME object). The run count is stored in the second *DWORD* and starts at 5; therefore, a run count of 6 means that the application was launched once. The FILETIME object is in the third and fourth *DWORDs*.

When you decrypt the value names, you'll see that many of them are preceded by *UEME_*, and then *RUNPATH, RUNPIDL, RUNCPL*, and so on. These tags can be relatively easy to sort out:

- **RUNPATH** Refers to an absolute path within the file system; occurs when you double-click an icon for an executable in Windows Explorer or type the name of the application in the Start | Run box.

- **RUNCPL** Refers to launching a Control Panel applet.

- **RUNPIDL** A *PIDL*, or pointer to an ID list, part of the internal Explorer namespace, is used to refer to an object. In the case of the UserAssist keys, these are most often shortcuts or LNK files, as when you choose Start | Documents and select a file.

For example, the system I'm writing this book on is a Dell Latitude D820, purchased in the beginning of August 2006. Whenever I purchase a new system, I reformat the hard drive and install the operating system all over again. For Dell systems, this means that I have to download and install several drivers (Dell makes it very easy to locate the necessary drivers). When I ran the uassist.pl script on my system, I saw the following entry:

```
UEME_RUNPATH:F:\D820\D820_A02_bios.EXE
        Mon Aug  7 16:35:39 2006 -- (1)
```

The script returns the FILETIME object in a local time, so we can see that the application D820_A02_bios.exe was executed one time, on August 7. Other entries include:

```
UEME_RUNCPL:"C:\WINDOWS\system32\desk.cpl",Display
        Thu Aug 24 21:27:45 2006 -- (1)
UEME_RUNCPL:"C:\WINDOWS\system32\powercfg.cpl",Power Options
        Thu Aug 24 21:27:07 2006 -- (1)
```

Here we can see that the Display and Power Options Control Panel applets were both executed on August 24, and that was the only time each was launched. Just for fun, on October 4, at about 10:55 P.M., I opened the Display applet in the Control Panel and then reran the Perl script to find that the date had been changed to Wed Oct 4 22:55:59 2006.

So, essentially, these keys record the number of times certain applications have been launched and the last time that action was taken. This information can be very helpful when you're working on a case. For example, seeing something like UEME_RUNCPL:timedate.cpl would indicate that the user had accessed the Date and Time Control Panel applet and possibly altered the system time.

The Perl script pnu.pl (found on the accompanying DVD) will assist you in collecting information from NTUSER.DAT files during an investigation. The Perl script uses the Parse::Win32Registry module to access the raw NTUSER.DAT file (which you've extracted from your case) and locate the UserAssist key that contains the GUID that points to ActiveDesktop. It gets the *LastWrite* time for the key and then parses through the key, extracting and decrypting value names. The output from the script, which follows, is sorted based on the timestamps found in the data for each of the values:

```
LastWrite time = Mon Sep 26 23:33:06 2005 (UTC)
Mon Sep 26 23:33:06 2005 (UTC)
        UEME_RUNPATH
        UEME_RUNPATH:C:\WINDOWS\system32\notepad.exe
Mon Sep 26 23:26:43 2005 (UTC)
        UEME_RUNPATH:Z:\WINNT\system32\sol.exe
Mon Sep 26 23:22:30 2005 (UTC)
        UEME_UISCUT
        UEME_RUNPATH:Downloads.lnk
Mon Sep 26 23:16:26 2005 (UTC)
        UEME_RUNPATH:C:\Program Files\Morpheus\Morpheus.exe
Mon Sep 26 23:16:25 2005 (UTC)
        UEME_RUNPATH:Morpheus.lnk
Mon Sep 26 23:15:04 2005 (UTC)
        UEME_RUNPATH:C:\Program Files\Internet Explorer\iexplore.exe
```

```
Mon Sep 26 23:04:08 2005 (UTC)
        UEME_RUNPATH:d:\bintext.exe
```

UAssist.pl, a ProScript for use with ProDiscover, is available on the accompanying DVD. This ProScript (version 0.11, 20060522) can be run against the Registry
once the Registry Viewer has been populated. The script parses through the
UserAssist Registry key entries for all users and extracts the information in a readable format, decrypting the value names and parsing the run count and last run
times from the data, where applicable. Once this is done, the script sorts all the
values with timestamps so that the information can be used for timeline analysis.
This version of the ProScript sends its results to the command window in
ProDiscover, where the investigator can then select, copy, and paste those results into
a file or report.

Are You Owned?

Case Study: Defragged?

I dealt with an incident in which an employee for the client might have known
that he was under suspicion, and while he was allowed access to his system he
might have deleted a number of files. The suspicious filenames were located
as deleted files, but the content simply wasn't there. There was the additional
suspicion that he'd not only deleted the files but also defragmented the hard
drive. The information in the UserAssist key showed that the employee had
run the Add/Remove Programs Control Panel applet. Information in the
Prefetch directory (more on that in Chapter 5) showed that the defrag utility
had been run, but there was nothing in the UserAssist key to indicate that the
employee had done so. This activity was determined to be part of the limited
defrag that Windows XP runs every three days.

TIP

If you've installed or are examining an image of a system on which
the user had installed Internet Explorer version 7, you will find a third
subkey beneath the UserAssist Registry key.

MRU Lists

Many applications maintain an MRU list, which is a list of files that have been most recently accessed. Within the running application, these filenames generally appear at the bottom of the drop-down menu when you select File on the menu bar.

Perhaps the most well-known (and all-inclusive) MRU list Registry key is the RecentDocs key:

```
\Software\Microsoft\Windows\CurrentVersion\Explorer\RecentDocs
```

This key can contain quite a number of values, all of which are binary data types. The values we are interested in are all of the ones that have names that are numbers and the one named MRUListEx. The numbered value names contain the names of the files accessed (in Unicode), and the MRUListEx key maintains the order in which they were accessed (as *DWORDs*). For example, on my system, the first *DWORD* in the MRUListEx value data is 0x26, or 38 in decimal. The value with the name 38 points to a directory that I opened. Given that adding a value and its associated data the key, as well as modifying the MRUListEx value, constituted modifying the key, the *LastWrite* time of the RecentDocs key will tell us when that file was accessed.

The RecentDocs key also has a number of subkeys, each one being the extension of a file that was opened (.doc, .txt, .html, etc.). The values within these subkeys is maintained in the same way as in the RecentDocs key: The value names are numbered, and their data contains the name of the file accessed as a binary data type (in Unicode). Another value called *MRUListEx* is also a binary data type and maintains the order in which the files were accessed, most recent first, as *DWORDs*.

Another popular MRUList can be found in the RunMRU key:

```
\Software\Microsoft\Windows\CurrentVersion\Explorer\RunMRU
```

This key maintains a list of all the values typed into the Run box on the Start menu. Figure 4.18 illustrates what the contents of this key might look like.

Figure 4.18 Excerpt from RunMRU Key

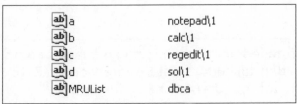

The RunMRU MRUList is maintained in clear text and is more easily readable than the RecentDocs key. As with the RecentDocs key, however, the most recently typed items are listed first. Entries are added to this key when a user clicks the **Start** button, chooses **Run**, and types a command, name of a file, or the like.

During investigations centered on user or employee activity, I have found entries in the RunMRU key that show accesses to remote systems as well as to applications and files on removable storage media.

Another key similar to the RunMRU key is the TypedURLs key:

```
\Software\Microsoft\Internet Explorer\TypedURLs
```

As with the RunMRU key, the TypedURLs key maintains a list of the URLs that the user types into the Address: bar in Internet Explorer. This information can be combined with the Temporary Internet Files to show which Web sites were visited by clicking a link and those that the user typed in by hand.

Yet another location for MRU lists can be found in the following key:

```
\Software\Microsoft\Windows\CurrentVersion\Explorer\ComDlg32\OpenSaveMRU[41]
```

This key maintains MRU lists of files opened via Open and SaveAs dialogs within the Windows shell. Similar to the RecentDocs key, the OpenSaveMRU key also maintains subkeys of specific file extensions that have been opened or saved. Like the RunMRU key, however, the data within these keys are string data types and easily read. The contents of this key can be very useful in several ways. First, some file extensions do not appear frequently during normal system use, so the subkey beneath the OpenSaveMRU key for that file extension may have only one entry, named *a*. In this case, the data for the MRUList value will have only *a* listed, as shown in Figure 4.19. The *LastWrite* time for the key will tell you when that file was opened or saved.

Figure 4.19 Excerpt from a Subkey of the OpenSaveMRU Key

| ab] a | REG_SZ | G:\book2\memory\pe_image.h.htm |
| ab] MRUList | REG_SZ | a |

Opening an image acquired from a Windows XP system in ProDiscover, I navigated to the OpenSaveMRU key for the user. The *LastWrite* time for the exe subkey is listed as August 17, 2004, at 11:18 A.M. The contents of the exe subkey are illustrated in Figure 4.20.

Figure 4.20 Excerpt from the exe Subkey of the OpenSaveMRU Key (Via ProDiscover)

a	REG_SZ	C:\Documents and Settings\Mr. Evil\Desktop\lalsetup250.exe
MRUList	REG_SZ	cdba
b	REG_SZ	C:\Documents and Settings\Mr. Evil\Desktop\netstumblerinstaller_0_4_0.exe
c	REG_SZ	C:\Documents and Settings\Mr. Evil\Desktop\ethereal-setup-0.10.6.exe
d	REG_SZ	C:\Documents and Settings\Mr. Evil\Desktop\WinPcap_3_01_a.exe

Figure 4.19 shows that the most recent file accessed was the Ethereal setup utility (Ethereal is a suite of network traffic capture and analysis tools, now called Wireshark), used to install the application. This information can then be correlated with the contents of the UserAssist key (using the UAssist.pl ProScript, version 0.11, 20060522). When the ProScript is run against the image, we see:

```
--> Fri Aug 27 15:34:54 2004
        --> UEME_RUNPATH:C:\Program Files\Ethereal\ethereal.exe
 --> Fri Aug 27 15:33:02 2004
        --> UEME_RUNPATH:C:\Program Files\Cain\Cain.exe
 --> Fri Aug 27 15:28:36 2004
        --> UEME_RUNPATH:C:\Documents and Settings\Mr.
Evil\Desktop\ethereal-setup-0.10.6.exe
 --> Fri Aug 27 15:15:08 2004
        --> UEME_RUNPATH:C:\Documents and Settings\Mr.
Evil\Desktop\WinPcap_3_01_a.exe
 --> Fri Aug 27 15:14:44 2004
        --> UEME_RUNCPL
        --> UEME_RUNCPL:"C:\WINDOWS\System32\appwiz.cpl",Add or Remove
Programs
 --> Fri Aug 27 15:12:35 2004
        --> UEME_RUNPATH:C:\Program Files\Network Stumbler\NetStumbler.exe
 --> Fri Aug 27 15:12:11 2004
        --> UEME_RUNPATH:C:\Documents and Settings\Mr.
Evil\Desktop\netstumblerinstaller_0_4_0.exe
```

As we can see, our user was quite busy on August 27, 2004. (*Note:* The ProScript extracts raw FILETIME data and translates it into UTC time, which is roughly equivalent to GMT time. The ProDiscover application shows all times relative to the examiner's system and TimeZoneInformation settings.) The TimeZoneInformation Registry key shows that when the system was running, it was set for the Central time zone, with automatic adjustments for Daylight Savings Time enabled. The ActiveTimeBias is 300 minutes (five hours), and ActiveTimeBias on my system (with ProDiscover open) is 240 minutes (four hours). From this information we see that about 10 minutes after saving the Ethereal setup application to his system, the "suspect" installed that application.

Another way that this information can be useful is to show the use of external storage devices. Not only will the *LastWrite* time of the subkey provide the date and time that the device was connected to the system, but the information can be correlated to the contents of the MountedDevices key to provide additional information about the device.

Yet another MRU list can be found beneath the following key:

```
Software\Microsoft\Windows\CurrentVersion\Explorer\FileExts
```

The subkeys beneath this key correspond to extensions for files that have been opened on the system. Beneath the file extension subkeys, you will find subkeys called OpenWithProgIDs and OpenWithList. These Registry entries tell the system what application to use to open a file with that extension when the user double-clicks the file.

Search Assistant

When a user clicks the **Start** button in Windows XP and chooses **Search**, then chooses **For Files and Folders**, the search terms entered into the dialog box are stored in the following Registry key:

```
Software\Microsoft\Search Assistant\ACMru
```

The ACMru key will generally have some combination of four subkeys: 5001, 5603, 5604, and 5647. The 5001 subkey contains the MRU list for the Internet Search Assistant, the 5603 subkey contains the MRU list for the Windows XP files and folders search, and the 5604 subkey contains the MRU list that corresponds to the "word or phrase in a file" dialog box. The 5647 subkey maintains the MRU list for the computers entered via the "for computers or people" selection in the Search Results dialog. The value names within the subkeys are three-digit numbers. The smallest number (i.e., 000) represents the most recent search, and the *LastWrite* time associated with the key will give you the time and date that the search was launched.

Knowing the purpose of the various subkeys and the way they are populated will give you insight into the user's activities on the system. This can be useful during investigations that concern what a user was doing and when.

Search information for "legacy" systems, such as Windows 2000, is maintained in different Registry keys and might be found on the system if it was upgraded from Windows 2000 to XP. The key in question is:

```
Software\Microsoft\Internet Explorer\Explorer Bars\{C4EE31F3-4768-11D2-BE5C-00A0C9A83DA1}
```

According to the contents of the HKEY_CLASSES_ROOT\CLSID key, that GUID refers to the File Search Explorer Band, contained in shell32.dll. Two subkeys beneath this key, FilesNamedMRU and ContainingTextMRU, correlate to the 5603 and 5604 subkeys (respectively) found on Windows XP systems.

Connecting to Other Systems

When a user uses the Map Network Drive Wizard (right-click the **My Computer** icon and choose **Map Network Drive…**) to connect to a remote system, an MRU list is created beneath the following key:

```
Software\Microsoft\Windows\CurrentVersion\Explorer\Map Network Drive MRU
```

Each entry is given a letter as the value name, and the MRUList value illustrates the order in which the user connected to each drive or share.

Whether the user uses the Map Network Drive Wizard or the *net use* command, the volumes the user added to the system will appear in the following key:

```
Software\Microsoft\Windows\CurrentVersion\Explorer\MountPoints2
```

As mentioned earlier, the MountPoints2 subkeys that appear as GUIDs can be mapped to the \??\Volume entries in the MountedDevices key. These GUIDs can also be mapped to the CPC\Volume subkey beneath the MountPoints2 key.

I've used the *net use* command on my system to perform testing, and when I connect to the C$ share on another system, I see subkeys such as ##192.168.1.22#c$ and ##192.168.1.71#c$.

These IP addresses (I have a flat test network that is not a domain, so the computer names are essentially the IP addresses) also appear in the following Registry key:

```
Software\Microsoft\Windows\CurrentVersion\Explorer\ComputerDescriptions
```

This key maintains descriptions of computers that are seen by the network browser. For systems that were part of a domain, it is normal to see several computer names listed in this key. However, for stand–alone systems, such as home users and other systems that are not part of a domain, you likely won't see values listed for this key. On my home system, only those systems that I have explicitly connected to using the *net use* command appear in this key. I use my work system to connect to my employer's intranet via a virtual private network (VPN), and several systems that I have connected to appear in the ComputerDescriptions key. One in particular has the description Samba 2.2.7a, indicating that it is a Linux system running Samba. Because this key is found in the NTUSER.DAT file, there could be different entries for different users on the same system.

IM and P2P

Instant messaging (IM) and peer-to-peer (P2P) file-sharing applications are immensely popular—a popularity that seems to cross all generations. Where people once wrote letters that took time to write and to get to the recipient, a quick e-mail can be sent and will be waiting for that person the next time they log on. Or you can be half a world away and receive a notification the instant your friend logs into her IM application. Or, using P2P file sharing, you can find any number of useful (or perhaps not so useful) files—music, movies, images, and more. The popularity of these applications has spawned a proliferation of various frameworks and client applications. Yahoo!, AOL, and Microsoft all have their own IM client applications, each with its own functionality and unique forensic "footprints" on a system. To top it off, there are various third-party applications that you can use to replace those clients or even combine them into a single interface. For example, Trillian (trillian.cc) allows users to combine other IM "identities" into a single application, so they only have to log into a single interface to access multiple IM networks. Meebo.com provides a similar, Web-based interface.

The same type of proliferation is true for P2P networks as well. Each has its own unique challenges when it comes to forensic analysis. For example, how does an investigator identify with whom a suspect was chatting (on IM) if the application does not log conversations by default? Or how does an investigator determine if a saved conversation was the result of the user specifically saving the conversation or the result of a third-party add-on for logging conversations? Regarding P2P, how does an investigator determine which search terms a suspect used, which files were retrieved from the sharing network, and from where the files originated?

The variation of clients for both IM and P2P is so great that they would require their own book to fully address the forensic analysis of each. When you consider that like other applications, IM and P2P clients will change between versions, including new functionality and creating new Registry keys and files, the issue of cataloguing the forensic artifacts of these applications becomes even more daunting. For example, when I was using older versions of the AOL Instant Messaging (AIM) client, there was a specific set of Registry keys within the user's profile that you could go to and see the user's encrypted password. This was the result of the user choosing to automatically log into the AIM network without having to retype his or her password. If, as part of your investigation, you found it necessary to gather information about this user's activities on AIM, you could use that encrypted password to set up a similar profile on another system, then log in as that user. I decided to try out the new AIM Triton client a while ago, and it works great, although it takes a little getting used to. One of the major interface changes was that instead of a different client window being opened for each conversation, each window is now tabbed in a single window. From a forensic perspective, however, I now open RegEdit and there are no entries for AOL or AIM beneath the HKEY_CURRENT_USER\Software hive.

To make matters worse, no effort has been made to publicly catalogue these artifacts. Over the years, forensic investigators and law enforcement have encountered situations requiring that they analyze IM and P2P artifacts, yet there haven't been any attempts to develop a database or online Wiki for these items. This is an area of research that needs to be developed.

TIP

There are other Registry keys that can be used to track user activity. For example, the ShellNoRoam\BagMRU[42] key maintains information about the user's view settings and customizations for folders. This means that the user has to have shell access (i.e., Windows Explorer, by default, either via the keyboard or a remote desktop application) to make these customizations. The Explorer\Streams[43] and StreamMRU keys maintain information about the size and location of a window when it's closed. This indicates that the user took specific actions to modify the size and/or location of the window on the desktop, which also indicates specific user interaction with the Windows Explorer shell.

Windows XP System Restore Points

Windows XP includes something called System Restore, which maintains a series of restore points so that should your system become unusable or start performing oddly, you can roll back the system to a previous configuration, when it was working properly. I'll readily admit to having had to do this several times myself. Every now and then I'll do ("do" usually means "install") something that ends up causing my system to start having fits. Or the installation might simply be a coincidence. Having the ability to "roll back" to a day when I know the system was working properly is great. I'm sure that many other users have found the same to be true.

This is an extremely useful utility for users as well as for forensic investigators. After all, here's a facility that operates in the background without the user's knowledge, silently creating backups of critical system configuration information. Restore points are created based on certain triggers, such as when applications or unsigned drivers are installed, or during AutoUpdate installations. Restore points can be created manually, and the System Restore service also creates restore points once a day by default.

To better understand how useful System Restore points can be for forensic analysis, we need to understand a bit about how System Restore works: what gets backed up, what doesn't get backed up, and what Registry keys control how System Restore behaves.

System Restore restores the following items:

- Registry
- Local (not roaming) profiles
- COM+ database
- Windows File Protection DLL cache
- WMI database
- IIS Metabase
- Files with extensions listed in the *<include>* portion of the Monitored File Extensions list in the System Restore section of the Platform SDK

System Restore *does not* restore the following:

- DRM settings
- SAM hive
- WPA settings (Windows authentication information is not restored)
- Specific directories/files listed in the Monitored File Extensions list in the System Restore section of the Platform SDK
- Any file with an extension not listed as *<included>* in the Monitored File Extensions list in the System Restore section of the Platform SDK
- User-created data stored in the user profile
- Contents of redirected folders

It is important to note that although the System Restore service does not *restore* the SAM hive, it does back it up—at least part of it, anyway. Checking the contents of the restore points, you will see copies of the SAM hive backed up, along with other Registry files.

For the purposes of this chapter, we are most interested in the System Restore points because they contain backups of certain Registry files, such as NTUSER.DAT, SYSTEM, SOFTWARE, and SAM. Figure 4.21 illustrates the contents of the snapshot directory of a restore point, as shown in ProDiscover.

Figure 4.21 Excerpt from ProDiscover Showing an RP Snapshot Directory

Select	File Name	File Exten...	Size
☐ 📁	Repository		
☐	ComDb	Dat	22512 bytes
☐	domain	txt	36 bytes
☐	_REGISTRY_MACHINE_SAM		24576 bytes
☐	_REGISTRY_MACHINE_SECURITY		45056 bytes
☐	_REGISTRY_MACHINE_SOFTWARE		9134080 bytes
☐	_REGISTRY_MACHINE_SYSTEM		4558848 bytes
☐	_REGISTRY_USER_	DEFAULT	241664 bytes
☐	_REGISTRY_USER_NTUSER_S-1-5-18		241664 bytes
☐	_REGISTRY_USER_NTUSER_S-1-5-19		229376 bytes
☐	_REGISTRY_USER_NTUSER_S-1-5-20		229376 bytes
☐	_REGISTRY_USER_NTUSER_S-1-5-21...		679936 bytes
☐	_REGISTRY_USER_USRCLASS_S-1-5-...		8192 bytes
☐	_REGISTRY_USER_USRCLASS_S-1-5-...		8192 bytes
☐	_REGISTRY_USER_USRCLASS_S-1-5-...		16384 bytes

As you can see, from a Registry analysis perspective the System Restore backs up quite a bit of very useful information. The Registry files that are backed up to the restore points are only a percentage of the size of those found in the system32\config directory, but they can still provide an investigator with valuable insight into the configuration of the system at points in the past.

We will address the files that are backed up by the System Restore service in Chapter 5, "File Analysis." In this chapter, we focus our attention on the Registry files.

Our analysis techniques, particularly using tools such as the Offline Registry Parser, are just as effective with the Registry files located in the restore points as they are with the raw Registry files that we find in the system32\config directory. In fact, many of the keys and values we discussed in this chapter are also found in the restore point backups of the Registry files. This allows the investigator to take a peek into the past and see some of the configuration settings and installed software on the system at that time.

Some caveats about System Restore are in order, though. By default, System Restore requires that there be 200MB of disk space available on the system. If this space requirement is not met, the System Restore service will go dormant until that space becomes available. This fact could be important during an investigation if you don't see the restore points you would expect to see on the system. Some investigators might suspect that someone was able to access the System Volume Information directory and intentionally delete the restore points when in fact they had not been created.

Another thing to be aware of when working with restore points is that the SYSTEM\ControlSet00x\Control\BackupRestore key also plays a role in determining what is and what isn't backed up or restored by the System Restore. This key has three subkeys (AsrKeysNotToRestore, FilesNotToBackup, and KeysNotToRestore) that are fairly self-explanatory. Beneath each subkey you'll see a list of Registry keys or files (in the case of the files, you'll see extensions listed with wildcards, meaning all files with that extension). These values and their data may also have an effect on what the investigator sees or has access to during a post-mortem investigation.

System Restore configuration information[44.] is maintained in the following Registry key:

```
HKEY_LOCAL_MACHINE\SOFTWARE\Microsoft\Windows NT\CurrentVersion\
SystemRestore
```

There are several important values beneath this key. The *RPGlobalInterval* value specifies how often restore points are created. The default value is 86400, which tells XP to create a restore point each calendar day (60 sec. × 60 sec/hr × 24 hrs/day = 86400, or 1 calendar day). If the *DisableSR* value is set to 1, the System Restore functionality was disabled. By default, this value is set to 0. The *RPLifeInterval* value specifies how long restore points will be retained (7776000 seconds = 90 days).

A simple way to access information about the System Restore on a live Windows XP system is via the SystemRestore[45.] and SystemRestoreConfig[46.] WMI classes. The sr.pl Perl script on the accompanying DVD provides an example of how these classes can be used. The Perl script will retrieve the System Restore configuration settings (essentially, Registry values) that are accessible via the SystemRestoreConfig WMI class and display information about each restore point (i.e., sequence number, creation date, and the string describing why the restore point was created). The information available via the SystemRestore class can be retrieved from files within the restore points and will be addressed in Chapter 5, "File Analysis."

Knowing this, how are the Registry files within the restore points useful from an investigative standpoint? The Registry files maintained in the restore points contain much of the same information as what is on the live system itself. If you don't have a system image available and want to see what these files look like, download a copy of psexec.exe from SysInternals to a Windows XP system, then type the command **psexec –s cmd**. This opens a command prompt running as SYSTEM. Change directories to the System Volume Information directory by typing:

```
cd \sys*
```

From there, proceed to the subdirectory that holds the restore points:

```
cd _restore*
```

At this point, if you request a directory listing, you should see several restore points, listed as directory names that start with *RP*. If you *cd* to one of these directories and then again to the snapshot subdirectory, you'll see the Registry files. From here, you can copy any of these files to another directory for analysis. One way to do that is with the Offline Registry Parser. Simply type the following command:

```
C:\tools>regp.pl <path>
```

If you don't have Perl installed on your system, you can use the stand-alone executable version of the script, compiled using Perl2Exe. The output will appear in ASCII format. Another way to view the information in the Registry file is to open RegEdit and select the **HKEY_USERS** hive. Click **File | Load Hive**, then navigate to the file you copied out of the restore point. When asked, give the hive a name, such as **test hive** or **test system** (if you're using the System file). Figure 4.22 illustrates a System hive loaded in this manner.

Figure 4.22 System Hive from Restore Point Loaded in RegEdit

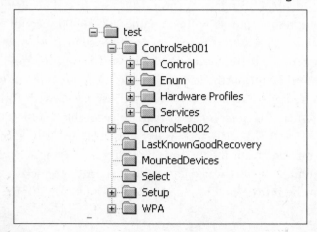

From here, you can view the contents of keys and even run tools against the Registry to extract the values and data, just as you would against a live system. You can also export values from within the hive.

As an example of how you can use this technique, say you are investigating a case and you suspect that a software program was deleted from the system. You've loaded the user's hive (NTUSER.DAT file) into RegEdit and used tools to extract from the hive information concerning the user's activities. You've parsed the UserAssist keys for that user, and you find that the Add/Remove Programs Control Panel applet had been run on a certain date. You also notice several restore points that were made prior to that date. By copying the Software hive files out of the restore points and examining the Software\Microsoft\Windows\CurrentVersion\ Uninstall subkeys, you can determine whether the software in question was installed prior to that date. In fact, depending on how the software was installed, you might even have a restore that was created when the software was removed.

Summary

Knowing how to navigate the Registry for specific information can prove an extremely valuable skill for administrators, consultants, and forensics analysts. The Registry will gladly spill forth its secrets to those who know where to look and how to interpret the information they find. Digging into the depths of the Registry is not unlike Indiana Jones tracking down ancient secrets in the shifting sands of time.

A comprehensive (I am extremely hesitant to use the word "complete") list of autostart locations and user MRU lists within the Registry can be found in the regref.xls spreadsheet included on the accompanying DVD. This list should be considered a starting point, albeit a comprehensive one, for the reader. The Registry keys listed were retrieved from online lists, applications such as AutoRuns, reports of malware on antivirus Web sites, and through personal experimentation.

This chapter should not be considered a complete reference of all the various Registry keys that might be of importance to a specific case. Registry keys with similar functionality differ in name and location between applications and, in some cases, between versions of the same application. No book can be considered a complete authoritative reference resource for Registry keys of interest; it would be far too large and expensive and then almost immediately out of date as soon as it was published. The purpose of this chapter is to illustrate what information is available and how to go about finding additional information.

DVD Contents

The DVD that accompanies this book includes a directory specifically for this chapter. That directory includes several subdirectories, one that contains the code presented in this chapter, including Perl scripts, as well as ProScripts, which are Perl scripts specifically written to be used with ProDiscover. The "spreadsheet" subdirectory includes a copy of the Registry reference spreadsheet that I compiled a bit ago. This spreadsheet lists several Registry keys and values of interest to forensic analysts as well as a brief description of their purpose and, where applicable, references. The spreadsheet is split up into different worksheets, each covering a specific area of functionality.

There is also a "samples" subdirectory that includes several Registry files from real systems—not only those found in the system32\config directory but also from restore points. I encourage you to look at these files, open them in a hex editor, and use any of the tools included in the "code" subdirectory for this chapter so that you can develop a familiarity with the tools as well as with the raw Registry files themselves.

Notes

1. For more information go to http://support.microsoft.com/kb/256986.
2. For more information go to
http://support.microsoft.com/default.aspx?scid=kb;en-us;141377.
3. For more information go to
http://support.microsoft.com/default.aspx?scid=kb;en-us;161678.
4. For more information go to
www.microsoft.com/technet/archive/winntas/tips/winntmag/inreg.mspx?mfr=true.
5. For more information go to http://home.eunet.no/pnordahl/ntpasswd/.
6. For more information go to www.sleuthkit.org/.
7. For more information go to http://pyflag.sourceforge.net/.
8. For more information go to
http://support.microsoft.com/default.aspx?scid=kb;en-us;188768.
9. For more information go to
http://msdn.microsoft.com/library/default.asp?url=/library/en-us/sysinfo/base/file-
timetosystemtime.asp.
10. For more information go to http://vil.nai.com/vil/Content/v_140546.htm.
11. For more information go to http://home.planet.nl/~pa0joz/pc_util.html.
12. For more information go to
www.microsoft.com/technet/sysinternals/SystemInformation/Regmon.mspx.
13. For more information go to http://liveview.sourceforge.net/.
14. For more information go to http://support.microsoft.com/kb/288164/en-us.
15. For more information go to
http://support.microsoft.com/default.aspx?scid=kb;EN-US;q246120.
16. For more information go to http://support.microsoft.com/kb/298931.
17. For more information go to http://support.microsoft.com/kb/310560.
18. For more information go to http://msdn.microsoft.com/library/
default.asp?url=/library/en-us/wmisdk/wmi/win32_startupcommand.asp.
19. For more information go to
www.microsoft.com/technet/prodtechnol/winxppro/reskit/c29621675.mspx.
20. For more information go to
http://support.microsoft.com/default.aspx?scid=kb;EN-US;137367.
21. For more information go to http://support.microsoft.com/kb/314866/EN-US/.
22. For more information go to http://liveview.sourceforge.net/.
23. For more information go to http://support.microsoft.com/?kbid=311446.
24. For more information go to http://support.microsoft.com/?kbid=310585.
25. For more information go to
www.microsoft.com/resources/documentation/Windows/2000/server/reskit/en-

us/Default.asp?url=/resources/documentation/Windows/2000/server/reskit/en-us/regentry/942.asp.

26. For more information go to http://support.microsoft.com/kb/197571.

27. For more information go to http://msdn.microsoft.com/library/default.asp?url=/library/en-us/secauthn/security/registry_entries.asp.

28. For more information go to http://support.microsoft.com/default.aspx?kbid=238788.

29. For more information go to http://support.microsoft.com/default.aspx?scid=kb;en-us;892894.

30. For more information go to http://silverstr.ufies.org/blog/archives/000809.html.

31. For more information go to www.sysinternals.com/ntw2k/freeware/autoruns.shtml.

32. For more information go to www.microsoft.com/whdc/device/stream/vidcap/UVCView.mspx.

33. For more information go to www.microsoft.com/whdc/system/bus/usb/USBFAQ_intermed.mspx.

34. For more information go to www.microsoft.com/whdc/device/storage/usbfaq.mspx#ERCAC.

35. For more information go to www.microsoft.com/technet/prodtechnol/windows2000serv/reskit/regentry/93502.mspx?mfr=true.

36. For more information go to www.hak5.org/wiki/USB_Hacksaw.

37. For more information go to http://support.microsoft.com/kb/157234/.

38. For more information go to www.accessdata.com/support/downloads/.

39. For more information go to http://search.cpan.org/~jmacfarla/Parse-Win32Registry-0.24/lib/Parse/Win32Registry.pm.

40. See http://computer.forensikblog.de/en/2006/02/list_members_of_a_windows_group.html.

41. For more information go to http://support.microsoft.com/default.aspx?scid=kb;en-us;322948.

42. For more information go to http://support.microsoft.com/kb/813711.

43. For more information go to http://support.microsoft.com/kb/235994.

44. For more information go to http://support.microsoft.com/kb/295659.

45. For more information go to http://msdn.microsoft.com/library/default.asp?url=/library/en-us/sr/sr/systemrestore.asp.

46. For more information go to http://msdn.microsoft.com/library/default.asp?url=/library/en-us/sr/sr/systemrestoreconfig.asp.

Solutions Fast Track

Inside the Registry

☑ The Windows Registry is a binary, hierarchal database of configuration information that not only controls various operating system and application configuration settings but also maintains information about various aspects of the user's interaction with the system.

☑ By understanding the format of the various Registry structures (i.e., keys and values), we can then parse and view portions of the Registry found in memory and unallocated space.

☑ Some portions of the Registry are volatile, created when the system is started, and will not be found in an acquired image of a system.

☑ Registry keys (and some values) have timestamps associated with them that can be used in timeline analysis. For this reason, the Registry can be considered a log file of sorts.

☑ There is no apparent standard for the way information is maintained in the Registry. Some MRU keys, for example, maintain their value data as binary types, others as ASCII strings (making searches for ASCII strings somewhat easy). Other Registry keys have their value names obfuscated with ROT-13 "encryption" or their value data maintained in such a way as to hamper string searches. You need to understand the structure of the specific key and value to parse the data stored in that location.

☑ There are tools available to track accesses and modifications to the Registry on a live system; this information can be used to locate Registry keys of interest as well as determine artifacts left by applications and user activity.

Registry Analysis

☑ A number of locations within the Registry contain information pertinent to most investigations. Other locations contain information pertinent to specific types of investigations, such as intrusions, fraud, or abuse of acceptable use policies.

☑ Some specific Registry keys and values can be of importance to an investigation, but often it is the correlation of several Registry keys and values that can provide the most complete picture.

☑ Windows XP System Restore Points maintain portions of the Registry that can be useful during an investigation. For example, examining the contents of the preserved SAM file, an investigator might be able to determine when a user's group membership changed (i.e., going from User to the Administrators group), if that is pertinent to the investigation. You might also be able to tell what applications were installed on the system in the recent past.

Q: How do I determine whether there are any browser helper objects (BHOs) installed and what they are?

Frequently Asked Questions

The following Frequently Asked Questions, answered by the authors of this book, are designed to both measure your understanding of the concepts presented   in this chapter and to assist you with real-life implementation of these concepts. To have your questions about this chapter answered by the author, browse to **www.syngress.com/solutions** and click on the **"Ask the Author"** form.

A: BHOs are maintained in the HKEY_LOCAL_MACHINE hive, which means that they affect all users on the system. The BHOs are listed under the Software\Microsoft\Windows\CurrentVersion\Explorer\Browser Helper Objects key. Beneath this key, each BHO will be listed as a GUID-named subkey. From there, go to the Software\Classes\CLSID key in the HKEY_LOCAL_MACHINE hive and locate each GUID. Once you locate the key with the same GUID as the BHO, check the *Default* value of that key for the name of the BHO. To get the DLL for the BHO, check the *Default* value of the InProcServer subkey. The Perl script bho.pl that is included on the accompanying DVD can be used to retrieve BHOs from a local system.

Q: During a search of a system, I found a Registry key in the user's hive (Software\Microsoft\Windows\CurrentVersion\Internet Settings\ZoneMap\Domains) that had a number of subkeys with the domains of Web sites. What is this key, and what do the subkeys represent?

A: These entries can be added to Internet Explorer by the administrator, by going to **Tools | Internet Options... | Restricted Sites** and clicking the **Sites...** button. However, look closely at the sites listed, since some malware will add sites to this key so that the user cannot access those Web sites. Although entries within this key might be indicative of Administrator activity or Group Policies, they could also be indicative of a malware infection.

Q: During an investigation, it became clear, based on information from a Windows XP system (installed software, etc.), that the user had Local Administrator rights on the system. In discussing this with the IT director, it was revealed that all users are provided with only User-level access to their systems. How can I track down when the user was added to the Administrators Group on the system?

A: This sort of information about users is maintained in the SAM file. The *LastWrite* time on the Registry key that maintains group membership information tion could provide you with some clues. In addition, there could be enough historical data in the Windows XP System Restore Points for you to locate that last time that the user's RID was associated with the User group and not the Administrators group.

Chapter 5

File Analysis

Solutions in this chapter:

- **Event Logs**
- **File Metadata**
- **Alternative Methods of Analysis**

☑ **Summary**

☑ **Solutions Fast Track**

☑ **Frequently Asked Questions**

Introduction

Windows systems maintain quite a number of files that are useful from a forensic perspective. In fact, many investigators might not realize the wealth of data that they can find within some of the files that Windows systems use to track various activity and functions. Knowing multiple locations where information is maintained within the system allows an investigator to corroborate information that is found in other areas and reduce the amount of uncertainty in their analysis.

In this chapter, we'll discuss some of the log files you can find on Windows systems as well as information about files in general, as along with specific files that could be of value to an investigator. We will discuss a number of apparently different aspects that are tied together by the fact that they all reside within files or the file system.

Event Logs

The Event Logs are perhaps the most well-known logs on Windows systems, the rough equivalent of syslog on Linux systems. The Event Logs record a variety of day-to-day events that occur on Windows systems and are configurable (as discussed in Chapter 4) to record a range of additional events. These events are split into categories that are implemented through the various Event Logs themselves, such as Security, System, and Application Event Logs. The Event Logs can provide a good deal of information that's useful for troubleshooting issues as well as for understanding events during forensic analysis.

TIP

On most Windows systems, the Resource Kit tool auditpol.exe can be used to query and set the audit policy. On Windows XPSP2 and 2003SP1, auditusr.exe allows for per-user audit policies. For example, logon auditing can be set for all users, but more detailed auditing can be enabled for a specific user. Changes made with auditusr.exe modify the HKEY_LOCAL_MACHINE\SYSTEM\CurrentControlSet\Control\Lsa\Audit\PerUserAuditing\System Registry key. The use of this tool can give the investigator an indication of the types of events she should expect to see in the Event Log as well as an indication of the technical skill level of the user or administrator.

Understanding Events

On the Windows NT family of operating systems, from Windows 2000 through XP and 2003, the Event Logs consist of a binary structure, with a header and a series of event records stored in the file. Based on the way the operating system was designed, when certain events, such as a user logging on or off, occur, a record of these events is generated. Some events are recorded by default; others are recorded based on the audit configuration maintained in the PolAdEvt Registry key, as discussed in Chapter 4. Other aspects of the event log configuration (file size, how long records are retained, and so on) are maintained in the following Registry key:

`HKEY_LOCAL_MACHINE\SYSTEM\CurrentControlSet\Services\Eventlog\<Event Log>`

By default, Windows 2000, XP, and 2003 all have Application, Security, and System Event Logs. Systems that are configured as domain controllers will also have File Replication and Directory Service Event Logs, and systems configured as domain name servers (DNS) will have DNS Event Logs.

Administrators are most familiar with interacting with the Event Logs through the Event Viewer, which is a GUI manager for the Event Logs. When the administrator views an event record on Windows XP, he will see something similar to what is illustrated in Figure 5.1.

Figure 5.1 Windows XP Event Record Viewed in the Event Viewer

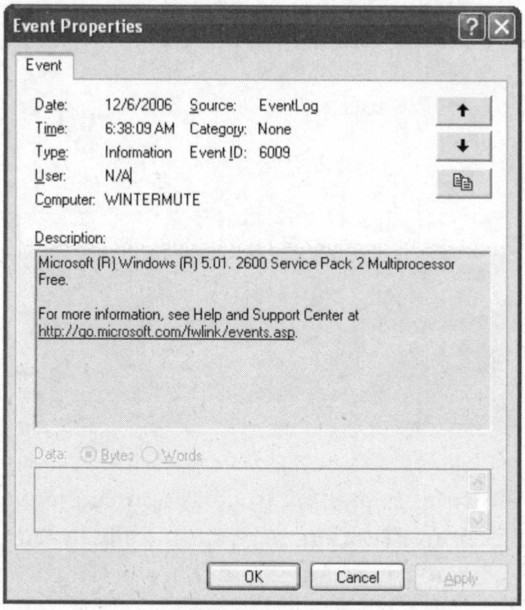

When the Event Viewer opens an event record, it populates the *Description:* field by reading the strings values from the event record, then locating the appropriate message file (DLL) on the system. The message files contain message strings that are used to support internationalization on the Windows operating systems, and the strings values from the event records are inserted into the appropriate locations within those strings. This allows for the internationalization of the Event Logs by providing event message strings in the language native to the system (English, German, French, or the like) and simply "filling in the gaps" with the necessary information (system name, date/time stamp, and so on). This shows a tight correlation among the Event Log, the Windows Registry, and many of the DLLs on the system. It also means that third-party applications that write to the Event Log will need to include their own message files.

Prior to Windows 2003, logon events would only contain the NetBIOS name of the system from which the logon originated. Beginning with Windows 2003, the Security Event Log records both the workstation name and the IP address of the system, as illustrated in Figure 5.2.

Figure 5.2 Windows 2003 Event Record Showing IP Address

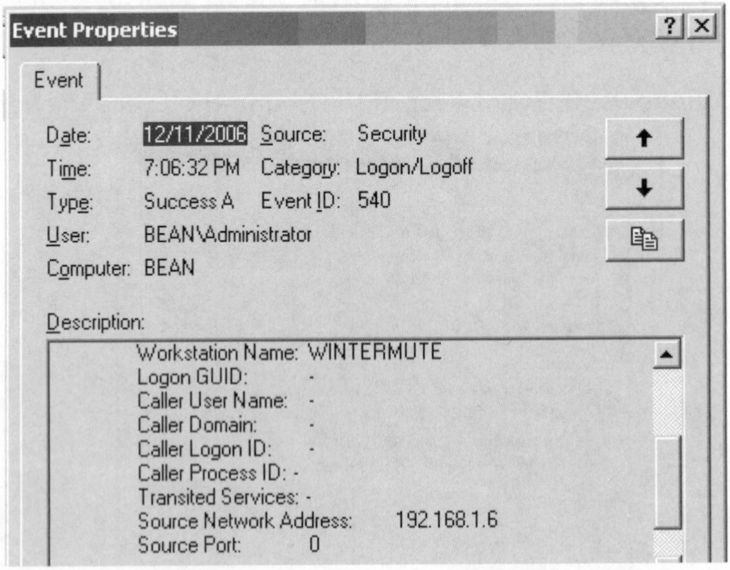

The information shown in Figure 5.2 (such as Source Network Address) can be extremely useful during an investigation, most specifically because the IP address of the remote system is visible in the event record. This information can be used to determine the source of logons and logon attempts.

Even without the DLL message files it is not difficult to tell what the different event records pertain to, since there is other identifying information in the record. In Figure 5.2, for example, we see an event ID, an event source, and other information we can use to sort on when analyzing event records. There is also a date/time stamp that we can use for timeline analysis; actually, there are two date/time stamps in an event record (as we'll discuss later in the chapter). Microsoft provides a good deal of information regarding some of the event records that you are likely to see. For example, if auditing and logging of logon/logoff events are enabled (see Chapter 4 for how to determine this from an acquired image), the investigator should see event IDs 528 (successful logon) and 538 (logoff) in the Security Event Log. If he sees several event records all with event ID 528, he will want to check the logon type, since there are nine different logon type codes. Table 5.1 lists the various security logon type codes[1] for successful logons and what they mean.

Table 5.1 Event Logon Types

Logon Type	Title	Description
2	*Interactive*	This logon type indicates that the user logged in at the console
3	*Network*	A user/computer logged into this computer from the network, such as via *net use*, accessing a network share, or a successful *net view* directed at a network share. (This has been replaced by Event ID 540)
4	*Batch*	Reserved for applications that run as batches.
5	*Service*	Service logon
6	*Proxy*	Not supported
7	*Unlock*	The user unlocked the workstation
8	*NetworkClearText*	A user logged onto a network, and the user's credentials were passed in an unencrypted form
9	*NewCredentials*	A process or thread cloned its current token but specified new credentials for outbound connections
10	*RemoteInteractive*	Logon using Terminal Services or a Remote Desktop connection

Continued

Table 5.1 continued Event Logon Types

Logon Type	Title	Description
11	*CachedInteractive*	A user logged onto the computer with credentials that were stored locally on the computer (domain controller may have been unavailable to verify credentials)
12	*CachedRemote Interactive*	Same as *RemoteInteractive*, used internally for auditing purposes
13	*CachedUnlock*	The logon attempt is to unlock a workstation

From a more general perspective, Microsoft provides two KnowledgeBase articles (299475[2] and 301677[3]) that list Windows 2000 Security Event descriptions. The security events are listed with a brief description as well as placeholders (%1, %2, etc.) where the strings from the event record are inserted.

TIP

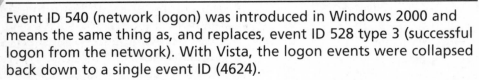

Event ID 540 (network logon) was introduced in Windows 2000 and means the same thing as, and replaces, event ID 528 type 3 (successful logon from the network). With Vista, the logon events were collapsed back down to a single event ID (4624).

For other event records, many sites provide detailed information regarding event record details, why the events are generated, and so on. For detailed information regarding specific entries in the Application Event Log, you might need to check with the vendor. One of the best sites I've found for gaining an understanding of what's in the event records is EventID.net. The site does require a subscription fee, but if you're spending a great deal of time investigating event records of different types, that fee is well worth the trouble saved in Googling. In many instances, you simply need to provide the event ID in question and you'll be treated information about the event, as generated by various sources, as well as links to references. For example, if I search for event ID 6009, I get four different event sources. From there, I can click on the details for the one I want (in this case, the event source is *EventLog*) and I get commentary from two authors as well as three links to the Microsoft site that provide detailed information regarding the event ID. In this case, in fairly short order, I see that the event ID is generated when a Windows system is booted (so the time that the event record was generated approximates to the time that the system was booted) and that information about the operating system version is written to the *Description* field of the event.

TIP

The event ID 6009 record from source *EventLog* can be used to determine or verify the operating system of the host system as well as the system name. The *Computer:* entry will contain the host name, and the *Description* of the event record will contain a string that identifies the version of the Windows operating system.

Besides EventID.net, an excellent source of information on Windows Event Logging is Eric Fitzgerald's Windows Security Logging and Other Esoterica blog.[4] Eric's blog contains a great deal of very useful information regarding Event Logs, including how they can be used to meet Visa's PCI compliance standards, as well as auditing tips and tricks. Microsoft also has the Events and Errors Message Center: Advanced Search[5] site that you can use to gather information about various Event Log entries.

TIP

Remember discussing artifacts of USB removable storage devices in Chapter 4? In Windows 2000, whenever a USB removable storage device was connected to a system, an event record with ID 134 was generated by the Removable Storage Service. When the device was removed, an event ID 135 was generated. These events are no longer visible as of Windows XP, and KB article 329463[6] provides a clue as to the reason. Once the hotfix is installed:

After you install the hotfix, Netshell no longer listens for Plug and Play device arrival notifications. Therefore, you are not notified about new devices.

So, you should not expect to see notifications in the Event Log that USB removable storage devices have been inserted or removed.

Also, you might want to drop by Randy Franklin's UltimateWindows Security.com site; he has pages dedicated specifically to the Windows Security Event Log, including an event ID reference sheet and an encyclopedia. With regard to the Security Event Log, this site is well worth a visit and a bookmark.

Event Log File Format

At times during an investigation you might need to examine the contents of an Event Log .evt file in an understandable format. (The Event Log format discussed in this section pertains to all operating systems except Vista.) So you extract the .evt file from an image, and you figure that you just open the file in the Event Viewer. However, when you attempt to do so, you get an error message telling you that the Event Log is "corrupt." At other times you might be searching through unallocated clusters in an image, looking for some information that could be useful to your case. In either situation, knowing the details of the structure of the Event Log file can be valuable.

The Windows Event Log (for Windows 2000, XP, and 2003) is a binary format with distinct, recognizable features that can assist an investigator in recognizing and interpreting Event Log files or simply event records on a system, either in files or located in unallocated space. Each Event Log consists of a header section and a series of event records, both of which we will discuss in detail. The Event Log is maintained as a circular buffer, so as new event records are added to the file, older event records are cycled out of the file.

Event Log Header

The Event Log header is contained in the first 48 bytes of a valid Event Log file. If the .evt file has not been corrupted in any way, the header will appear similar to the sample Event Log header in Figure 5.3.

Figure 5.3 Event Log Header

```
00000000h: 30 00 00 00 4C 66 4C 65 01 00 00 00 01 00 00 00 ; 0...LfLe........
00000010h: 30 00 00 00 F0 A9 00 00 AD 00 00 00 01 00 00 00 ; 0...ð©.........
00000020h: 00 00 01 00 09 00 00 00 80 3A 09 00 30 00 00 00 ; ........€:..0...
```

The Event Log header consists of 12 distinct *DWORD* values. Table 5.2 lists nine of those values and provides a brief description of each.

Table 5.2 Event Log Header Structure

Offset	Size	Description
0	4 bytes	Size of the record; for an .evt file header, the size is 0x30 (48) bytes. Event record sizes are 56 bytes
4	4 bytes	Magic number ("LfLe")
16	4 bytes	Offset within the .evt file of the oldest event record
20	4 bytes	Offset within the .evt file to the next event record to be written
24	4 bytes	ID of the next event record
28	4 bytes	ID of the oldest event record
32	4 bytes	Maximum size of the .evt file (from the Registry)
40	4 bytes	Retention time of event records (from the Registry)
44	4 bytes	Size of the record (repeat of *DWORD* at offset 0)

The value of importance in the header is the "magic number," which appears as *LfLe* beginning at the fourth byte (the second *DWORD*) in the header. This value is unique to the Windows Event Log (for Windows 2000, XP, and 2003) and is associated with event records. Microsoft refers to this value as the *ELF_LOG_SIGNATURE*. (A description of the event record structure at the Microsoft site states that this is "a *DWORD* value that is always set to *ELF_LOG_SIGNATURE*.") Notice that the size of the record (for the header, 0x30, or 48 bytes) brackets the header, appearing at the beginning and the end of the header. This allows the investigator to either programmatically (using code) or manually (using a hex editor) locate the header (or an event record), whether looking at an Event Log file, unallocated space, or a file of unknown type. The ID numbers for the next event record to be written and the oldest event record can be used to determine the total number of event records that the investigator should expect to see.

NOTE

When we're working with files, we use the term *magic number* to refer to a specific series of bytes within the file that are unique to that file or file type. These magic numbers are used in performing file signature analysis, a technique used to determine whether a file has the correct file extension based on its magic number. In the case of Event Log files, the magic number is 0x654c664c, or as shown in Figure 5.3, 4C 66 4C 65. Even though this series of bytes translates to the string *LfLe"* when the endianness is reversed, it is still referred to as a magic number.

The values for the maximum size of the Event Log file and the retention time of event records are taken from the Registry of the system where the Event Logs are maintained.

Event Record Structure

Event records have some structure values in common with Event Log header, but event records contain much more information, as illustrated in Figure 5.4. However, the basic header for an event record is somewhat larger than the header, weighing in at 56 bytes. Although the record size provided in the event record (0xF4, or 244 bytes) is larger than 56 bytes, the first 56 bytes of the event record constitute an event record header.

Figure 5.4 Sample Event Record Structure

```
00000030h: F4 00 00 00 4C 66 4C 65 01 00 00 00 3D E1 20 43 ; ô...LfLe....=á C
00000040h: 3D E1 20 43 64 02 00 00 08 00 15 00 06 00 00 00 ; =á Cd...........
00000050h: 00 00 00 00 72 00 00 00 1C 00 00 00 56 00 00 00 ; ....r.......V...
00000060h: 00 00 00 00 EE 00 00 00 53 00 65 00 63 00 75 00 ; ....î...S.e.c.u.
```

As you can see, the Event Log magic number appears in the second *DWORD* value of the event record, just as it does for the header. Table 5.3 provides details of the content of the first 56 bytes of an event record.

Table 5.3 Event Record Structure

Offset	Size	Description
0	4 bytes	Length of the event record, or size of the record in bytes
4	4 bytes	Reserved; magic number
8	4 bytes	Record number
12	4 bytes	Time generated; measured in Unix time, or the number of seconds elapsed since 00:00:00 1 Jan 1970, in Universal Coordinated Time (UTC)
16	4 bytes	Time written; measured in Unix time, or the number of seconds elapsed since 00:00:00 1 Jan 1970, in Universal Coordinated Time (UTC)
20	4 bytes	Event ID, which is specific to the event source and uniquely identifies the event; the event ID is used along with the source name to locate the appropriate description string within the message file for the event source
24	2 bytes	Event type (0x01 = Error; 0x10 = Failure; 0x08 = Success; 0x04 = Information; 0x02 = Warning)
26	2 bytes	Number of strings
28	2 bytes	Event category
30	2 bytes	Reserved flags
32	4 bytes	Closing record number
36	4 bytes	String offset; offset to the description strings within this event record
40	4 bytes	Length of the user SID; size of the user SID in bytes (if 0, no user SID is provided)
44	4 bytes	Offset to the user SID within this event record
48	4 bytes	Data length; length of the binary data associated with this event record
52	4 bytes	Offset to the data

Table 5.3 lists the first 56 bytes of an event record. Keep in mind that the actual length of the record itself is listed in the first and last *DWORDs* of the record. (The size of the record brackets the actual record, just as it does with the file header.) With this information in hand, it is a relatively straightforward process to parse through the contents of an Event Log file, extracting and displaying the event records.

Having the event record structure definition also makes it possible to reassemble partial event records found in unallocated space. Using the magic number as a guide post, an analyst can search through unallocated space; should she locate the magic number, all she has to do is read the preceding *DWORD* for the size of the event record, then extract that number of bytes for the full event record. Even if the entire event record is not available, the first 56 bytes will provide a road map for reconstructing portions of an event record.

Tools & Traps…

Reading Event Logs

Once I was assisting with a case in which an analyst who is extremely familiar with Linux was using PyFlag[7] as his forensic analysis tool. He decided that he wanted me to open the Event Logs and retrieve available records; he'd tried to do so, but when he copied the .evt files to his Windows desktop system and tried to open the .evt files with Event Viewer, he received a message that the files were corrupted.

I had already been researching the Event Log and event record structure, so I tweaked my Perl script just a bit and parsed through the Event Log files, retrieving all the event records with no problems whatsoever. However, I found a disparity between the information I was receiving from the header of one of the Event Logs and what I was seeing in the output of the event records; no matter how I approached the situation, I always had one more complete event record than the header information was telling me I should have. After investigating this issue for some time, I determined that according to the API, a section of the Event Log just preceding the first record was a buffer area left over from when the Event Log was cleared. This buffer area was not read by the API, and if the system had been allowed to continue normally, it would have been flushed out of the circular buffer as new event records were written to the file. However, this buffer contained one complete event record; since the tool I was using did not use the API to retrieve event records but instead read through the file in binary mode, parsing the information it found, the tool didn't recognize this buffer area.

Although the "lost" event record did not have a significant impact on the case, it did show the usefulness (with regard to forensic analysis) of understanding the format of certain files on Windows systems, and where possible, developing tools that parse through the information in those files in a manner that does not rely on the Windows API. Not only does this provide the investi-

Continued

gator with the possibility of discovering "hidden" information, it also allows the investigator to perform analysis on platforms other than Windows (particularly on Linux); investigators are not restricted to analyzing Windows images on a Windows platform.

Three Perl scripts in the ReadEvt directory of the accompanying DVD allow you to collect information from Event Log files from Windows 2000, XP, and 2003 systems. The first, evtstats.pl, displays simple statistics collected from an .evt file, as shown here:

```
G:\>evtstats.pl d:\cases\appevent.evt

Max    Size of the Event Log file          = 65536 bytes
Actual Size of the Event Log file          = 65536 bytes
Total number of event records (header info) = 200
Total number of event records (actual count) = 206
Total number of event records (rec_nums)    = 206
Total number of event records (sources)     = 206
Total number of event records (types)       = 206
Total number of event records (IDs)         = 206
```

The script parses the header of the Event Log file and determines the number of records that should exist, then parses through the contents of the Event Log file itself and, using various tags from within each event record, performs an actual count of the number of records found.

The second Perl script, lsevt.pl, uses the File::ReadEvt Perl module to parse through the Event Log file and display event records in a simple listing format, as illustrated here:

```
Record Number : 198
Source    : SecurityCenter
Computer Name : PETER
Event ID   : 1800
Event Type  : EVENTLOG_INFORMATION_TYPE
Time Generated: Mon Sep 19 21:07:32 2005
Time Written : Mon Sep 19 21:07:32 2005
```

The third Perl script, lsevt2.pl, provides a bit more flexibility than lsevt.pl in that it allows you to choose to output the format as comma-separated values. This way, the investigator can run the script against a Windows Event Log file using the following command line:

```
C:\Perl>perl lsevt2.pl -f d:\cases\appevent.evt -c > testevt.csv
```

He can then open the resulting testevt.csv file in Excel for sorting, searching, and analysis. Further, lsevt2.pl does not require the use of the File::ReadEvt Perl module.

All three Perl scripts parse through the Event Log files in binary mode, bypassing the Windows API all together. This way, not only can the Event Log files be parsed on a platform other than Windows (Mac OS X, Linux, and so on) but an investigator can still parse the Event Log files even if the Event Viewer gives him error messages that the file is somehow corrupted. Both files do require the use of the File::ReadEvt Perl module that is also included on the accompanying DVD. Installation of this module is trivial; simply copy the ReadEvt.pm file to the site\lib\File directory in your Perl installation. Once you've done this, you'll be able to use the module from within Perl scripts.

Another option for dealing with Event Logs that the Event Viewer reports as corrupted involves using a hex editor to make modifications to the header of the Event Log file. Stephen Bunting, a captain with the University of Delaware Police, has a detailed listing[8] of the steps that can be used to modify the Event Log header so that the file can be opened and viewed in the Event Viewer as well as other applications that use the Windows API to access.evt files.

WARNING

In February 2007, Andreas Schuster blogged[9] about a special condition regarding Event Log records, in which a record is written to the end of the .evt file but wraps around to the beginning of the file so that part of the record follows the header. This record will be incorrectly read by tools (such as the Perl scripts listed in this chapter) that look for the event record magic number, because only part of the record will be identified. Andreas was kind enough to provide an example .evt file so that parsers can be tested (and improved) against this condition.

Vista Event Logs

A lot about the Windows operating system has changed with the advent of Vista, including the Event Log structure used by the operating system. For example, this service is now referred to as Windows Event Log rather than Event Logging and takes on a whole new format. Vista uses an XML format for storing events, and Vista now supports central collection of event records.

Other changes include the fact that although Vista still maintains the three main categories of event log (Application, Security, and System), it now has a wide range of categories under which different events can be logged, as illustrated in Figure 5.5.

Figure 5.5 Vista Event Viewer

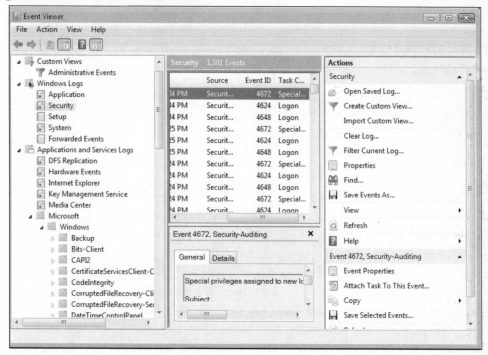

As illustrated in Figure 5.5, there are now more Event Logs, including one for Internet Explorer as well as Hardware Events. (Installing the new IE version 7 also adds an Internet Explorer Event Log to Windows XP and 2003.) Also notice on the lower right-hand side of Figure 5.5, under Actions, there is an item called Attach Task To This Event.... As tools are developed for parsing through Vista Event Logs and as those tools are used by incident responders and forensics analysts, this particular item will be of interest.

Andreas Schuster and Eric Fitzgerald have posted some information in their respective blogs about the structure used to store event records.

On a live Vista system, the wevtutil.exe command can be used to retrieve information about the Windows Event Log that isn't readily apparent via the Event

Viewer UI. For example, the following command will display a list of the available Event Logs on the system:

```
C:\>wevtutil el
```

From there you can use the next command to list configuration information about a specific Event Log, including the name and path to the file:

```
C:\>wevtutil gl log name
```

Much of the information displayed by this command is also available in the following Registry key on a Vista system:

```
HKEY_LOCAL_MACHINE\System\ControlSet00x\Services\EventLog\log name
```

This will be useful information for incident responders and forensic analysts alike. Tools and techniques need to be developed that allow incident responders and forensic analysts to extract relevant and pertinent information from the Windows Event Logs on Vista systems.

IIS Logs

Microsoft's Internet Information Server (IIS) is a Web server platform that's popular with both users and attackers. It is easy for administrators to install—to the point that sometimes they aren't even aware that they have a Web server running on their system. It is also a very popular target for attackers, and with good reason. Many times there are vulnerabilities to the Web server due to coding or configuration issues that when left unaddressed, leave not only the Web server software but the entire platform open to exploitation. One of the best ways to uncover attempts to compromise the IIS Web server or details of a successful exploit is to examine the logs generated by the Web server.

The IIS Web server logs are most often maintained in the %WinDir%\System32\LogFiles directory. Each virtual server has its own subdirectory for log files, named for the server itself. In most situations, only one instance of the Web server might be running, so the log subdirectory will be W3SVC1. During an investigation, you might find multiple subdirectories, named W3SVC*n*, where *n* is the number of the virtual server. However, the location of the logs is configurable by the administrator and can be modified to point to any location, even a shared drive. By default, the log files are ASCII text format (this is also configurable by the administrator), meaning that they are easily opened and searchable. In many cases, the log files can be quite large, particularly for extremely active Web sites, so opening and searching the file by hand isn't going to be feasible or effective. Searches can be scripted using Perl scripts or *grep* searches, or if you're looking for something specific, the find/search capability found in whichever editor you choose to use might also work.

While we are discussing searches, one of the biggest questions investigators face is, how do we cull through voluminous Web server logs to find what might be the proverbial needle in a haystack? On a high-volume server, the log files can be pretty large, and searching through them for relevant data can be an arduous task. Sometimes using a victim's incident report can help an investigator narrow the time-frame of when the attack occurred, allowing for a modicum of data reduction. However, this doesn't always work. It is not uncommon for an investigator to find a system that had been compromised weeks or even months before any unusual activity was reported. So what do you do?

A while back—a long while in Internet years, all the way back to 1997[10]—Marcus Ranum developed an outline for what he referred to as "artificial ignorance" (AI). The basic idea is that if you remove all legitimate activity from the Web server logs, what you have left should be "unusual."

Tools & Traps...

Implementing "AI"

I've used the "artificial ignorance" method for filtering various items, and it has been a very useful technique. I had written a Perl script that would reach out across the enterprise for me (I was working in a small company with between 300 and 400 employees) and collect the contents of specific Registry keys from all the systems that were logged into the domain. I could run this script during lunch and come back to a nice log file that was easy to parse and open in Excel. However, it was pretty large, and I wanted to see only those things that required my attention. So I began examining some of the entries I found, and as I verified that each one of the entries was legitimate, I would add it to a file of "known-good" entries. Then I would collect the contents of the Registry keys and log only those that did not appear in the known-good file. In a short time, I went from several pages of entries to less than half a page of items I needed to investigate.

With Web server logs, it is a fairly straightforward process to implement this type of AI. For example, assume that you're investigating a case in which a Web server might have been compromised, and there are a very small number of files on the server—the index.html file and perhaps half a dozen other HTML files that contain supporting information for the main site (about.html, contact.html, links.html, and so forth).

IIS Web server logs that are saved in ASCII format (which is the default) have a rather simple format, so it is a fairly simple task to use your favorite scripting language to open the file, read each log entry in, one line at a time, and perform processing. IIS logs will generally have column headers located at the top of the file, or that information might be somewhere else in the file if the Web server was restarted. Using the column headers as a key, you can then parse each entry for relevant information, such as the request verb (*GET, HEAD, POST*), the page requested, and the status or response code[11] that was returned. If you find a page that was requested that is not on your list of known-good pages, you can log the filename, date/time of the request, source IP address of the request, and the like to a separate file for analysis.

WARNING

I am not providing code for this technique simply due to the fact that not all IIS Web logs are of the same format. The information that is logged is configurable by the Web server administrator, so I really cannot provide a "one size fits all" solution. Further, the exact specifications of a search may differ between cases. For example, in one case you might be interested in all pages that were requested that are not part of the Web server; in another case, you might be interested only in requests issued from a specific IP address or address range. In yet another case, you might be interested only in requests that generated specific response codes.

"Artificial ignorance" is one approach to take when searching Web server logs; this technique is very flexible and can be implemented on a wide range of logs and files. Another technique you can use is to look for specific artifacts left behind by specific attacks. This technique can be very useful in cases where more information about the infrastructure, the level of access the attacker obtained, and other specifics are known. Also, if there seems to be a particular vulnerability that was released around the time of the intrusion or there is an increase in reported attempts against a specific exploit, searching for specific artifacts could be an effective technique.

For example, if an IIS Web server uses an MS SQL database server as a back end, one attack to look for is SQL injection. An attacker may use queries submitted to the Web server to be processed by the back-end database server to extract information, upload files to the server, or the like. A telltale sign of a SQL injection attack is the existence of *xpcmdshell* in the log file entries. *Xpcmdshell* is an extended stored procedure that is part of the MS SQL server that can allow an attacker to run commands on the database server with the same privileges as the server itself (which is usually System-level privileges).

There are a number of other issues that one can search for based on various keywords or phrases. For example, the existence of *vti_auth\author.dll* in the Web server logs can be indicative of the issue[12.] with the permissions on FrontPage extensions that can lead to Web page defacements. Other signatures I have used in the past to look for the Nimda[13.] worm (see the "System Footprint" section in the CERT advisory) included attempts to execute cmd.exe and tftp.exe via URLs submitted to the Web browser.

Analysis of IIS (and other Web server) logs can be an expansive subject, one suitable for an entire chapter all on its own. However, as with most log files, the principles of data reduction remain the same: Remove all the entries that you know should be there, accounting for legitimate activity. Or, if you know or at least have an idea of what you're looking for, you can use signatures to look for indications of specific activity.

Notes from the Underground...

FTP Logs

I was assisting with an investigation in which someone had access to a Windows system via a remote management utility (such as WinVNC or PCAnywhere) and used the installed Microsoft FTP server to transfer files to and from the system. Similarly to the IIS Web server, the FTP server maintains its logs in the LogFiles directory, beneath the MSFTPSVCx subdirectory. There were no indications that the individual did anything to attempt to hide or obfuscate his presence on the system, and we were able to develop a timeline of activity using the FTP logs as an initial reference. Thanks to the default FTP log format, we not only had the date/time stamp of his visits and the username he used, but also the FTP address from which his connections originated. We correlated that information to date/time stamps from activity in the Registry (i.e., UserAssist keys and so on) and the Event Logs (several event ID 10 entries stated that the FTP connection had timed out due to inactivity) to develop a clearer picture of this individual's activity on the system.

Internet Explorer Browsing History

On the opposite end of the Web server logs is the Internet Explorer (IE) Web browsing history. IE is installed by default on Windows systems and is the default browser for many users. In some cases, as with corporate users, some corporate intranet Web sites (for submitting timecard information or travel expenses) could be specifically designed for use with IE; other browsers (such as Firefox or Opera) are not supported. When IE is used to browse the Web, it keeps a history of its activity that the investigator can use to develop an understanding of the user's activity as well as to obtain evidence. The IE browser history files are saved in the user's profile directory, beneath the Local Settings\Temporary Internet Files\Content.IE5 subdirectory. Beneath this directory path, the investigator might find several subdirectories with names containing eight random characters. The structure and contents of these directories, including the structure of the index.dat files within each of these directories, has been covered at great length via other resources, so we won't repeat that information here. For live systems, investigators can use the WebHistorian tool (version 1.3 is available from Mandiant.com at the time of this writing) to parse the Internet browser history. When examining an image, the investigator can use tools such as ProDiscover's Internet History Viewer to consolidate the browser history information into something easy to view and understand. The index.dat file from each subdirectory (either from a live system or when extracted from an image) can be viewed using tools such as Index Dat Spy[14.] and Index.dat Analyzer.[15.]

TIP

Often when you're conducting an investigation, there are places you can look for information about what you should expect to see. For example, if the auditing on a system is set to record successful logons and you can see from the Registry when various users last logged on, you should expect to see successful logon event records in the Security Event Log. With regard to Internet browsing history, IE has a setting for the number of days it will keep the history of visited URLs. That setting is found in the user's hive (NTUSER.DAT file, or HKEY_CUR-RENT_USER hive if they're logged on), in the \Software\ Microsoft\Windows\CurrentVersion\Internet Settings\URL History key. The value in question is *DaysToKeep*, and the default setting is 0x014, or 20 in decimal notation. If the data associated with the value is not the default setting, one can assume that the value has been changed, most likely by choosing **Tools** from the IE menu bar and selecting

Internet Options, then looking in the **History** section of the **General** tab. The *LastWrite* time for the Registry key will tell you when the value was changed.

Many investigators are familiar with using the Internet browsing history as a way of documenting a user's activities. For example, you could find references to sites from which malicious software tools may be downloaded, MySpace.com, or other sites that the user should not be browsing. As with most aspects of forensic artifacts on a system, what you look for as "evidence" really depends on the nature of your case. However, nothing should be overlooked; small bits of information can provide clues or context to your evidence or to the case as a whole.

Other Log Files

Windows systems maintain a number of other, less well-known log files, during both the initial installation of the operating system and day-to-day operations. Some of these log files are intended to record actions and errors that occur during the setup process. Other log files are generated or appended to only when certain events occur. These log files can be extremely valuable to an investigator who understands not only *that* they exist but also what activities cause their creation or expansion and how to parse and understand the information they contain. In this section, we're going to take a look at several of these log files.

Setuplog.txt

The setuplog.txt file, located in the Windows directory, is used to record information during the setup process, when Windows is installed. Perhaps the most important thing to an investigator about this file is that it maintains a timestamp on all the actions that are recorded, telling you the date and time that the system was installed. This information can help you establish a timeline of activity on the system.

An excerpt of a setuplog.txt file from a Windows XP SP2 system is shown here:

```
08/07/2006
16:14:22.921,d:\xpsprtm\base\ntsetup\syssetup\syssetup.c,6434,BEGIN_SECTION,
Installing Windows NT
08/07/2006
16:14:24.921,d:\xpsprtm\base\ntsetup\syssetup\wizard.c,1568,,SETUP:
Calculating registery size
08/07/2006
16:14:24.921,d:\xpsprtm\base\ntsetup\syssetup\wizard.c,1599,,SETUP:
Calculated time for Win9x migration = 120 seconds
```

```
08/07/2006
16:14:24.937,d:\xpsprtm\base\ntsetup\syssetup\syssetup.c,6465,BEGIN_SECTION,
Initialization
08/07/2006
16:14:24.984,d:\xpsprtm\base\ntsetup\syssetup\syssetup.c,6585,BEGIN_SECTION,
Common Initialiazation
08/07/2006
16:14:25.000,d:\xpsprtm\base\ntsetup\syssetup\syssetup.c,1674,BEGIN_SECTION,
Initializing action log
08/07/2006 16:14:25.046,d:\xpsprtm\base\ntsetup\syssetup\log.c,133,,GUI mode
Setup has started.
08/07/2006
16:14:25.078,d:\xpsprtm\base\ntsetup\syssetup\syssetup.c,1679,END_SECTION,In
itializing action log
08/07/2006
16:14:25.093,d:\xpsprtm\base\ntsetup\syssetup\syssetup.c,1764,BEGIN_SECTION,
Creating setup background window
```

WARNING

While writing this book, I made sure to take a look at the various versions of Windows in regard to the setuplog.txt file. On Windows 2000, the file had timestamps, but no dates were included. On Windows XP and 2003, the contents of the file were similar in that each entry had a timestamp with a date. I did not find a setuplog.txt file on Vista.

As you can see from the excerpt of the setuplog.txt file from an XP system, the date and timestamp are included with each entry. Even if the file's creation and last modification times are altered or the file is deleted, the contents of the file can provide valuable information for the investigator.

WARNING

If you're analyzing an image from a system and the timestamps that you see in the setuplog.txt file don't seem to make sense (for example, the timeline doesn't correspond to other information you've collected), the system might have been installed via a ghosted image or restored from backup. Keep in mind that the setuplog.txt file records activity during an installation, so the operating system must be installed on the system for the file to provide useful information.

Setupact.log

The setupact.log file, located in the Windows directory, maintains a list of actions that occurred during the graphical portion of the setup process. On Windows 2000, XP, and 2003, this file has no timestamps associated with the various actions that are recorded, but the dates that the file was created and last modified will provide the investigator with a clue as to when the operating system was installed. On Vista, this file contains entries that do include time and date stamps on many of the actions that are recorded.

SetupAPI.log

The setupapi.log file (maintained in the Windows directory) maintains a record of device, service pack, and hotfix installations on a Windows system. Logging on Windows XP and later versions of Windows is more extensive than on previous versions, and although Microsoft uses this file primarily for troubleshooting purposes, the information in this file can be extremely useful to an investigator.

Microsoft maintains a document called *Troubleshoooting Device Installation with the SetupAPI Log File* that provides a good deal of extremely useful information about the setupapi.log file. For example, the setupapi.log file contains a Windows installation header section that lists operating system version along with other information. If the setupapi.log file is deleted for any reason, the operating system creates a new file and inserts a new Windows installation header.

Device installations are also recorded in this file, along with timestamps that an investigator can use to track this sort of activity on the system. In Chapter 4 we saw that when a USB removable storage device (thumb drive, iPod, or the like) is attached to a Windows system, changes are recorded in the Registry. When the device is first attached to the system, a driver has to be located and loaded to support the device. Take a look at this excerpt from a setupapi.log file:

```
[2006/10/18 14:11:53 1040.8 Driver Install]
#-019 Searching for hardware ID(s):
usbstor\disksony____sony_dsc_____5.00,usbstor\disksony____sony_dsc_____
_,usbstor\disksony____,usbstor\sony____sony_dsc_____5,sony____sony_dsc___
_____5,usbstor\gendisk,gendisk
#-018 Searching for compatible ID(s): usbstor\disk,usbstor\raw
#-198 Command line processed: C:\WINDOWS\system32\services.exe
#I022 Found "GenDisk" in C:\WINDOWS\inf\disk.inf; Device: "Disk drive";
Driver: "Disk drive"; Provider: "Microsoft"; Mfg: "(Standard disk drives)";
Section name: "disk_install".
#I023 Actual install section: [disk_install.NT]. Rank: 0x00000006. Effective
driver date: 07/01/2001.
```

```
#-166 Device install function: DIF_SELECTBESTCOMPATDRV.
#I063 Selected driver installs from section [disk_install] in
"c:\windows\inf\disk.inf".
#I320 Class GUID of device remains: {4D36E967-E325-11CE-BFC1-08002BE10318}.
#I060 Set selected driver.
#I058 Selected best compatible driver.
#-166 Device install function: DIF_INSTALLDEVICEFILES.
#I124 Doing copy-only install of
"USBSTOR\DISK&VEN_SONY&PROD_SONY_DSC&REV_5.00\6&1655167&0".
```

From this log file excerpt, we can see that a USB removable storage device man-ufactured by Sony was first connected to the system on October 18, 2006. Based on what we covered in Chapter 4, we can see from the last log entry in our excerpt that the device had no serial number. However, the date and timestamp from the "Driver Install" section shows us the date that the device was first plugged into the system, which we can use along with the *LastWrite* time of the appropriate Registry key to determine a timeline of when the device was used on the system.

Netsetup.log

The netsetup.log file is created during system setup; on Windows XP it can be found in the Windows\Debug folder. The file records information about workgroup and domain membership for the system, maintaining timestamps on all the messages it records. The timestamps within the netsetup.log file occur within the same timeframe as those within the setuplog.txt file. Additional entries will be added to the file if the workgroup or domain of the system is changed. For example, I installed the Windows XP operating system for my personal laptop on August 7, 2006, as evidenced by the timestamps in the netsetup.log and setuplog.txt files. On November 19, 2006, I modi-fied the workgroup membership (moved from workgroup WorkGroup to workgroup Home) of the system by enabling file sharing. This information was recorded in the netsetup.log file, along with the appropriate timestamps. Log entries will also be added to the file if the system is added to or removed from a domain.

Task Scheduler Log

Not many folks are familiar with the Task Scheduler service on Windows systems, which can be accessed through at.exe or Scheduled Tasks Wizard in the Control Panel. This service allows a user with Administrator privileges to schedule a task to be run at some point in the future or to be run repeatedly at specific times each day, week, or month. This is a very beneficial for administering and managing a system or an entire network. Fortunately, in a file called SchedLgU.txt, this service keeps a log of the tasks that have been run. This log file is actually the default name associated with the *LogFile* value located in the following Registry key:

```
HKEY_LOCAL_MACHINE\SOFTWARE\Microsoft\SchedulingAgent
```

On Windows XP, the schedlgu.txt log is located in the Windows directory by default (C:\Windows), whereas on Vista, the schedlgu.txt file is located (by default) in the Tasks directory (C:\Windows\Tasks).

If the Task Scheduler isn't used by the administrator, the investigator should expect to see entries stating that the Task Scheduler service started and exited on specific dates and times. Since the Task Scheduler service is usually set to start up along with the system, this information can give the investigator a view of when the system was started and shut down.

If a task was scheduled and executed, you will see entries in the schedlgu.txt file that look like the following (excerpted from a Windows XP schedlgu.txt file):

```
"At1.job" (regedit.exe)
      Started 9/26/2006 4:35:00 PM
"At1.job" (regedit.exe)
      Finished 9/26/2006 4:35:04 PM
      Result: The task completed with an exit code of (0).
"Pinball.job" (PINBALL.EXE)
      Started 9/26/2006 4:36:00 PM
"Pinball.job" (PINBALL.EXE)
      Finished 9/26/2006 4:36:07 PM
      Result: The task completed with an exit code of (0).
```

The first job was set up via at.exe, and the second job (Pinball.job) was set up via the Scheduled Tasks Wizard. These .job files are kept in the Windows\Tasks directory.

Notes from the Underground…

Hiding Scheduled Tasks

There's an effective method for hiding Scheduled Tasks. Create a Scheduled Task via either at.exe or the Scheduled Tasks Wizard. Go to the Control Panel and open the **Scheduled Tasks** applet and see that the task you just created is listed. Now close the applet, open a command prompt, navigate to the

Continued

> **Windows\Tasks** directory, and use **attrib.exe** to set the hidden bit on the .job file. Once you've done this, go back to the **Scheduled Tasks** applet and you won't see the task listed any longer. Of course, the usual caveats apply to the command prompt (you must use the right switch with the *dir* command) and Windows Explorer (by default, it will not show files with the hidden attribute set). However, the task will run when you scheduled it to do so.
>
> I actually caught myself with this while writing my first book. I did some writing while on vacation and ran through the preceding procedure with the Solitaire card game. However, I never deleted the file, so when I got home I was working away one weekend and took a break. When I returned to my office, Solitaire was open on my desktop and at first I thought someone had been in my office! Then it struck me as to what happened, and I deleted the .job file.

Unfortunately, the full path to the executable run by the task is not recorded in the log file, but an indication of when a program was run via the Task Scheduler service is provided.

XP Firewall Logs

Most of us are familiar with the firewall components shipped with Windows XP, perhaps from the news media and issues that were addressed in the release of Windows XP Service Pack 2. Most users don't even see or interact with the XP firewall, and it is enabled by default. The firewall can be disabled,[16] and this may be part of a corporate configuration scheme to ease management of those systems. The firewall can also be manually configured[17] to allow specific applications to have network access.

The Windows XP firewall has a log file in which it records various activities that occur, but by default, no logging occurs. Figure 5.6 illustrates the default settings via the Log Settings dialog for the firewall.

As you can see, the logging options are pretty limited. Logging is not enabled by default, so you might not find the firewall log pfirewall.log on most systems. The lack of a log file does not mean that the firewall was not enabled. However, should you find a copy of the log file on the system, the firewall log format is straightforward and easy to understand. An excerpt from an example firewall log appears as follows:

Figure 5.6 Configure Windows XP Firewall Logging

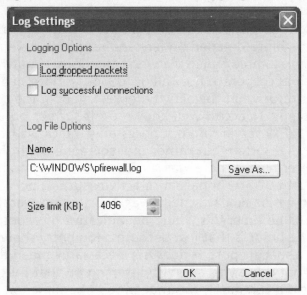

```
#Version: 1.0
#Software: Microsoft Internet Connection Firewall
#Time Format: Local
#Fields: date time action protocol src-ip dst-ip src-port dst-port size
tcpflags tcpsyn tcpack tcpwin icmptype icmpcode info

2003-10-10 10:21:11 DROP ICMP 131.107.0.2 131.107.0.1 - - 60 - - - - 8 0 -
2003-10-10 10:21:16 DROP ICMP 131.107.0.2 131.107.0.1 - - 60 - - - - 8 0 -
2003-10-10 10:21:21 DROP ICMP 131.107.0.2 131.107.0.1 - - 60 - - - - 8 0 -
2003-10-10 10:21:26 DROP ICMP 131.107.0.2 131.107.0.1 - - 60 - - - - 8 0 -
2003-10-10 10:21:34 DROP TCP 131.107.0.2 131.107.0.1 1045 21 48 S 1226886480
0 16384 - - -
2003-10-10 10:21:37 DROP TCP 131.107.0.2 131.107.0.1 1045 21 48 S 1226886480
0 16384 - - -
2003-10-10 10:21:43 DROP TCP 131.107.0.2 131.107.0.1 1045 21 48 S 1226886480
0 16384 - - -
```

The *Fields* tag in the firewall log header tells us what the various portions of the log entries refer to and how to interpret the information in the log file. We can see from the entries listed in the excerpt from pfirewall.log that several ICMP packets (perhaps from the ping.exe application) were dropped, as were several attempts to connect to the computer on port 21, which is the default port for FTP servers.

WARNING

Often it might be difficult to interpret the activity in a pfirewall.log file without a more detailed understanding of the system and its environment. For example, when viewing other logs of network-based activity, such as corporate firewall or IDS logs, I have been asked by the administrator what the activity represented. In the case of a single system, attempts to access well-known ports such as port 80 (Web server) or 21 (FTP server) are not necessarily indicative of something running on that system but rather that someone might have been trying to determine if there was something running on that port. This can be indicative of reconnaissance activity such as port scanning. If the logs show that similar activity was directed at several systems, all around the same time, this would be indicative of widespread port scanning. The point is that just because a log entry shows activity directed at a specific port, it does not necessarily mean that the port was open (that there was a service listening on that port) on the system. This is a commonly misunderstood phenomenon, particularly when it comes to widespread scanning activity directed toward ports used by Trojan backdoor applications.

For ease of viewing, a number of freely available utilities will parse this file and make it easier to interpret, even to the point of color coding certain entries. You can Google for various combinations of *XP* and *firewall* and *viewer* to locate one that will meet your needs.

TIP

The accompanying DVD includes a subdirectory within the Chapter 5 directory called *samples*. This subdirectory contains a file named nmap_scan_XP.txt, which contains the command line used to launch an nmap scan against a Windows XP SP2 system (with the firewall enabled),as well as the results of the scan that were sent to STDOUT. Another file named pfirewall_nmap_scan.txt contains a portion of the logged packets that were sent to the target system. For ease of viewing, the nmap scan was launched from 192.168.1.28, and the target system was 192.168.1.6.

Dr. Watson Logs

The Dr. Watson tool[18.] has shipped with versions of Windows for quite some time, but generally it doesn't come up in conversation these days. When a program error occurs on a system, the Dr. Watson tool collects information about the system and the program error in a text log file that can then be sent to support personnel for troubleshooting and program resolution. This information can also be useful when you're investigating an issue on a system.

The text log file produced by Dr. Watson is named drwtsn32.log and is maintained in the following directory:

```
C:\Documents and Settings\All Users\Application Data\Microsoft\Dr Watson
```

The configuration information for the Dr. Watson tool is maintained in the following Registry key:

```
HKEY_LOCAL_MACHINE\SOFTWARE\Microsoft\DrWatson
```

This Registry key contains a number of values that are visible in the Dr. Watson GUI, which is visible when you click on **Start | Run** and type **drwtsn32**. By default, the log file will maintain information from 10 program exceptions. These values will indicate to the investigator what she should expect to see if any exceptions have occurred on the system.

When an error occurs, the information saved by the Dr. Watson tool is appended to the drwtsn32.log file. Dr. Watson first writes as section that begins with *Application exception occurred:* to the file. This section contains information about the program that caused the error, along with the date and time that the error occurred:

```
App: C:\Perl\bin\perl.exe (pid=4040)
When: 8/21/2006 @ 10:17:35.859
```

Notice that the name of the program that caused the error can include the full path to the executable image along with a date/timestamp. As we've seen in previous chapters, this information can be useful to an investigator, particularly in instances in which the program in question is malware or something placed on the system as a result of an intrusion or misuse. Dr. Watson then writes some system information, a list of running processes, a list of modules (DLLs) loaded by the program, and stack dumps to the log file that can be used to troubleshoot the program exception. An investigator can use this information to demonstrate the user that was logged into the system on a certain date, what processes were running (which could show applications that were installed), and what DLLs were loaded by the program that caused the exception (which might show browser helper objects installed via Internet Explorer, any DLLs that were injected into a process to subvert that process, and so on).

NOTE

The Dr. Watson log can be extremely beneficial in demonstrating or corroborating a timeline of activity on a system. In one case, an individual who had accessed a system had uploaded tools to that system and, when attempting to run some of those tools, had generated application exceptions. We found logs of his access to the system, logs showing when he'd uploaded the tools (including the IP address from which his connection originated), Event Log entries showing the application exception popup message, and the Dr. Watson log that showed the application that had crashed. In addition to this information, we also had the user context for the application when it crashed as well as a list of other applications that were running at the time of the crash. All this information helped solidify our view of what applications were already in place prior to this person accessing the system, what application he had added to the system, and when he had used them.

Dr. Watson also produces a crash dump file (user.dmp) that is located in the same directory as the text-based log file. This dump file contains private pages used by the process at the time of the exception and does not contain code pages from executable files (EXE, DLL, or the like). The user.dmp file can be opened in the WinDbg tool, which is part of the Microsoft Debugging Tools. However, the user.dmp file is overwritten with each exception, so you will see only the user.dmp file from the last exception.

Crash Dump Files

Crash dump files were discussed in Chapter 3. I thought it would be a good idea to reference them in this chapter, too, for the sake of completeness.

In Chapter 3 we discussed ways to configure and generate crash dump files, but in most cases, I've found that the systems themselves haven't been modified at all. During some incidents or investigations, if you do find a crash dump file, it might be a good idea to take a look at it and see what it holds. You can use tools such as dumpchk.exe (for Windows 2000/2003[19.] and XP[20.]) to verify the dump file and ensure that it is valid. You can then load the file into a debugging tool (such as WinDbg) and use commands such as *!process 0 0* to view the list of running processes at the time of the crash or *lm kv* to view a list of loaded kernel mode drivers.

Further, you can use tools such as strings.exe, BinText.exe, and *grep* expressions to locate specific information.

Recycle Bin

Most forensics investigators are aware of the old adage that when a file is deleted, it isn't really gone. This is even more true with the advent of the Recycle Bin on the Windows desktop. The Recycle Bin exists as a metaphor for throwing files away, as though you're crumpling them up and tossing them into a wastebasket. The Recycle Bin also allows us to retrieve and restore files that we've "accidentally" thrown away. We can open the Recycle Bin, select files that we've previously thrown away, and restore them to their previous location.

So when something is deleted through the shell—that is, when a user selects a file on the desktop or through Windows Explorer and "deletes" it—it isn't really gone. The file is simply moved to the Recycle Bin, which appears by default in the file structure as the Recycler directory at the root of each drive. In many cases, this directory can provide a significant amount of information relevant to an investigation.

To better understand how information in this directory can be used as evidence, let's take a look at what happens when a user deletes a file through the shell. Once each user on a system begins to delete files through the shell (as opposed to using the *del* or *erase* commands at the command line), a subdirectory is created for that user within the Recycler directory; that subdirectory is named with the user's security identifier, or SID. For example, from the command prompt, the subdirectory will look something like this:

```
C:\RECYCLER\S-1-5-21-1454471165-630328440-725345543-1003>
```

When you open the Recycle Bin from the desktop, the user's subdirectory is automatically opened for his or her view. So if you were to sit down at a user's laptop with a user's account logged in and you opened the Recycle Bin to view the contents, you would see the files that the user had "deleted." If you were to switch accounts and repeat the process, you would automatically see the files deleted within the active user account.

When viewing the Recycler directory via an image, you should expect to see a subdirectory for each active user on the system that has deleted files via the shell, as illustrated in Figure 5.7.

Figure 5.7 Example of a Recycle Bin Viewed via ProDiscover

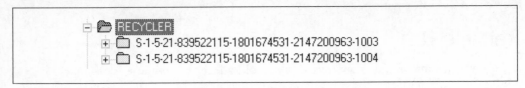

Within each subdirectory, you might see a number of files, depending on the user's activity and how often the user has emptied the Recycle Bin. Files sent to the Recycle Bin are maintained according to a specific naming convention,[21.] which, once you understand that convention, makes it relatively easy to identify certain types of files and which ones might be of interest. When the file is moved to the Recycle Bin, it is renamed using the following convention:

```
D<original drive letter of file><#>.<original extension>
```

The filename starts with the letter *D* and is followed by the letter of the original drive from which the file was deleted, then a zero-based index for the number of the file (in other words, the fifth file deleted will have the number 4). The file maintains the original extension. Further, a record is added to the INFO2 file within the directory, which is a log file of all files that are currently in the Recycle Bin. The index number of the deleted file serves as a reference to the original filename (and path) maintained in the INFO2 file.

Fortunately, Keith Jones (formerly of Foundstone, now with Mandiant) was able to document the format of the INFO2 file so that this information would be more useful to forensic analysts. The INFO2 file contains records that correspond to each deleted file in the Recycle Bin; each record contains the record number, the drive designator, the timestamp of when the file was moved to the Recycle Bin, the file size, and the file's original name and full path, in both ASCII and Unicode.

The INFO2 file begins with a 16-byte header, of which the final *DWORD* value is the size of each record. This value is 0x320 (little endian), which translates to 800 bytes. The first record begins immediately following the header and is a total of 800 bytes in length.

The first *DWORD* (4 bytes) of the record can be disregarded. The file's original full path and name, in ASCII format, is a null-terminated string beginning after the first *DWORD* and taking up the first 260 bytes of the record. Opening an INFO2 file, you'll see that most of the space consumed by the ASCII format of the filename is zeros. These zeros can be stripped out to retrieve only the filename. The rest of the items within the record appear as follows:

- The record number is the *DWORD* located at offset 264 within the record.

- The drive designator is the *DWORD* located at offset 268 within the record. The drive designator is used to determine which drive the file was deleted from; 2 = C:\, 3 = D:\, and so on.

- The timestamp for when the file was moved to the Recycle Bin is the 64-bit FILETIME object located at offset 272 within the record.

- The size of the deleted file (in increments of a cluster size) is the *DWORD* located at offset 280 within the record.

The original filename in Unicode format consumes the rest of the record, from offset 284 within the record to the end (516 bytes). Simply stripping out the null bytes will give you the path and name of the file in English ASCII format. (*Note:* The Unicode format is 2 bytes wide, and removing the null bytes from the second half of the Unicode format will leave you with just the ASCII format, in English.)

The recbin.pl Perl script located on the accompanying DVD will retrieve the various elements from each record, displaying the record number, the timestamp telling when the file was moved to the Recycle Bin (in UTC format; the time zone settings for the system are not taken into account), and the original name and path of the file. The script takes the path to an INFO2 file as its only argument, and the output can be easily manipulated to provide any structure and format that the investigator requires.

Keith Jones has also provided a tool called *rifiuti* (the name means *trash* in Italian) for parsing the contents of an INFO2 file. Rifiuit.exe is freely available from Foundstone.com and will parse the INFO2 file in a format that is easily opened for viewing in spreadsheet format.

Notes from the Underground...

Looking Closely in the Recycle Bin

Investigators should also be on the lookout for files that have been added to the Recycler directory but are not stored within one of the user SID subdirectories, as well as files that do not meet the naming convention for files moved to the Recycle Bin. This could indicate malicious activity by a user or by malware, intending to purposely hide a file. Investigators should also be aware that applications such as Norton AntiVirus might use the Recycle Bin; Norton's Recycle Bin Protector will place a file called nprotect.log in the directory. Datalifter, a company that produces forensic analysis tools, has an NProtect Viewer[22.] that will parse the contents of the nprotect.log file. The NProtect Viewer is part of the Datalifter .Net Bonus Tools pack.

One of the things I do when digging into an image is to check the last modification time on the INFO2 file. This will tell me when the last record was added to the INFO2 file, which approximates to the time that the file in question was moved to the Recycle Bin. If the user's subdirectory within the Recycler directory contains only the desktop.ini and INFO2 files and the INFO2 file is small, the last modification time refers to the time at which the user cleared the Recycle Bin (that is, right-clicked the **Recycle Bin** and choose **Empty Recycle Bin** from the context menu).

System Restore Points

The Registry files maintained in system restore points were discussed in Chapter 4. In this chapter we will address the log files maintained within restore points.

Rp.log Files

Rp.log is the restore point log file is located within the restore point (RPxx) directory. This restore point log contains a value indicating the type of the restore point, a descriptive name for the restore point creation event (i.e, application or device driver installation, application uninstall, or the like), and the 64-bit FILETIME object indicating when the restore point was created. The restore point type is a 4-byte (*DWORD*) value starting at the fourth byte of the file. The description of the restore point is a null-terminated Unicode string that starts at offset 16 (0x10) within the file, and the creation date/time is the 8-byte (*QWORD*) value located at offset 528 (0x210) within the file.

The Perl script sr.pl (located on the accompanying DVD; this is the same sr.pl Perl script that was discussed in Chapter 4) can be run on a live system to collect information about restore points. The script implements the SystemRestore WMI class to access the *RestorePointType*, *Description*, and *CreationTime* values for each restore point and display them to the user.

The SysRestore.pl Perl script (located on the accompanying DVD) is a ProScript that can be used with ProDiscover to retrieve information from the rp.log files located in the restore point directories of an image of a Windows XP system (that is open in ProDiscover). The script opens the rp.log file within each directory and retrieves the description of the restore point and the date that the restore point was created.

The description for the restore point can be useful to the investigator, particular if he's looking for information regarding the installation or removal of an application. System restore points will be created when applications and unsigned drivers are installed, when an autoupdate installation is performed, and when a restore operation is performed. Restore points can also be created manually. When a restore point is created, a description of the event that caused the restore point creation is written to the rp.log file. Many times, you'll see the description *System Checkpoint*, which is the restore point that is created by Windows XP every 24 hours (default setting). The description *Software Distribution Service* refers to Windows Updates being installed. I've also seen descriptions such as *Installed QuickTime, Removed ProDiscover 4.8a,* and *Installed Windows Media Player 11* on systems. The description might tell the investigator the date that a particular application was installed or removed.

The creation date of the restore point could also be useful to the investigator. Not only does it add information to the timeline of activity on the system, but the investigator can also use the creation date to determine whether changes were made to the system time. If successive restore points (successive based on the number of the restore point, such as RP80, RP81, RP82, and so on) have nonsequential creation dates, it could indicate that someone modified the system time.

Change.log.x Files

Once the restore point has been created, key system and application files continue to be monitored so that the system can be restored to a particular state. File changes are recorded, and if necessary, the entire file is preserved so that the system can be restored. These changes are recorded in the change.log files, which are located in the restore point directories. As changes to the monitored files are detected by the restore point file system driver, the original filename is entered into the change.log file along with a sequence number and other necessary information, such as the type of change that occurred (file deletion, change of file attributes, or change of content). If the monitored file needs to be preserved (as with a file deletion operation), the file is copied to the restore point directory and renamed to the format Axxxxxxx.*ext*, where *x* represents a sequence number and .*ext* is the file's original extension.

When the system is restarted, the first change.log file is appended with a sequence number (the name of the change.log file is changed to change.log.1) and a new change.log file is created. However, you won't find a file named change.log in the restore point directories; rather, you'll find several files named change.log.*x*, where *x* is the number of the change.log file.

Each change.log.*x* file consists of a number of change log records. I was able to locate a Web site[23] that contained detailed information regarding the binary format of these records (to include the 0xABCDEF12 "magic number" for identifying change log records in unallocated space). Using the information on this site, I was able to create a Perl script that parses and interprets the contents of the change.log.*x* files. The lscl.pl (for *LiSt Change Log*) Perl script is located on the accompanying DVD.

TIP

Fifo.log is another file maintained by (and located in the root of) the System Restore. As the System Restore reaches 90 percent of its capacity, it will delete restore points on a first-in, first-out (FIFO) basis, reducing the capacity to 75 percent of the maximum size (either the default or a user-defined value). The fifo.log file maintains a list of restore points that were "fifoed" or deleted from a monitored drive, as well as the date and time that they were deleted. Restore points will also be "fifoed" when they are 90 days old.[24]

Prefetch Files

Beginning with Windows XP, the Microsoft operating systems began using something called "prefetching" to improve performance of the systems. XP, Windows 2003, and Vista perform boot prefetching by default, and XP and Vista also perform application prefetching by default as well.

For boot prefetching, the Cache Manager monitors hard page faults (require that data be read from disk) and soft page faults (require that data in memory be added to a process's working set) during whichever occurs first—the first 2 minutes of the boot process, the first minute after all Windows services have started, or the first 30 seconds following the start of the user's shell. The fault data is processed along with references to files and directories that are accessed, which ultimately allows all this data to be accessed from a single file rather than requiring that data be retrieved from different files and directories scattered across the hard drive. This, in turn, decreases the amount of time required to boot the system.

During application prefetching, the Cache Manager monitors the first 10 seconds after a process is started. Once this data is processed, it is written to a .pf file in the Windows\Prefetch directory. This file's name is created using the application's name followed by a dash and then by a hexadecimal representation of the hash of the path to the application. For example, on a Windows XP system, two different .pf files will be created when Notepad is run from the C:\Windows directory and from the C:\Windows\system32 directory. (For some reason, Windows XP has a copy of Notepad in each directory.)

Prefetching is controlled by the following Registry key:

```
HKEY_LOCAL_MACHINE\SYSTEM\ControlSet00x\Control\Session Manager\Memory
Management\PrefetchParameters
```

Within this key is a value named *EnablePrefetcher*. The data associated with this value will tell you which form of prefetching the system uses:

- 0: Prefetching is disabled
- 1: Application prefetching is enabled
- 2: Boot prefetching is enabled
- 3: Both application and boot prefetching are enabled

On Windows XP and Vista, the default value for EnablePrefetcher is 3; it is 2 on Windows 2003. One of the interesting things about application prefetching is that Windows XP has a limit of 128 .pf files.

Some information in the .pf files in the Prefetch directory can be extremely useful to an investigator. At offset 144 within the file is a *DWORD* (4-byte) value that corresponds to the number of times the application has been launched. At offset 120 within the file is a 64-bit value that is a FILETIME object that corresponds to the last time that the application was run. This value is stored in UTC format, which is analogous to GMT time. The Prefetch.pl Perl script on the accompanying DVD is a ProScript that will parse the Prefetch directory for .pf files and then extract the run count and last run times from the .pf files. The pref.pl Perl script will run through the Prefetch directory on a live system and retrieve the MAC times (more on MAC times in the next section) and the last run time from .pf files, sending its output to the console in a comma-delimited format (suitable for opening in an Excel spreadsheet).

Although the contents of the .pf files won't tell you who launched the application, the filename will tell you which application was run (in the case of multiple copies of the same application in different directories, you'll have to do some testing to figure out which .pf file was generated for which application), how many times it was run, and the last time it was run.

The path to the application that was run is saved in a Unicode string within the .pf file (along with a range of other strings), as illustrated in Figure 5.8.

Figure 5.8 Example of a File Path in a .pf File

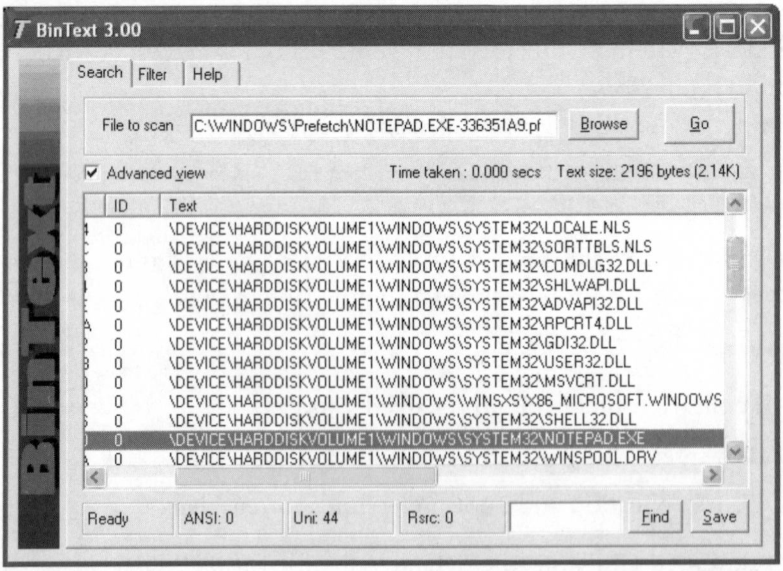

The various information from within a .pf file can be correlated with information from the Registry (refer back to Chapter 4) or the Event Log to determine who was logged on to the system, who was running which applications, and so on. One of the benefits of this correlation is that if the user installs an application and runs it, then deletes the application, traces of that application could be left in the Prefetch directory. When I've spoken to law enforcement officers about issues such as steganography applications used in online crime, they've all said that they don't usually look for steganography unless there's something to indicate that such an application was used. The existence of a .pf file with the name of a particular application can be that indication.

Shortcut Files

Shortcut files can prove useful during an investigation. Think of the way shortcuts (those files with .lnk extensions) are created and accessed in normal day-to-day use. A user accesses a document on her hard drive, a removable storage device, or a network share, and a shortcut is created on the system in the Recent folder (the Recent folder is a hidden folder within the user's profile directory). Shortcuts can provide information about files (or network shares) that the user has accessed as well as devices that the user might have had attached to her system at one point. Several commercial forensic analysis tools such as AccessData's Forensic Toolkit (FTK) and EnCase from Guidance Software provide the ability to parse the contents of the .lnk files to reveal information embedded within the file. Also, the Windows File Analyzer[25.] (WFA) from MiTeC is a freeware tool that will parse information from within a .lnk file. Not long ago, Jesse Hager published a white paper, *The Windows Shortcut File Format* (at the time of this writing, available from I2S-LaB[26.]), in which he documented the offsets and sizes of the various components of a shortcut file. Nathan Weilbacher[27.] wrote an article for the ForensicFocus.com site that referenced Jesse's paper and detailed the evidentiary value of Windows shortcut files.

The Perl script lslnk.pl (found on the accompanying DVD) implements much of Jesse's white paper and allows an investigator to view the internals of Windows shortcut files, displaying information such as the MAC times of the target file, various flag and attribute settings, and local volume information, an example of which is shown here:

```
Shortcut file is on a local volume.
Volume Name = C-DISK
Volume Type = Fixed
Volume SN   = 0x303d30de
```

If the target file is on a network share, lslnk.pl will extract the path to the share, as illustrated here:

```
File is on a network share.
Network Share name = \\192.168.1.22\c$ Z:
```

The lslnk.pl script opens the shortcut file in binary mode, parsing the contents without using the Windows API. The Perl script can be used on any system that supports Perl. Jake Cunningham has made a similar Perl script named lnk-parse.pl available on his JAFAT[28.] Web site.

File Metadata

The term *metadata* refers to *data about data.* The most commonly known metadata about files on Windows systems are the file MAC times; *MAC* stands for *modified, accessed, and created.* The MAC times are timestamps that refer to the time at which the file was last modified in some way (data was either added to the file or removed from it), last accessed (when the file was last opened), and when the file was originally created. How these times are managed by the operating system depends on the file system used. For example, on the FAT file system, times are stored based on the local time of the computer system, whereas the NTFS file system stores MAC times in Coordinated Universal Time (UTC) format, which is analogous to Greenwich Mean Time (GMT). When applications such as Windows Explorer display the MAC times, time zone and daylight savings settings need to be taken into account. Further, MAC time resolution for the FAT file system is 10 milliseconds for the creation time, 2 seconds for the modification time, and one day for the last access time (the date, really). For the NTFS file system, the last access time has a resolution of one hour.

WARNING

On Windows systems, the *NtfsDisableLastAccessUpdate* Registry value (located in the HKEY_LOCAL_MACHINE\System\CurrentControlSet\Control\FileSystem key) will allow you to disable (a *DWORD* value of 1 disables the functionality) the updating of last access times within the operating system. Although this is a recommended setting for high-volume file servers (to optimize performance and increase overall response time), it can make things difficult for a forensic analyst, particularly when determining file access times is an important part of the case. This value can be set via the *fsutil* command on Windows XP and 2003 and comes set (that is, updating of last access times is disabled) by default on Vista. This means that forensic analysts will need to develop additional analysis techniques and methodologies and rely on other sources of evidence.

Another aspect of file and directory MAC times that an investigator might be interested in is the way the timestamps are displayed,[29.] based on various move and copy actions. For the FAT16 file system:

- **Copy myfile.txt from C:\ to C:\subdir** Myfile.txt keeps the same modification date, but the creation date is updated to the current date and time.

- **Move myfile.txt from C:\ to C:\subdir** Myfile.txt keeps the same modification and creation dates.

- **Copy myfile.txt from a FAT16 partition to an NTFS partition** Myfile.txt keeps the same modification date, but the creation date is updated to the current date and time.

- **Move myfile.txt from a FAT16 partition to an NTFS partition** Myfile.txt keeps the same modification and creation dates.

For the NTFS file system:

- **Copy myfile.txt from C:\ to C:\subdir** Myfile.txt keeps the same modification date, but the creation date is updated to the current date and time.

- **Move myfile.txt from C:\ to C:\subdir** Myfile.txt keeps the same modification and creation dates.

In a nutshell, regardless of the file system in use, if the file is copied, the creation date for the file is updated to the current date and time; if the file is moved, the creation date stays the same. The modification date is updated when a change is made to the file.

Notes from the Underground...

Modifying MAC Times

As useful as file MAC times can be to an investigation, you need to keep in mind that there are people out there who might be actively attempting to hide data on a system by modifying the MAC times of the files. I have demonstrated the use of tools that allow the user to modify the MAC times on a file at conferences, using Perl scripts to access the necessary (and thoroughly documented) Windows APIs to first create a file, then change the creation date to six years in the future and make the modification date two years in the past. That sort of thing can throw off an investigation, and when you see something like that, how are you to trust *any* MAC times?

Continued

> But that's not all. The MetaSploit Project has an Anti-Forensics project[30.] that includes a tool called timestomp.exe that allows the user to modify not only the MAC times of a file but also the "entry modified" date/timestamp, which indicates when file attributes were modified.
>
> As a side note, the MetaSploit Anti-Forensics Project also contains a tool called slacker.exe that reportedly allows the user to hide data in the slack space of a file.

The rest of this section addresses metadata embedded in various file formats.

Word Documents

Metadata contained within Word documents has long been an issue. Word documents are compound documents, based on the Object Linking and Embedding (OLE) technology that defines a "file structure within a file." Besides formatting information, Word documents can contain quite a bit of additional information that is not visible to the user, depending on the user's view of the document. For example, Word documents can maintain not only past revisions but also a list of up to the last 10 authors to edit a file. This has posed an information disclosure risk to individuals and organizations. Perhaps one of the most visible was made public in mid-2003 by Richard M. Smith, in relation to a document released by British Prime Minister Tony Blair.[31.] The Blair government had released a dossier of Iraq's security and intelligence organizations as a Word document on the Web in February 2003. A lecturer in politics at Cambridge University recognized portions of the content of this document as having originally been written by a U.S. researcher in Iraq. This caused quite a number of people to look much more closely at the document. In his discussion of the information disclosure issue, the lecturer illustrated information he was able to extract from the Word document, which consists of a list of the last 10 authors to modify the document. This information proved quite embarrassing to Prime Minister Blair's staff.

On his Web site, the lecturer mentions a utility that he wrote to extract this information from Word documents, yet this utility is not provided for others to use. I wrote a Perl script called wmd.pl, included on the accompanying DVD, which parses through the binary header of the Word document to extract some information. The script uses Perl modules (the script does not use the MS Word API, so the Perl script can be run on any system that supports Perl and has the necessary modules, as listed in the *use* pragmas for the script, installed) to retrieve additional information. The output of the script run against the Blair document appears as follows:

```
C:\Perl>wmd.pl g:\book2\ch5\blair.doc
```

```
--------------------
Statistics
--------------------

File    = g:\book2\ch5\blair.doc
Size    = 65024 bytes
Magic   = 0xa5ec (Word 8.0)
Version = 193
LangID  = English (US)


Document was created on Windows.


Magic Created : MS Word 97
Magic Revised : MS Word 97


--------------------
Last Author(s) Info
--------------------

1 : cic22 : C:\DOCUME~1\phamill\LOCALS~1\Temp\AutoRecovery save of Iraq -
security.asd
2 : cic22 : C:\DOCUME~1\phamill\LOCALS~1\Temp\AutoRecovery save of Iraq -
security.asd
3 : cic22 : C:\DOCUME~1\phamill\LOCALS~1\Temp\AutoRecovery save of Iraq -
security.asd
4 : JPratt : C:\TEMP\Iraq - security.doc
5 : JPratt : A:\Iraq - security.doc
6 : ablackshaw : C:\ABlackshaw\Iraq - security.doc
7 : ablackshaw : C:\ABlackshaw\A;Iraq - security.doc
8 : ablackshaw : A:\Iraq - security.doc
9 : MKhan : C:\TEMP\Iraq - security.doc
10 : MKhan : C:\WINNT\Profiles\mkhan\Desktop\Iraq.doc


--------------------
Summary Information
--------------------

Title      : Iraq- ITS INFRASTRUCTURE OF CONCEALMENT, DECEPTION AND
INTIMIDATION
Subject    :
Authress   : default
LastAuth   : MKhan
RevNum     : 4
```

```
AppName      : Microsoft Word 8.0
Created      : 03.02.2003, 09:31:00
Last Saved   : 03.02.2003, 11:18:00
Last Printed : 30.01.2003, 21:33:00


-------------------
Document Summary Information
-------------------
Organization : default
```

As you can see, some of the information "hidden" in Word documents can be quite revealing and potentially quite embarrassing. In addition to the last 10 authors, the script will reveal the platform (Windows or Mac) that the document was created on as well as which version of Word was used to create and later revise the document. The script also extracts summary information from the document (discussed further in the "NTFS Alternate Data Streams" section of this chapter).

I have also included another small utility on the accompanying DVD called oledmp.pl. This utility uses the same Perl modules as wmd.pl but performs a slightly different function. Oledmp.pl will list the OLE streams and trash bins embedded in a Word document as well as the same summary information that wmd.pl extracts, as illustrated in the following sample output:

```
C:\Perl>oledmp.pl blair.doc¶
ListStreams¶
Stream ::@CompObj¶
Stream ::WordDocument¶
Stream ::♣DocumentSummaryInformation¶
Stream ::ObjectPool¶
Stream ::1Table¶
Stream ::♣SummaryInformation¶
¶
Trash Bin·······Size¶
BigBlocks·······0¶
SystemSpace·····940¶
SmallBlocks·····0¶
FileEndSpace····1450¶
¶
Summary Information¶
subject¶
lastauth········MKhan¶
```

```
lastprinted      30.01.2003, 21:33:00
appname          Microsoft Word 8.0
created          03.02.2003, 09:31:00
lastsaved        03.02.2003, 11:18:00
revnum           4
title            Iraq- ITS INFRASTRUCTURE OF CONCEALMENT, DECEPTION AND
INTIMIDATION
authress         default


1Table
1   cic22          C:\DOCUME~1\phamill\LOCALS~1\Temp\AutoRecovery save of
Iraq - security.asd
2   cic22          C:\DOCUME~1\phamill\LOCALS~1\Temp\AutoRecovery save of
Iraq - security.asd
3   cic22          C:\DOCUME~1\phamill\LOCALS~1\Temp\AutoRecovery save of
Iraq - security.asd
4   JPratt         C:\TEMP\Iraq - security.doc
5   JPratt         A:\Iraq - security.doc
6   ablackshaw     C:\ABlackshaw\Iraq - security.doc
7   ablackshaw     C:\ABlackshaw\A;Iraq - security.doc
8   ablackshaw     A:\Iraq - security.doc
9   MKhan          C:\TEMP\Iraq - security.doc
10  MKhan          C:\WINNT\Profiles\mkhan\Desktop\Iraq.doc
```

The *ListStreams* information displays the names of the various OLE streams that make up the Word document. Microsoft refers to OLE as "a file system within a file," and these stream names refer to the "files" in the document.

WARNING

Sometimes it can pretty shocking how much information is revealed in Word document metadata. Try a little experiment: Look around a file server at work (with permission, of course) and find some Word documents, such as something that might have been sent to clients, and see what the hidden metadata says about the documents. I tried something similar, only I used Google instead of a corporate file server. Due to the number of responses I received, I restricted my searches to .mil and .gov domains, but I still found more documents than I really knew what to do with.

Interestingly enough, as I was writing my first book, one of the technical reviewers did not want me to know his name and specifically

requested that the publisher not share any of the reviewer's information with me. Taking things a step further, this reviewer would complete the review forms in Word documents but save the content as a
straight ASCII text document, removing all metadata. I guess he *really*
didn't want me to know who he was!

Not only can this metadata pose an information disclosure risk to an individual
or organization, but it can also be useful to an investigator who is looking for specific information regarding documents. This can be particularly important during e-
discovery cases, particularly if searches for keywords or phrases are confined to the
visible text of the documents.

For the sake of completeness on this topic, I need to add a couple of things
before moving on to the next topic. First, Microsoft provides information to users
regarding metadata in Word documents and ways to minimize the available metadata. Second, Word documents are not the only Office files that have an issue with
metadata. To both of these items, Microsoft provides the following KnowledgeBase
articles:

- 223790: WD97: *How to Minimize Metadata in Microsoft Word Documents*

- 223396: OFF: *How to Minimize Metadata in Microsoft Office Documents*

- 223789: XL: *How to Minimize Metadata in Microsoft Excel Workbooks*

- 223793: PPT97: *How to Minimize Metadata in Microsoft PowerPoint Presentations*

- 290945: *How to Minimize Metadata in Word 2002*

- 825576: *How to Minimize Metadata in Word 2003*

In addition to these KnowledgeBase articles, Microsoft also provides the
Remove Hidden Data tool[32.] as a plugin to Office 2003 and XP. Authors can use this
tool to remove a great deal of metadata from documents. This is an excellent tool to
ensure that the amount of available metadata is minimized, even if your authoring
process includes saving the file in a different format, such as PDF.

Notes from the Underground...

The MergeStreams Utility

A utility called MergeStreams,[33.] available from NTKernel.com, implements an interesting aspect of Office OLE documents. In a nutshell, it allows you to "merge" an Excel spreadsheet into a Word document. The utility has a simple GUI that allows you select a Word document and an Excel spreadsheet and merge the two together. Say you have one of each document in a directory. If you run the utility and merge the two documents, you will be left with a Word document that is larger than the original Word document as well as being larger than the original Excel spreadsheet. However, if you were to delete the Excel spreadsheet, change the file extension of the Word document to .xls, and then double-click the file, you would see the Excel spreadsheet opened on the desktop, with no evidence of the original Word document or its contents. Changing the file extension back to .doc allows you to open the Word document with no apparent evidence of the Excel spreadsheet.

When presenting on this subject at conferences, I generally include a demonstration of the tool. Most often I demonstrate it from the aspect of a corporate user trying to smuggle a spreadsheet of financial forecasts or contract information pertinent to an important bid out of an organization. All the "user" has to do is merge the Excel spreadsheet into the Word document (something harmless, such as a letter) and then copy the Word document to a thumb drive. If anyone stops the user on the way out the front door and inspects the contents of the thumb drive, all they will see is the Word document.

When talking to law enforcement officers, however, I take a slightly different approach. Suppose a corporate employee has some illicit images that he'd like to share with his buddies. He copies the images into a Word document, then locates an Excel spreadsheet on the file server that all of them have access to (as well as a legitimate need to access) and merges them. He then renames the Word document to the original name and extension of the spreadsheet and lets his buddies know what he's done. This way, he can distribute the images without leaving any traces.

Detecting the use of a utility like MergeStreams isn't necessarily an overly difficult task. Using scripts that include functionality similar to oledmp.pl, as mentioned previously in this chapter, you can list the OLE streams that make up the Word document. If you see any stream names (Workbook, Worksheet, or the like) that would indicate the presence of an Excel spreadsheet, the Word document is definitely worth examining.

PDF Documents

Portable document format (PDF) files can also contain metadata such as the name of the author, the date that the file was created, and the application used to create the PDF file. Often the metadata can show that the PDF file was created on a Mac or that the PDF file was created by converting a Word document to PDF format. As with Word documents, this metadata can pose a risk of information disclosure. However, depending on the situation, this information can also be useful to an investigator, either to assist in e-discovery or to show that a particular application had been installed on the user's system.

On the accompanying DVD I've included two Perl scripts (pdfmeta.pl and pdfdmp.pl) that I have used to extract metadata from PDF files. The only difference between the two scripts is that they use different Perl modules to interact with PDF files. To be honest, I've had varying amounts of success with the scripts; in some instances, both scripts will successfully retrieve metadata from a PDF file, whereas in other cases, one or the other will fail for some reason. As a test, I used Google to search for some sample PDF files and found two, one at from the Federal Trade Commission and another from the IRS. The PDF file from the FTC was called idtheft.pdf, and pdfmeta.pl returned the following information:

```
C:\Perl>pdfmeta.pl d:\pdf\idtheft.pdf
Author          FTC
CreationDate    D:20050513135557Z
Creator         Adobe InDesign CS (3.0)
Keywords        identity theft, id theft, idtheft, credit
ModDate         D:20050513151619-04'00'
Producer        Adobe PDF Library 6.0
Subject         Identity Theft
Title           Take Charge: Fighting Back Against Identity Theft
```

The PDF file downloaded from the IRS site was a copy of the 2006 Form W-4, called fw4.pdf. Pdfmeta.pl returned the following information:

```
C:\Perl>pdfmeta.pl d:\pdf\fw4.pdf
Author          SE:W:CAR:MP
CreationDate    D:20051208083254-05'00'
Creator         OneForm Designer Plus
Keywords        Fillable
ModDate         D:20060721144654-04'00'
Producer        APJavaScript 2.2.1 Windows SPDF_1112 Oct  3 2005
```

Subject	Employee's Withholding Allowance Certificate
Title	2006 Form W-4

Both of these examples are fairly innocuous, but it should be easy to see how the metadata in PDF files can be used in e-discovery or should at least be considered in keyword searches. If you have trouble retrieving metadata with either of the two Perl scripts provided with this book, the old standby is to open the file in Adobe Reader (freely available from Adobe.com) and click **File | Document Properties**. The **Description** tab of the Document Properties dialog box contains all the available metadata. Figure 5.9 illustrates the document properties for idtheft.pdf.

Figure 5.9 Idtheft.pdf Document Properties

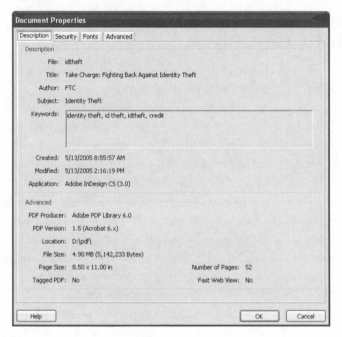

Image Files

Word processing files aren't the only ones that maintain internal metadata. In February 2006, an article about a bot-herder (someone who infects systems with bots and then manages and even rents those networks) in the *Washington Post Magazine* included a JPEG image in the online version of the story. Though the author of the story took pains to keep the bot-herder's identity a secret, the JPEG image included notes from the photographer that stated the location (city and state) where the photo was taken.

The metadata available in a JPEG image depends largely on the application that created or modified it. For example, digital cameras embed Exchangeable Image File Format (EXIF) information in images, which can include the model and manufacturer of the camera (unfortunately, no serial number seems to be either used or stored), and can even store a thumbnail or audio information (EXIF uses the TIFF image file directory format). Applications such as Adobe's Photoshop have their own set of metadata that they add to JPEG files.

Tools such as Exifer,[34] IrfanView,[35] and the Image::MetaData::JPEG[36] Perl module allow you to view, retrieve, and in some cases modify the metadata embedded in JPEG image files. ProDiscover can also display EXIF data found in a JPEG image. Chris Brown (of Technology Pathways) provides a white paper[37] that describes the EXIF data and, to a small degree, the format of a JPEG file.

File Signature Analysis

During an investigation, you might come across files with unusual extensions or files with familiar extensions that are in unusual locations. In such cases, we can use *file signature analysis* to determine the nature of these files as well as gain some insight into an attacker's technical abilities. One way to determine the true nature of files, regardless of their extension, is through file signature analysis.

File signature analysis pertains to collecting information from the first 20 bytes of a file and looking for a specific signature or "magic number" that will tell you the type and function of the file. Different file types have different signatures, and these signatures are independent of the file extension. In fact, often the bad guy will change the extension of a file so that when it's viewed in Windows Explorer, the file will appear with an icon that effectively masks the contents and intent of the file. Once, long ago, on a system far, far away, I was analyzing an IRCbot that I dubbed the russiantopz[38] bot. This IRCbot deposited a number of files on the infected system and gave those files .drv and .dll extensions, so when an administrator viewed those files, they would appear to be ominous files that most administrators simply do not open. After all, in most cases when an administrator opens a file with one of those extensions in a hex editor, all they see is a bunch of binary "stuff." During my analysis, I actually opened those files and was able to see that they contained text information, specifically configuration information and actions that the bot would perform when sent a command.

Forensic analysis tools such as ProDiscover allow the investigator to readily perform file signature analysis and easily view the results. When such tools perform the analysis, they get the file's extension and compare the signature associated with that extension to the information contained in the first 20 bytes of the file. For example,

Windows Portable Executable (PE) files will begin with the letters *MZ* (a reference to Mark Zbikowski,[39.] a Microsoft architect), which are located at the first two bytes of the PE file. Executable files can have .exe, .dll, .sys, .ocx, or .drv (to name a few) file extensions, as seen in the headersig.txt[40.] file used by ProDiscover as its "database" of file extensions and signatures. In short, if a file has an executable extension, we should expect to see a valid executable signature. Files that do not have valid signatures that match their extensions are flagged for further investigation.

Image files such as JPEG and GIF files also have their own signatures. The signature for a JPEG file is JFIF, and the signature for a GIF file is GIF87a or GIF89a. Figure 5.10 illustrates the signature for a PDF document, or %PDF-, followed by the version of the Portable Document Format for the file.

Figure 5.10 PDF File Signature

```
00000000h: 25 50 44 46 2D 31 2E 35 0D 25 E2 E3 CF D3 0D 0A ; %PDF-1.5.%âãÏÓ..
```

The sigs.pl Perl script located on the accompanying DVD will allow you to perform file signature analysis on live systems. The script will examine a file, a directory of files or all the files in a directory structure to determine whether the file signatures match the file extensions. The script uses that headersig.txt file from Technology Pathways as its default "database" of file signatures; however, other listings of the same format can be used. As the script parses through the files, it will determine whether the file signature matches the extension, but it will also alert the investigator if the file extension is not found in its "database." If this is the case, the script will provide the extension and the signature so that the investigator can update her database, if she deems it necessary to do so. By default, the script sends its output to the console in comma-separated value (.csv) format so that it can be redirected to a file and opened in Excel for easy analysis.

NTFS Alternate Data Streams

An NTFS alternate data stream (ADS) is a feature of the NTFS file system that is neither well known nor understood among members of the system administration community. After all, why would it be? On the surface, ADSes are used "behind the scenes" by several Microsoft applications, so they can't be bad. Right?

Let me put it another way. What if I were to tell you that there is a way to create legitimate files on a Windows system, files that can contain data as well as scripts or executable code, and that these files can be created or launched but that there are no native tools within the operating system distribution that will allow you to detect the presence of arbitrary files? That's right. The Windows operating system has all the native tools to create, modify, and manipulate ADSes, but there are no native tools available to view the existence of arbitrary ADSes. Well, that's not completely true, since beginning with Vista, the *dir* command now has a switch to let you see ADSes. We'll address this in a moment.

So, what are alternate data streams, where do they come from, and how are they used? ADSes are a feature of the NTFS file system that were introduced beginning with Windows NT 3.1. ADSes were added to the file system to support the Hierarchal File System (HFS) used by the Macintosh. HFS employs resource forks so that the file system can maintain metadata about the file, such as icons, menus, or dialog boxes. This functionality was incorporated into the NTFS file system but was never something that was widely discussed. In fact, for the longest time, there was very little discussion of ADSes and very little information available on the topic, even from Microsoft. Although there are Microsoft applications and functionality in the shell that allow for the creation of specific ADSes, the fact remains that there is very little operational, day-to-day use for ADSes. Bad guys have picked up on this and have used ADSes to hide tools, even as part of rootkits. This is an effective approach because some antivirus utilities either do not scan ADSes or do not do so by default. Therefore, malware that is dropped onto a system in an ADS might not be detected or removed/quarantined by the antivirus application.

Notes from the Underground...

Using ADSes

In the late 1990s, as a consultant, I was involved in a number of penetration tests and vulnerability assessments. During a penetration test, if we gained access to a Windows system and had authorization to do so, we'd leave an ADS on the system. This had no effect other than to consume a few bytes, since we only left a text message. However, this was our way of telling the system administrator, "Tag, you're it!" and to provide proof that we'd gotten as far as we said we had. I have spoken to other pen testers who will copy all their tools over to a compromised system into ADSes.

Creating ADSes

Creating an ADS is relatively simple; heck, there are even some Microsoft applications that do it automatically. Any user can do it, as long as the user has the ability to create a file. For example, the simplest way to create an ADS is to type the following command:

```
D:\ads>notepad myfile.txt:ads.txt
```

You'll initially see a dialog box that will ask you if you want to create a new file. Click **Yes**, add some text to the window, save the file, and then close the Notepad window. At this point, if you type **dir**, you'll see that the file myfile.txt is zero bytes in size, although you just typed a bunch of text into Notepad.

Another way to create an ADS is to use the *echo* command:

```
D:\ads>echo "This is another ADS test file" > myfile.txt:ads2.txt
```

Okay, so we've created two ADSes, and whether you type **dir** or view the contents of the directory in Windows Explorer, you'll see a single file in the directory, and that file will be zero bytes in size.

Yet another way to create an ADS is to use the *type* command to copy another file into an ADS:

```
D:\ads>type c:\windows\system32\sol.exe > myfile.txt:ads3.exe
```

So now what we've done is copied the contents of the file called sol.exe (which is the Solitaire card game on Windows 2000, XP, and 2003) into an ADS. These same commands can be run on Vista to create ADSes, although for some applications (such as the Solitaire game) the paths to the executable files might be different.

ADSes can be added to directory listings as well, using the following syntax:

```
D:\ads>echo "This is an ADS attached to a directory" > :ads.txt
```

Notice that no specific filename was provided. This causes the ADS to be attached to the directory listing; in this case, D:\ads.

ADSes will also be created in other ways, often without you ever being aware of it. When you right-click a file and choose **Properties**, one of the tabs you see is called Summary (interestingly enough, this tab doesn't seem to be available on Vista). You can enter just about anything in the various text fields, and when you save the information by clicking **OK**, the information is saved in an ADS (unless you're working with an Office document, in which case the information you entered saved within the structured storage or OLE document itself).

Further, as of Windows XP SP2, Internet Explorer and Outlook will add an ADS to files downloaded from the Internet or retrieved as file attachments from an e-mail. When you download a file through IE, the file will be written to whichever location you choose and to an ADS named Zone.Identifier. The ADS is added to the file so that when the user attempts to execute or open the file, he is presented with a warning dialog box that notifies him that the file might not be safe to open.

Enumerating ADSes

Now that we've created several ADSes, how do we go about detecting them? As I mentioned before, there are no tools native to Windows systems that allow you to enumerate arbitrary ADSes. You can't see them through Windows Explorer, and the *dir* command is equally useless. Well, that last statement isn't exactly true; Vista has a switch that allows you to enumerate ADSes with *dir* using the */r* switch, as illustrated in Figure 5.11.

Figure 5.11 An Example of Enumerating ADSes on Vista

```
C:\ads>dir /r
 Volume in drive C has no label.
 Volume Serial Number is 98A5-80D5

 Directory of C:\ads

11/20/2006  07:17 PM    <DIR>          .
11/20/2006  07:17 PM    <DIR>          ..
11/20/2006  07:33 PM                 0 myfile.txt
                                    23 myfile.txt:ads.txt:$DATA
                                    34 myfile.txt:ads2.txt:$DATA
                               982,528 myfile.txt:ads3.exe:$DATA
                1 File(s)              0 bytes
                2 Dir(s)  14,823,571,456 bytes free
```

Figure 5.11 shows the results of running the *dir /r* command on Vista after creating several ADSes in a similar manner as we did in the "Creating ADSes" section (in that section, we created ADSes on XP).

With the other Windows operating systems (2000, XP, and 2003), you need to get outside help to enumerate ADSes. My personal favorite is lads.exe,[41] from Frank Heyne. Lads.exe is a CLI tool that you can run against any directory.

```
D:\tools>lads d:\ads


LADS - Freeware version 4.00
```

```
(C) Copyright 1998-2004 Frank Heyne Software (http://www.heysoft.de)
This program lists files with alternate data streams (ADS)
Use LADS on your own risk!

Scanning directory d:\ads\

      size   ADS in file
----------   --------------------------------
         0   d:\ads\myfile.txt:ads.txt
        34   d:\ads\myfile.txt:ads2.txt
   1032192   d:\ads\myfile.txt:ads3.exe


   1032226 bytes in 3 ADS listed
```

Lads.exe is just one of the available tools that allow you to enumerate ADSes on Windows. There are others that are also CLI tools, there are GUI tools, and there are even some that install as shell plugins so that you can enumerate ADSes via the Windows Explorer UI.

ADSes added to a file by adding summary information to the file (mentioned in the previous section) appear somewhat differently than the ADSes we've already added. For example, if we add summary information to myfile.txt and then run lads.exe again, we see:

```
······size··ADS·in·file¶
----------··-------------------------------¶
········120··d:\ads\myfile.txt:♣DocumentSummaryInformation¶
········232··d:\ads\myfile.txt:♣SummaryInformation¶
··········0··d:\ads\myfile.txt:ads.txt¶
·········34··d:\ads\myfile.txt:ads2.txt¶
···1032192··d:\ads\myfile.txt:ads3.exe¶
··········0··d:\ads\myfile.txt:{4c8cc155-6c1e-11d1-8e41-00c04fb9386d}¶
```

From the output of lads.exe, we can see that there have been three additional ADSes added to myfile.txt: one that appears as a GUID (and is 0 bytes in size) and two others that start with the club symbol. These last two are where the information entered into the Properties | Summary tab is saved.

There may be times when you see an ADS named AFP_AfpInfo or AFP_Resource. If you see an ADS named in such a manner, check to see if the File Services for Macintosh service is installed and enabled on the system. If so, it might be the case that the unnamed stream was copied from a Macintosh system via the

AppleTalk protocol. When this occurs, the data fork for the file is saved to a file-name, such as myfile.txt. The resource fork is then saved to myfile.txt:AFP_Resource, and the finder or attribute information is saved to myfile.txt:AFP_AfpInfo.

As previously mentioned, other tools exist for enumerating ADSes. Streams.exe (available from SysInternals.com), lns.exe (from Arne Vidstrom, at NTSecurity.nu), and sfind.exe (part of the Forensic Toolkit available from Foundstone.com) are CLI tools similar to lads.exe. ADSDetector is a shell (i.e., Windows Explorer) plugin from CodeProject.com that allows for "visual real-time viewing of a nonencrypted file's alternative data streams." Finally, CrucialADS (from CrucialSecurity.com) and ADSSpy (from SpyWareInfo.com) are GUI-based tools for enumerating ADSes. ADSSpy, illustrated in Figure 5.12, also allows the user to delete selected ADSes.

Figure 5.12 ADSSpy GUI

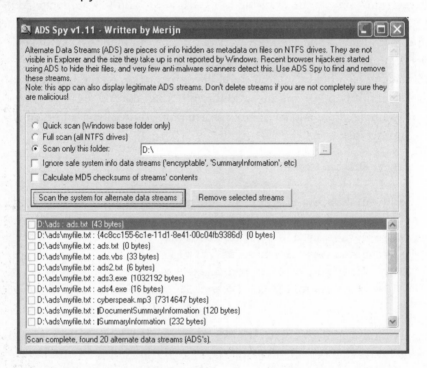

Once you've located an ADS, you can view the contents of the file by opening it in Notepad or by using the *cat* utility, part of the UnxUtils package on SourceForge.net. You can use *cat* to view the contents of an ADS at the console (i.e., *STDOUT*) or by redirecting the output of the command to a separate file.

WARNING

!

In 2000, Benny and Ratter, then of the virus-writing group known as 29A (the hexadecimal representation for 666), released a virus named W2K.Stream that used ADSes. The virus would infect a file, replace it, and then copy the original file into an ADS. For example, if the virus infected Notepad.exe, it would replace the executable file and copy the original Notepad into Notepad.exe:STR. This only worked on NTFS-formatted systems. If the file system was formatted FAT, there was no ADS and all you were left with was the infected file.

In June 2006, the F-Secure antivirus company blog contained an entry that described the Mailbot.AZ (a.k.a. Rustock.A) kernel-mode rootkit driver (more about rootkits in Chapter 7, "Rootkits and Rootkit Detection") that makes detection especially difficult by hiding itself in an ADS. Further, the ADS reportedly cannot be enumerated by tools that detect ADSes, since it is hidden by the rootkit. Very tricky!

Using ADSes

So, you're probably wondering, what can ADSes be used for besides hiding data? As it turns out, it can be used for a number of things. For example, you can put an executable file into an ADS and run it from there. Use the *type* command, just as we did before, to place an executable in an ADS, like so:

```
D:\ads>type c:\windows\system32\sol.exe > myfile.txt:ads4.exe
```

In this case, we've placed the Solitaire game in an ADS. This is a good example to use because when run, it results in a nice GUI that lets us see that things are working properly. To execute the program, type the following command:

```
D:\ads>start .\myfile.txt:ads4.exe
```

As you can see, we're presented with the Solitaire GUI. And this isn't restricted to executables, because scripts (Windows Scripting Host, Perl, etc.) can be hidden in ADSes and launched just as easily. The Windows Scripting Host tools (cscript.exe, wscript.exe) will run scripts hidden in ADSes with no trouble, as will Perl; even the IIS Web server will serve up HTML and script files hidden in ADSes (which is a great way to grade "capture the flag" events).

Attempting to execute an ADS on Vista returns a different result, as illustrated in Figure 5.13.

Figure 5.13 Dialog Box Returned When You Attempt to Execute an ADS on Vista

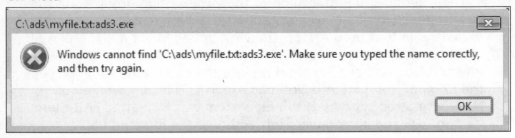

Attempts to launch the ADS (myfile.txt:ads3.exe contains the Vista version of Solitaire) were all met with the same result, including variations of the *start* command as well as using Start | Run. However, launching WSH scripts from within an ADS worked without any issues on Vista.

Another interesting use for ADSes is in hiding media. Movies and podcasts can be hidden in ADSes, and then the Windows Media Player can be launched from the command line to open the media:

```
wmplayer d:\ads\myfile.txt:cyberspeak.mp3
```

I listed to an edition of the CyberSpeak podcast this way. Interestingly enough, although the podcast was launched from the command line, the filename appeared in the following Registry key:

```
HKEY_CURRENT_USER\Software\Microsoft\MediaPlayer\Player\RecentFileList
```

The entry was listed in the data associated with the *File0* value, indicating that whenever a new file is added to this list, the filename is added to the top of the list and the older filenames are pushed down the list; the smaller the file number, the more recent the file. As we learned in Chapter 4, getting the *LastWriteTime* from the Registry key will tell us when that file was accessed via the Windows Media Player.

WARNING

When looking at a sample case in ProDiscover, I noticed that there were several ADSes in the Recycle Bin. ProDiscover displays ADSes with a red-colored font so they stand out and are obvious. I had deleted some files I'd been working with, one of which I downloaded from the Internet. I noticed that the ZoneIdentifier ADS was visible for the file (I had downloaded the file via IE) but that the record count for the total number of files via the INFO2 file did not reflect the existence of the ADS.

Removing ADSes

Now that we've seen how ADSes can be created and used, what can we do about removing them? There are several ways to go about this, and the way you choose to use simply depends on your needs and preferences.

One way to remove an ADS is to simply delete the file to which the ADS is attached. However, the obvious result is that if the original file was important to you (document, spreadsheet, image file), you lose that data.

To save your original data, you might want to use the *type* command to copy the contents of the original unnamed stream (in our example, myfile.txt) to another file-name and then delete the original file. Another option is to copy the file to a non-NTFS media. Remember, ADSes are an NTFS feature, so copying the file to a floppy disk (remember those?), thumb drive, or another partition formatted in FAT, FAT32, or some other file system (FTP file to a Linux system formatted ext2 and then back again) will effectively remove the ADS.

But what if the ADS you've detected is attached to a directory listing, such as C:\ or C:\windows\systm32? You can't just delete the directory, and copying it to and from another file system is going to be a bit cumbersome. So what do you do? Using the *echo* command, you can reduce the ADS to a harmless text file, regardless of its contents. From our previous example of copying the Solitaire game into an ADS, we can run lads.exe and get information about that ADS:

```
56832  d:\ads\myfile.txt:ads4.exe
```

Okay, so we have an ADS that is 56,832 bytes in size, and we already know that this is an executable file. So, type in the following command:

```
D:\ads>echo "deleted ADS" > myfile.txt:ads4.exe
```

Rerunning lads.exe, we see that the file size has changed:

```
16  d:\ads\myfile.txt:ads4.exe
```

So, we've effectively "taken care of" the ADS; although we didn't delete it, we rendered it harmless. You can even write a message to the ADS stating the nature of the ADS you'd located, your name, and when you deleted it.

Finally, another option is to use the ADSSpy GUI application mentioned previously.

ADS Summary

At this point, we've covered a lot of information about ADSes, discussing how they are created and how they can be used and removed. This information is important to keep in mind when you're performing either incident response or computer forensics activities. ADSes are unusual enough that commercial forensic analysis tools such as ProDiscover display ADSes in red. However, not all ADSes are malicious in nature; we have seen how some applications use ADSes simply as part of how they operate.

One thing investigators should keep in mind is to view the contents of an ADS. Just because an ADS is named using one of the naming schemes employed by known, legitimate applications doesn't mean that what's in the ADS isn't malicious. That is to say, do not simply write off the ADS as benign because it's named AFP_AfpInfo. Bad guys love to hide malware in plain sight by naming it something an administrator or forensic analyst will most likely overlook.

Alternative Methods of Analysis

There might be times when you're conducting a post-mortem computer forensic analysis (say, after you've acquired an image) that you might need to perform analysis that is simply more cumbersome when you're working with an image. For example, you might decide that you want to scan the system for malware, such as Trojans, backdoors, or spyware. When you're working with an image of the system, you've got what amounts to a single file (or, as is often the case, multiple files that add up to the size of the original hard drive), and you need a way to scan the files within the image. So, rather than pulling all the files out of the image, there are some tools that you can use to convert the image into a format suitable for scanning.

One such tool is available via ProDiscover. Beginning with version 4.85 of ProDiscover, the tool has the ability to either convert an image from the native ProDiscover format or the *dd* format to an ISO format. ProDiscover also has the ability to create files needed to boot the image in VMware. These new options are illustrated in Figure 5.14.

Figure 5.14 ProDiscover Menu Showing New Tools

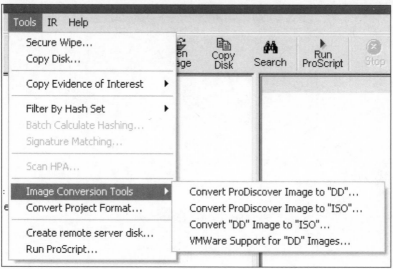

As you can see in Figure 5.14, you can use ProDiscover to convert from the native ProDiscover .eve file format to *dd* format or from either a ProDiscover or *dd* image to an ISO 9660 Joliet specifications image. You can also use ProDiscover to create the necessary files required to boot the image in VMware, which is similar to what the VMware P2V (which stands for "physical to virtual") Assistant tool allows you to do. Using tools like this, you can boot the system to perform additional analysis, such as antivirus and antispyware scanning, or to simply see what the system "looked like" when it was running. Sometimes this can be very useful when you're investigating a case, because it is so difficult to determine the nature of a running system (given the interactions between various configuration settings, installed software, and so on) during a post-mortem analysis.

A technical Webinar available at the Technology Pathways Resource Center[42.] Web site walks you through the details of how to use the ProDiscover tools to ultimately boot an image in VMware. The Webinar requires the appropriate client software from WebEx.com.

Another tool that is free and extremely easy to use to boot an acquired image in VMware is LiveView,[43.] which is available from CERT. LiveView uses an easy-to-understand GUI (as illustrated in Figure 5.15) to walk you through many of the configuration options required to configure an image to be booted in VMware, and it automates the creation of the necessary files.

Figure 5.15 LiveView GUI

Running LiveView is a straightforward and intuitive process. LiveView supports most versions of Windows and has limited support for Linux. I've used the tool successfully several times to boot and log into acquired images.

NOTE

Once you get the image to boot, there are a variety of things you can do. If you're using the VMware Workstation product and have it configured as a bridged network, you can enable the network interface for your newly booted image and scan it just as though you were doing a remote port scan and/or vulnerability scan. You might also want to log into the running system, so unless the Administrator or user password is blank, you're going to need to get the user's or the organization's IT department's cooperation to obtain the password.

Another excellent (albeit not free) tool is Mount Image Pro[44] (MIP). MIP is a great tool that allows you to mount an image as a read-only drive on your current system. Figure 5.16 illustrates two images mounted as drives F:\ and H:\ via the 30-day evaluation version of Mount Image Pro.

Figure 5.16 Images Mounted As Drive Letters via Mount Image Pro v2.02

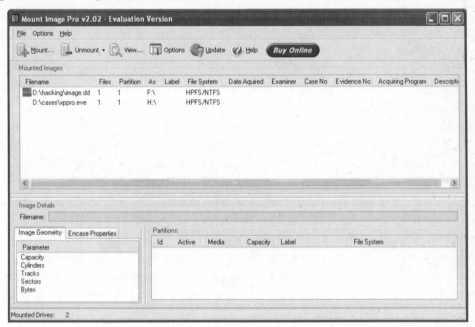

MIP does not boot the image and allow you to access the image as a running system; you will not be able to extract running processes for that system from physical memory. Rather, it mounts the image as a drive letter so that you can access the files within the image just as you would any other drive letter, and it does so in read-only mode so that no changes are made to the image. To verify this, I used md5deep.exe[45] to compute a cryptographic hash for an image of an acquired system that was contained in a single file. I then used MIP to mount the image as a drive letter, and I accessed several files and copied several files from the mounted drive to another partition on my system. Once I had completed several actions, including running several Perl scripts against files in the mounted drive, I dismounted the drive letter and shut the MIP application down completely. I then reran md5deep.exe against the image file and the returned hash was identical to the first hash that I had calculated, verifying that the image is mounted read-only. Creating and verifying cryptographic hashes using a known and accepted algorithm should be part of your standard operating procedure if you're using tools such as Mount Image Pro. (Several freely available tools such as MD5, SHA-1, and SHA-256 implement many of the accepted algorithms.)

Mounting images as read-only drive letters has a lot of advantages, particularly in the areas of data reduction and analysis. For example, you can run any number of tools, such as antivirus and spyware detectors, file signature analysis, and tools for enumerating NTFS alternate data streams, against images in an automated fashion. Rather than enumerating through an image and then having to copy files of interest out of the image for more detailed analysis, many of these methodologies can be automated via Perl scripts.

One laborious analysis task is locating malware on a system. In one instance, I was examining an image of a system on which the user had reported suspicious events. I eventually located malware that was responsible for those events, but using a tool like Mount Image Pro would not only allow me to locate the specific malware much more quickly, but I could also automate scans across several images to locate malware. This would have been beneficial to me in one particular case where the initial infection to the system occurred two years prior to the image being acquired.

Because MIP provides access to the files within an image, you can access those files just like regular files on a system. As such, scripting languages such as Perl will return file handles when you open the files and directories, making restore point and Prefetch directory analysis a straightforward process. Perl scripts used on live systems to perform these functions need only to be "pointed to" the appropriate locations.

Summary

Most of us know, or have said, that no two investigations are alike. Each investigation we undertake seems to be different from the last, much like snowflakes. However, some basic concepts can be common across investigations, and knowing were to look for corroborating information can be an important key. Too often we might be tugged or driven by external forces and deadlines, and knowing where to look for information or evidence of activity, beyond what is presented by forensic "analysis" GUIs, can be very important. Many investigations are limited due to time and resources for merely a search for keywords or specific files, whereas there could be a great deal of information available if only we knew where to look and what questions to ask. Besides the existence of specific files (illicit images, malware), there are number of undocumented (or poorly documented) file formats that we can examine to develop a greater understanding of what occurred on the system and when.

Knowing where to look and where evidence should exist based on how the operating system and applications respond to user action are both very important aspects of forensic analysis. Knowing where log files should exist, as well as their format, can provide valuable clues during an investigation—perhaps more so if those artifacts are absent.

A lack of clear documentation of various file formats (as well as the existence of certain files) has been a challenge for forensic investigations. The key to overcoming this challenge is thorough, documented investigation of these file formats and sharing of this information. This includes not only files and file formats from versions of the Windows operating system currently being investigated (Windows 2000, XP, and 2003) but also newer versions such as Vista.

Notes

1. For more information on event logon codes, go to http://msdn2.microsoft.com/en-us/library/aa380129.aspx.
2. For more information go to http://support.microsoft.com/kb/299475/.
3. For more information go to http://support.microsoft.com/kb/301677/EN-US/.
4. For more information go to http://blogs.msdn.com/ericfitz/default.aspx.
5. For more information go to www.microsoft.com/technet/support/ee/ee_advanced.aspx.
6. For more information go to http://support.microsoft.com/kb/329463/en-us.
7. For more information go to http://pyflag.sourceforge.net/.
8. To read Stephen Bunting's steps for modifying the Event Log header, go to http://128.175.24.251/forensics/repaireventlogfile.htm.

9. To read Andreas Schuster's blog, go to
http://computer.forensikblog.de/en/2007/02/a_common_misconception.html.

10. For more information go to http://www.ranum.com.

11. For more information go to http://support.microsoft.com/?id=318380.

12. For more information go to http://xforce.iss.net/xforce/xfdb/3682.

13. For more information go to www.cert.org/advisories/CA-2001-26.html.

14. For more information go to www.stevengould.org/software/indexdatspy/screen-shots.html.

15. www.systenance.com/indexdat.php.

16. For more information go to http://support.microsoft.com/kb/283673.

17. For more information go to http://support.microsoft.com/kb/308127.

18. For more information go to http://support.microsoft.com/kb/308538/.

19. For more information go to http://support.microsoft.com/kb/156280/.

20. For more information go to http://support.microsoft.com/kb/315271/.

21. For more information go to http://support.microsoft.com/kb/136517.

22. For more information go to
www.datalifter.com/tutorial/bt/NProtect_Using_NProtect.htm.

23. For more information go to www.ediscovery.co.nz/wip/srp.html.

24. For more information go to http://support.microsoft.com/kb/301224.

25. For more information go to www.mitec.cz/wfa.htm.

26. For more information go to www.i2s-lab.com/Papers/
The_Windows_Shortcut_File_Format.pdf.

27. For more information go to forensicfocus.com/link-file-evidentiary-value.

28. For more information go to http://jafat.sourceforge.net/files.html.

29. For more information go to http://support.microsoft.com/?kbid=299648.

30. For more information go to www.metasploit.org/projects/antiforensics/.

31. For more information go to www.computerbytesman.com/privacy/blair.htm.

32. For more information go to http://support.microsoft.com/kb/834427.

33. For more information go to www.ntkernel.com/w&p.php?id=23.

34. For more information go to www.friedemann-schmidt.com/software/exifer/.

35. For more information go to www.irfanview.com/.

36. For more information go to http://search.cpan.org/~bettelli/Image-MetaData-JPEG-0.15/.

37. For more information go to http://toorcon.techpathways.com/cs/
forums/storage/8/11/EXIF.pdf.

38. For more information go to www.securityfocus.com/infocus/1618.

39. For more information go to http://en.wikipedia.org/wiki/Mark_Zbikowski.

40. For more information go to www.techpathways.com/uploads/headersig.txt.

41. For more information go to www.heysoft.de/Frames/f_sw_la_en.htm.

42. For more information go to
www.techpathways.com/DesktopDefault.aspx?tabindex=8&tabid=14.
43. For more information go to http://liveview.sourceforge.net/.
44. For more information go to www.mountimage.com/.
45. For more information go to http://md5deep.sourceforge.net/.
46. For more information go to
http://blogs.technet.com/robert_hensing/default.aspx.
47. For more information go to www.mandiant.com/webhistorian.htm.
48. For more information go to http://support.microsoft.com/?id=235162.

Solutions Fast Track

Event Logs

- ☑ A good deal of traditional computer forensic analysis revolves around the existence of files or file fragments. Windows systems maintain a number of files that can be incorporated into this traditional view to provide a greater level of detail of analysis.

- ☑ Many of the log files maintained by Windows systems include timestamps that can be incorporated into the investigator's timeline analysis of activity on the system.

File Metadata

- ☑ The term *metadata* refers to data about data. This amounts to additional data about a file that is separate from the actual contents of the file (i.e., where many analysts perform text searches).

- ☑ Many applications maintain metadata about a file or document within the file itself.

Alternative Methods of Analysis

- ☑ In addition to the traditional means of computer forensic analysis of files, additional methods of analysis are available to the investigator.

☑ Booting an acquired image into a virtual environment can provide the investigator with a useful means for both analysis of the system as well as presentation of collected data to others (such as a jury).

☑ Accessing an image as a read-only file system provides the investigator with the means to quickly scan for viruses, Trojans, and other malware.

Frequently Asked Questions

The following Frequently Asked Questions, answered by the authors of this book, are designed to both measure your understanding of the concepts presented in this chapter and to assist you with real-life implementation of these concepts. To have your questions about this chapter answered by the author, browse to **www.syngress.com/solutions** and click on the **"Ask the Author"** form.

Q: I was performing a search of Internet browsing activity in an image, and I found that the "Default User" had some browsing history. What does this mean?

A: Although we did not discuss Internet browsing history in this chapter (this subject has been thoroughly addressed through other means), this is a question I have received, and in fact, I have seen it myself in investigations. Robert Hensing (a Microsoft employee) addressed this issue in his blog.[46] In a nutshell, the Default User does not have any Temporary Internet Files or browsing history by default. If a browsing history is discovered for this account, it is indicative of someone with SYSTEM level access making use of the WinInet API functions. I have seen this in cases where an attacker was able to gain SYSTEM level access and run a tool called wget.exe to download tools to the compromised system. Since the wget.exe file uses the WinInet API, the "browsing history" was evident in the Temporary Internet Files directory for the Default User. Robert provides an excellent example to demonstrate this situation by using launching Internet Explorer as a Scheduled Task, so that when it runs it does so with SYSTEM credentials. The browsing history will then be populated for the Default User. Analysis can then be performed on the browsing history/index.dat file using the Internet History Viewer in ProDiscover, or WebHistorian[47] from Mandiant.com.

Q: I've acquired an image of a hard drive, and at first glance, there doesn't seem to be a great deal of data on the system. My understanding is that the user who "owned" this system has been with the organization for several years and has recently left under suspicious circumstances. The installation date maintained in the Registry is for approximately a month ago. What are some approaches I can take from an analysis perspective?

A: This question very often appears in the context that while analyzing a system, the investigator believes that the operating system was reinstalled just prior to the image being acquired. This could end up being the case, but before we go down that route, there are places the investigator can look to gather more data about the issue. The date/timestamp for when the operating system is written to the *InstallDate* value in the following Registry key during installation:

```
HKEY_LOCAL_MACHINE\SOFTWARE\Microsoft\Windows NT\CurrentVersion
```

The data associated with the *InstallDate* value is a *DWORD* that represents the number of seconds since 00:00:00, January 1, 1970. MS KB article 235162[48.] indicates that this value may be recorded incorrectly. Other places that an investigator can look for information to confirm or corroborate this value are the date/timestamps on entries in the setuplog.txt file, in *LastWrite* times for the Service Registry keys, and so on. Also be sure to check the *LastWrite* times for the user account Registry keys in the SAM file. Refer to Chapter 4, "Registry Analysis," for more information regarding extracting information from the Registry (UserAssist keys and the like). Other areas the investigator should examine include the Prefetch directory on Windows XP systems and the MAC times on the user profile directories.

Q: I've heard talk about a topic called *antiforensics*, where someone makes special efforts and uses special tools to hide evidence from a forensic analyst. What can I do about that?

A: Forensic analysts and investigators should never hang a theory or their findings on a single piece of data. Rather, wherever possible, findings should be corroborated by supporting facts. In many cases, attempts to hide data will create their own sets of artifacts; understanding how the operating system behaves and what circumstances and events cause certain artifacts to be created (note that if a value is changed, that's still an "artifact") allows an investigator to see signs of activity. Also keep in mind that the absence of an artifact where there should be one is itself an artifact.

Chapter 6

Executable
File Analysis

Solutions in this chapter:

- **Static Analysis**
- **Dynamic Analysis**

- ☑ **Summary**
- ☑ **Solutions Fast Track**
- ☑ **Frequently Asked Questions**

Introduction

At times during an investigation you might come across a suspicious file and decide that you'd like to perform some analysis of that file to get an idea of what it does or what function it performs. Often an intruder leaves behind scripts or configuration files, generally text files that can be opened and viewed. In the case of scripts, some knowledge of programming might be necessary to fully understand the function of the file.

In Chapter 5 we discussed file signature analysis, a method for determining whether a file had the correct file extension based on the file's type. This is one of the most simple means of obfuscation used by an attacker to hide or mask the presence of files on a compromised system; by changing the filename and extension, the attacker can (often correctly) assume that if the administrator discovers a file with an extension such as .dll, he won't be very eager to access it and determine its true nature.

In this chapter, we'll discuss ways in which you, the investigator, can attempt to determine the nature of an executable file. We will present tools and techniques you can use to gather information about an executable file and get clues about the purpose it serves. This discussion will not be simply about malware analysis; rather, we will present techniques for analyzing executable files in general, of which malware might be just one class. We'll discuss several analysis techniques, but we will stop short of any discussion of disassembling the code or using tools such as IDAPro.[1] The use of disassembler applications is a completely separate topic unto itself, more than sufficient to fill several volumes. Here we'll stick to methods and techniques that most administrators and forensic analysts will be able to perform.

Static Analysis

Static analysis is a process that consists of collecting information about and from an executable file without actually running or launching the file in any way. When most people open an executable file in Notepad (I've done this many times to illustrate something for a client) or even a hex editor, all they see is a bunch of binary data that appears to be just meaningless garbage. Now and again, you might see a word that you recognize, but for the most part, that word has no context; it could be anything. Investigators need to keep in mind that executable files have to follow certain rules with regard to their format; we expect to see specific things in an executable file found on a Windows system. Understanding those rules lets us delve into the apparent gobbledygook of executable files to extract meaningful information.

Before we dig into an executable file, however, there are a couple of things that we need to do first.

Documenting the File

Before analyzing or digging into the executable file in any way, the first thing you should do is document it. However, it's a widely held belief (almost to the point of being an urban legend) that technically oriented folks hate to document anything. Like most legends, this is due to the fact that it's true, at least in part. I can't tell you the number of times that I've responded to an incident (on-site or remote) and been told by the responders, "We found a file." When asked, "Where did you find the file?" the responders replied with wide-eyed, thousand-yard stares. Where the file was found can be extremely useful in adding context to other information and helping you figure out what happened.

So, the very first thing you need to do is document the full path and location of the file you found; the system it was on, the complete path to the file, and who found it and when.

WARNING

Consider this: One thing that many technical folks do not seem to realize is that on a computer system (not just on Windows), a file can be named just about anything. Monitor any of the public listservs for a period of time and you'll find posts in which someone will say, "I found this file on my system and a Google search tells me that it's harmless …" Searching for information about a file based solely on the name of the file can turn up some interesting or useful information, but that information should not be considered the end of the investigation. I responded to an incident once where the on-site IT staff had located several files on an infected system and then Googled for information about each file. Typing in the name of one of the files they found, they saw that the file was legitimate, provided by Microsoft, and they ended their investigation there. However, by examining the file further using techniques presented in this chapter, I was able to determine that the file was, in fact, the malware that I was investigating.

Depending on how the suspicious file was originally located, you might already have the documentation for the file available. If you responded to a live system, for example, and used one (or more) of the response techniques mentioned in Chapter 1, it is likely that you already have documentation, such as the full path to the file. The same is true if you located the file in a system image using ProDiscover or some other forensic analysis tool or technique.

Another aspect of the file that is important to document is the operating system and version on which it was located. Windows operating systems vary between versions and even between service packs within the same version. The effect of the malware on a target might depend on, or even vary depending on, the version of Windows on which it was located. For example, the Teddy Bear virus hoax e-mail identified the jdbgmgr.exe file as being malware (it was referred to as the "Teddy Bear" virus because the icon for this file is a teddy bear) and told the reader to immediately delete the file. If this was done on Windows NT 4.0, the file would be deleted. However, on Windows 2000, Windows File Protection (WFP) would have immediately replaced the file. The set of files protected by WFP differs between Windows 2000 and Windows XP. Back in 2000, Benny and Ratter released the W32.Stream proof-of-concept virus that used NTFS Alternate Data Streams (see Chapter 5 for a detailed explanation of alternate data streams). If the virus made its way onto a Windows system with the file system formatted FAT/FAT32, the virus appeared to behave differently, but only because the FAT file system does not support alternate data streams.

Besides noting in your response procedures where within the file system the file was found and on which version of Windows, you should also collect additional information about the file, such as the file's MAC times or any references to that file within the file system (shortcuts in a user's StartUp folder, for example) or Registry, that you notice during your initial examination.

WARNING

Investigators need to be very careful when initially approaching a system, particularly one that is still running. Earlier in this book, Locard's Exchange Principle was discussed, as was the fact that ASCII and Unicode text searches do not always work on searches of the Registry because some values are stored in binary format. Anything an investigator does on a system will leave artifacts on that system, so if an unusual file is found, limit your searches for extra information about the file as much as possible. Any activities you do engage in should be thoroughly documented.

The more complete your documentation, the better. It's a good idea to make a habit of doing this for every investigation because it will save you a great deal of heartache in the future. Further, this constitutes a "best practices" approach.

Another step you need to follow to document the file is to calculate crypto-graphic hashes for it. Cryptographic hashes are used in information security and computer forensics to ensure the integrity of a file—that is, that no changes have been made to it. One popular hash algorithm is the MD5 function, which takes input of arbitrary length and produces a 128-bit output hash that is usually repre-sented in 32 hexadecimal characters. Any changes to the input, even switching a single bit, will result in a different MD5 hash. Although deficiencies in the MD5 algorithm that allow for collisions have been noted,[2] the algorithm is still useful for computer forensics. Another popular hash algorithm is SHA-1.[3] Organizations such as the National Software Reference Library (NSRL) at NIST use the SHA-1 algo-rithm in computing cryptographic hashes for the Reference Data Set (RDS) CDs. Reference sets such as this allow investigators a modicum of data reduction by fil-tering out "known-good" (legitimate operating system and application files) and "known-bad" (known malware files) files from the data set.

Another useful hashing algorithm was implemented by Jesse Kornblum in his tool called ssdeep[4] (which is based on SpamSum by Dr. Andrews Tridgell). Ssdeep.exe computes "context-triggered piecewise hashes,"[5] which means that instead of computing a cryptographic hash across the entire file, start to finish, it computes a hash using a piecewise approach, hashing randomly sized sections (for example, 4KB) at a time. Not only does this technique produce a hash that can then later be used to verify the integrity of the original file, it can also be used to see how similar two files are. For example, if a Word document is hashed using ssdeep.exe and then modified slightly (adding/removing text, changing formatting, or the like) and the hash recomputed, ssdeep.exe will be able to show how similar the files are. This technique can be used with other file types as well, such as image, video, and audio files.

Once you've documented information about the file, you can begin gathering information from within the file itself.

Analysis

One of the first steps of static analysis that most investigators engage in is to scan the suspicious file with antivirus software. This is an excellent way to start, but do not be surprised if the antivirus scan comes up with nothing definitive. New malcode is being released all the time. In fact, one antivirus company released a report in January 2007, looking back over the previous year, in which there were a total of

207,684 different threats that the antivirus product protected against, and 41,536 new pieces of malcode detected by their product. Scanning the suspicious file might provide you with insight as to the nature of the file, but don't be overly concerned if the response you receive is "no virus detected." Scanning with multiple antivirus engines could provide a more comprehensive view of the file as well.

The next step that most investigators take with a suspicious executable file is to run it through strings.exe,[6] extracting all ASCII and Unicode strings of a specific length. This can be very helpful in that the investigator can get an idea of the file's nature from the strings within the file. The latest version of strings.exe (as of this writing) allows you to search for both ASCII and Unicode strings as well as print the offset of where within the file the string is located. This offset will tell you which section the string appears in and provides context to the string. (Sections and section headers are discussed later in this chapter.) The strings.exe program can even be run to search for specific strings in all files, using the example command line listed at the Web site for the application.

> **NOTE**
>
> Back "in the day," I was assisting with an investigation of a file taken from a system that was spewing traffic out onto the Internet from within a corporate infrastructure. The file turned out to be the IE0199[7] virus that would infect a system and start sending traffic to the Bulgarian telecommunications infrastructure. We found ASCII strings within the file that made up a "manifesto." Fortunately someone on our team had received Russian language training in the U.S. Army and was able to interpret what we'd found. Evidently, the author was upset with the prices charged for Internet access in Bulgaria and wanted to conduct a denial-of-service (DoS) attack against the infrastructure.

Another useful utility for searching for strings in a binary file is BinText, which used to be available from FoundStone (owned by McAfee Inc.). BinText would locate all ASCII, Unicode, and resource strings within a binary file and display them within a nice GUI, along with the offset with the binary file where the string was found. Figure 6.1 illustrates several of the strings found in notepad.exe.

Figure 6.1 Notepad.exe Open in BinText

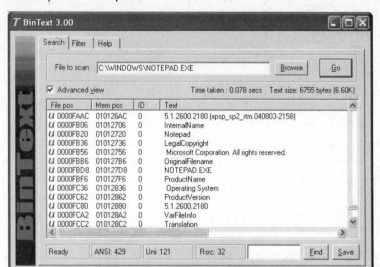

The strings found in the file do not paint a complete picture of what the file does, but they can give the investigator clues. Further, the strings might be out of context, other than their location. For example, in Figure 6.1, we see that the strings are Unicode (see the red "U" on the left of the interface) and they appear to be part of the file-versioning information (more on this later in this chapter). Other strings might not have this same level of context within the file. Another option is that strings that appear odd or unique within the file can be used for searches in other files as well as on the Internet. The results of these searches could provide you with clues to assist in further analysis (either static or dynamic) of the executable file. (In all seriousness, I actually found the string *supercalifragilisticexpialidocious* in a file once. Honest.)

A great many Web sites are available on reverse engineering malware or even legitimate applications, and oddly enough, they all point to some of the same core techniques for collecting information from executables, as well as using some of the very same tools. Two of the tools that we'll use throughout the next sections of this chapter are pedump.exe and PEview.exe.

In February 2002, the first of two articles by Matt Pietrek, "An In-Depth Look into the Win32 Portable Executable File Format,"[8.] was published. In these articles Matt not only described the various aspects of the PE file format in detail but also provided a CLI tool called pedump.exe (found at www.wheaty.net) that can be used to extract detailed information from the header of a PE file.[9.] The information extracted by pedump.exe is sent to STDOUT so it can be easily viewed at the console or redirected to a file for later analysis.

Another useful tool for exploring the internals of Windows PE files is PEview.exe,[10.] from Wayne Radburn. PEview.exe is a GUI tool that allows you to see the various components of the PE header (and the remaining portions as well) in a nicely laid-out format. The most current version of PEview.exe available at the time of this writing is version 0.96, which does not include the ability to save what is viewed in the GUI to a file.

Neither of these tools is provided on the accompanying DVD due to licensing and distribution issues. Besides, going to the Web sites to obtain the tools will ensure that you have the latest available versions. The DVD does, however, contain Perl code for accessing the PE file structures. The Perl script pedmp.pl uses the File::ReadPE Perl module to access the contents of the PE header and to parse the various structures. The Perl script and module are provided for educational and instructional purposes so that you can see what actually goes on behind the scenes with the other tools. Also, the Perl code is written to be as platform-independent as possible; that is, when byte values are retrieved from the executable file, the Perl *unpack()* function is used with *unpack* strings that force the values into little-endian order. This way, the scripts can be run on Windows, Linux, and even on Mac OS X (which is beneficial for analysis, since it is unlikely that on Linux or Mac OS X you will "accidentally" execute Windows malware and infect the system), and so the investigator is not restricted to performing analysis on a single platform.

The PE Header

Microsoft has thoroughly documented[11.] the format of portable executable (PE) files (as well as the Common Object File Format, or COFF, found on VAX/VMS systems) and made that documentation public. Microsoft has also made most of the structures used within the file headers publicly available, as part of the documentation for the ImageHlp[12.] API structures. With these and other resources, we are able to understand the structure of a PE file, delve into its depths, and extract information that could be of use to us during an investigation.

A PE file can be broken down into several areas of interest (I hesitate to say "sections," since we're actually going to be using this term for a specific purpose later in our discussion). The first and perhaps most important part of a PE file (if not the most important, then one of the best bits of geek trivia) is the file signature. For executable files on Windows systems, the file signature consists of the letters *MZ*, found in the first 2 bytes of the file. These two letters are actually the initials of Mark Zbikowski,[13.] the Microsoft architect credited with designing the executable file format. However, as we'll see, it takes much more than those two letters and an .exe at the end of the filename to make a file executable.

Mark's initials are the signature for a 64-byte structure called the IMAGE_DOS_HEADER. The important elements of this structure are the first 2 bytes (the "magic number" 0x5a4d in little-endian hexadecimal format, or *MZ*) and the last *DWORD* (4-byte) value, which is referred to as *e_lfanew*. This value is defined in the ntimage.h header file as the file address (offset) of the new EXE header—that is, the offset at which we should find the signature for the beginning of the IMAGE_NT_HEADERS structure. The *e_lfanew* value points to the location of the PE header, enabling Windows to properly execute the image file. Figure 6.2 illustrates these values from an executable file opened in a hex editor.

Figure 6.2 IMAGE_DOS_HEADER Structure Viewed in a Hex Editor

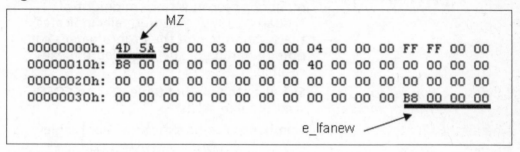

In the example illustrated in Figure 6.2, the IMAGE_NT_HEADERS structure should be located at offset 0xB8 (184 in decimal notation) within the file. The IMAGE_NT_HEADERS structure consists of a signature and two additional structures, IMAGE_FILE_HEADER and IMAGE_OPTIONAL_HEADER. The signature for a PE header is, sensibly enough, PE followed by two zero values (the signature value is a *DWORD*, or 4 bytes in length, and appears as PE\00\00), illustrated in Figure 6.3.

Figure 6.3 IMAGE_NT_HEADERS Signature Value

```
000000b0h: 00 00 00 00 00 00 00 00 50 45 00 00 4C 01 03 00
000000c0h: C2 E1 C2 40 00 00 00 00 00 00 00 00 E0 00 0F 01
000000d0h: 0B 01 06 00 00 80 07 00 00 30 00 00 00 00 00 00
```

The IMAGE_FILE_HEADER[14] structure is contained in the 20 bytes immediately following the PE\00\00 signature and contains several values that can be useful to investigators. Table 6.1 lists the values and descriptions of the IMAGE_FILE_HEADER structure.

Table 6.1 IMAGE_FILE_HEADER Structure Values

Size	Name	Description
2 bytes	*Machine*	Designates the architecture type of the computer; the program can only be run on a system that emulates this type
2 bytes	*Number of Sections*	Designates how many sections (IMAGE_SECTION_HEADERS) are included in the PE file
4 bytes	*TimeDateStamp*	The time and date that the image was created by the linker; UNIX time format (i.e, number of seconds since midnight of January 1, 1970). This normally indicates the system time on the programmer's computer when he or she compiled the executable
4 bytes	*Pointer to Symbol Table*	Offset to the symbol table (0 if no COFF symbol table exists)
4 bytes	*Number of Symbols*	Number of symbols in the symbol table
2 bytes	*Size of Optional Header*	Size of the IMAGE_OPTIONAL_HEADER structure; determines whether the structure is for 32-bit or 64-bit architecture
2 bytes	*Characteristics*	Flags designating various characteristics of the file

Figure 6.4 illustrates the IMAGE_FILE_HEADER of a sample application opened in PEview.

Figure 6.4 IMAGE_FILE_HEADER Viewed in PEview

pFile	Data	Description	Value
000000BC	014C	Machine	IMAGE_FILE_MACHINE_I386
000000BE	0003	Number of Sections	
000000C0	40C2E1C2	Time Date Stamp	2004/06/06 Sun 09:20:02 UTC
000000C4	00000000	Pointer to Symbol Table	
000000C8	00000000	Number of Symbols	
000000CC	00E0	Size of Optional Header	
000000CE	010F	Characteristics	
	0001		IMAGE_FILE_RELOCS_STRIPPED
	0002		IMAGE_FILE_EXECUTABLE_IMAGE
	0004		IMAGE_FILE_LINE_NUMS_STRIPPED
	0008		IMAGE_FILE_LOCAL_SYMS_STRIPPED
	0100		IMAGE_FILE_32BIT_MACHINE

For forensic investigators, the *TimeDateStamp* value might be of significance in investigating an executable file, because it shows when the linker created the image file. (Investigators should also be aware that this value can be modified with a hex editor without having any effect on the execution of the file itself.) This normally indicates the system time on the programmer's computer when he or she compiled the executable and could be a clue as to when this program was constructed. When you're performing analysis of the file, the number of sections that are reported in the IMAGE_FILE_HEADER structure should match the actual number of sections within the file. Also, if the file extension has been altered, the *Characteristics* value will provide some clues as to the true nature of the file; if the IMAGE_FILE_DLL flag (0x2000) is set, the executable file is a dynamic link library and cannot be run directly. One class of file that usually occurs as a DLL is browser helper objects, or BHOs (presented in Chapter 3). These are DLLs that are loaded by Internet Explorer and that can provide all manner of functionality. In some instances, these DLLs are legitimate (such as the BHO used to load Adobe's Acrobat Reader when a PDF file is accessed via the browser), but in many cases they might be spyware or adware.

The value that gives the size of the IMAGE_OPTIONAL_HEADER[15.] structure is important for our analysis of the file because it lets us know whether the optional header is for a 32-bit or a 64-bit application. This value corresponds to the "magic number" of the IMAGE_OPTIONAL_HEADER structure, which is located in the first 2 bytes of the structure; a value of 0x10b indicates a 32-bit executable image, a value of 0x20b indicates a 64-bit executable image, and a value of 0x107 indicates a ROM image. In our discussion, we will focus on the IMAGE_OPTIONAL_HEADER32 structure for a 32-bit executable image. Figure 6.5 illustrates the IMAGE_OPTIONAL_HEADER of a sample application viewed in PEview.

Figure 6.5 IMAGE_OPTIONAL_HEADER Viewed in PEview

pFile	Data	Description	Value
00000108	0007C000	Size of Image	
0000010C	00001000	Size of Headers	
00000110	0007F430	Checksum	
00000114	0002	Subsystem	IMAGE_SUBSYSTEM_WINDOWS_GUI
00000116	0000	DLL Characteristics	
00000118	00100000	Size of Stack Reserve	
0000011C	00001000	Size of Stack Commit	
00000120	00100000	Size of Heap Reserve	
00000124	00001000	Size of Heap Commit	
00000128	00000000	Loader Flags	
0000012C	00000010	Number of Data Directories	

The values visible in Figure 6.5 indicate that the sample application was designed for the Windows GUI subsystem, and a *DLL Characteristics* value of 0000 indicates that the sample application is not a DLL.

As we saw earlier, the size of the IMAGE_OPTIONAL_HEADER structure is stored in the IMAGE_FILE_HEADER structure. The IMAGE_OPTIONAL_HEADER structure contains several values that could be useful for certain detailed analyses of executable files. This level of analysis is beyond the scope of this chapter.

However, a value of interest within the IMAGE_OPTIONAL_HEADER is the *SubSystem* value, which tells the operating system which subsystem is required to run the image. Microsoft even provides a KnowledgeBase article (KB90493) that describes how to determine the subsystem of an application and includes sample code. Note that the MSDN page of the IMAGE_OPTIONAL_HEADER structure provides several more possible values for the *SubSystem* than the KB article.

Another value that investigators will be interested in is the *AddressofEntryPoint* value within the IMAGE_OPTIONAL_HEADER. This is a pointer to the entry point function relative to the image base address. For executable files, this is where the code for the application begins. The importance of this value will become apparent later in this chapter.

Immediately following the IMAGE_OPTIONAL_HEADER structure are the IMAGE_DATA_DIRECTORY[16.] structures. These data directories, illustrated in Figure 6.6, act as a directory structure for information within the PE file, such as the Import Name and Import Address Tables (listings of DLL functions that are imported into and used by the executable file), the Export Table (for DLLs, the location of functions that are exported), the starting address and size of the Debug Directory[17.] (if there is one), and the Resource Directory, to name a few of the 16 possible directories. Each of the data directories is listed as a relative virtual address (RVA) and size value and is listed in a specific, defined order.

Figure 6.6 Excerpt of IMAGE_DATA_DIRECTORIES Viewed in PEview

00000138	00078004	RVA	IMPORT Table
0000013C	00000028	Size	
00000140	0007A000	RVA	RESOURCE Table
00000144	0000114C	Size	
00000148	00000000	RVA	EXCEPTION Table
0000014C	00000000	Size	
00000150	00000000	Offset	CERTIFICATE Table
00000154	00000000	Size	

Figure 6.6 shows four of the 16 data directories available in the sample application. The values listed are the locations or offsets within the PE file where the information is located (such as 0x138), the value at that location (0x78004), and the name of the value (RVA). From the information visible in Figure 6.6, we can see that the sample application has both an import table and a resource table.

TIP

An RVA, or relative virtual address, is used within an executable file when an address of a variable (for example) needs to be specified but hard-coded addresses cannot be used. This is due to the fact that the executable image will not be loaded into the same location in memory on every system. RVAs are used because of the required ability to specify locations in memory that are independent of the location where the file is loaded. An RVA is essentially an offset in memory, relative to the location of the loaded file. To compute the RVA:

```
RVA = (Target Address) - (Load Address)
```

To obtain the actual memory address (the Virtual Address, or VA), simply add the Load Address to the RVA.

The final portion of the PE file that is of interest to us at this point is the IMAGE_SECTION_HEADER[18.] structure. The IMAGE_FILE_HEADER structure contains a value that specifies the number of sections that should be in a PE file and therefore the number of IMAGE_SECTION_HEADER structures that need to be read. The IMAGE_SECTION_HEADER structures are 40 bytes in size and contain the name of the section (8 characters in length), information about the size of the section both on disk and in memory (we saw reference to this in Chapter 4), and the characteristics of the section (whether the section can be read, written to, executed, and so on). Figure 6.7 illustrates the structure of an IMAGE_SECTION_HEADER.

Figure 6.7 IMAGE_SECTION_HEADER Viewed in PEview

pFile	Data	Description	Value
000001B0	2E 74 65 78	Name	.text
000001B4	74 00 00 00		
000001B8	000776EC	Virtual Size	
000001BC	00001000	RVA	
000001C0	00078000	Size of Raw Data	
000001C4	00001000	Pointer to Raw Data	
000001C8	00000000	Pointer to Relocations	
000001CC	00000000	Pointer to Line Numbers	
000001D0	0000	Number of Relocations	
000001D2	0000	Number of Line Numbers	
000001D4	60000020	Characteristics	
	00000020		IMAGE_SCN_CNT_CODE
	20000000		IMAGE_SCN_MEM_EXECUTE
	40000000		IMAGE_SCN_MEM_READ

TIP

One thing to keep in mind when viewing the section names is that there are no hard and fast requirements as to what section names should or can be. The section name is nothing more than a series of characters (up to eight) that can be anything. Rather than .*text*, the section name could be *timmy*. Changing the name does not affect the functionality of the PE file. In fact, some malware authors will edit and modify the section names, perhaps to throw off inexperienced malware analysts. Most "normal" programs have names like .code, .data, .rsrc, or .text. System programs could have names like PAGE or PAGEDATA. Although these names are normal, a malware author can easily rename the sections in a malicious program to appear innocuous. Some section names can be directly associated with packers and cryptors. For example, any program with a section name beginning with *UPX* has been processed using one of those programs. This will be discussed at greater length later in this chapter.

All the PE file information is also available via pedump.exe. The section information in Figure 6.7 appears as follows when viewed via pedump.exe:

```
01 .text     VirtSize: 000776EC  VirtAddr:  00001000
   raw data offs:    00001000  raw data size: 00078000
```

```
relocation offs:  00000000   relocations:    00000000
line # offs:      00000000   line #'s:       00000000
characteristics:  60000020
   CODE   EXECUTE   READ   ALIGN_DEFAULT(16)
```

As you can see, there is no significant difference in the information available via the two tools. The virtual size and address information determines how the executable image file will "look" when in memory, and the "raw data" information applies to the executable image file as it exists on disk. As we saw in Chapter 3, this information also provides us with a road map for extracting the executable image from a memory dump.

Import Tables

It's very rare these days that an application is written completely from scratch. Most programs are constructed by accessing the Windows application programming interface (API) though various functions made available in libraries (DLLs) on the system. Microsoft provides a great number of DLLs that give access to ready-made functions for creating windows, menus, dialog boxes, sockets, and just about any widget, object, and construct on the system. There is no need to create any of these completely by hand when we're creating an application or program.

That being the case, when programs are written and then compiled and linked into executable image files, information about the DLLs and functions accessed by that program needs to be available to the operating system when the application is running. This information is maintained in the import table and the import address table of the executable file.

NOTE

A while back I had the opportunity to work on a project that involved determining whether an executable file had network capabilities. I had done some work examining applications to determine whether they had either network server capabilities (listened for connections, like a Trojan backdoor) or client capabilities (made connections to servers, like an IRCbot), but with this project, the goal was to automate the process. So we started by examining available DLLs to determine which of them provided networking functionality, and then we determined which functions provided the core functionality in question. Once we had that information, we could then automate the process by parsing the PE file structures, locating the import table, and determining which DLLs and functions were used.

The pedump.exe tool provides easy access to the import table information by locating the import data directory and parsing the structures to determine the DLLs and their functions that the application uses. Example output from pedump.exe appears as follows:

```
KERNEL32.dll
 OrigFirstThunk:    0000D114  (Unbound IAT)
 TimeDateStamp:     00000000 -> Wed Dec 31 19:00:00 1969
 ForwarderChain:    00000000
 First thunk RVA:  0000B000
 Ordn  Name
  448   GetSystemTimeAsFileTime
   77   CreateFileA
  393   GetNumberOfConsoleInputEvents
  643   PeekConsoleInputA
  571   LCMapStringW
  570   LCMapStringA
  443   GetSystemInfo
```

As you can see, the sample application imports several functions from kernel32.dll. The DLL actually provides a great deal of functions that are available for use (see the Export Table section), but this example executable imports functions such as *GetSystemTimeAsFileTime()* and *CreateFileA()* for use. Microsoft provides a good deal of information regarding many of the available functions, so you can do research online to see what various functions are meant to do. For example, the *GetSystemTimeAsFileTime()* function retrieves the current system time as a 64-bit FILETIME object, and the returned value represents the number of 100-nanosecond intervals since January 1, 1601, in UTC format.

TIP

Microsoft API functions can be looked up via the Microsoft Developer's Network (MSDN). I keep a link the Microsoft Advanced Search[19.] page on my browser toolbar for quick access. Typing the name of the function I'm interested in, such as **GetSystemTimeAsFileTime**, provides me not only with information about the API function but also ancillary information as well.

Seeing what functions an application imports gives you something of a general clue as to what it does (and does not) do. For example, if the application does not import any of the DLLs that contain networking code, either as low-level socket functions or higher-level Internet APIs, it is unlikely that the application is a backdoor or can be used to transmit information off the system and onto the Internet. This is a useful technique, one that I have used to provide information and answer questions about an application. I was once given an executable image and asked whether it was or had the capability of being a network backdoor. After documenting the file, I took a look at the import table and saw that there were no DLLs imported that provided networking capabilities. I took my analysis a step further by looking at the functions that were imported and found that although there were several that provided mathematic functionality, none provided networking capability.

Another useful tool for viewing the information regarding DLLs and functions required by an application is to use the Dependency Walker tool, also known as depends.exe, available from the Web site of the same name. Figure 6.8 illustrates an excerpt of the Dependency Walker GUI, with the sample application dcode.exe open in the Dependency Walker.

Figure 6.8 Excerpt from Dependency Walker GUI

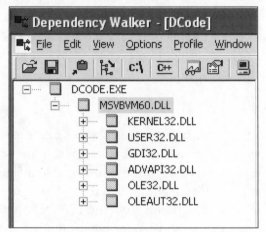

As illustrated in Figure 6.8, the dcode.exe application relies on functions from MSVBVM60.DLL, which in turn relies on functions from six other DLLs. (Each of these DLLs ships with most current Windows distributions.) Figure 6.9 illustrates a portion of the functions exported by MSVBVM60.DLL, as reported by the Dependency Walker tool.

Figure 6.9 Functions Exported by MSVBVM60.DLL

E	Ordinal ^	Hint	Function	Entry Point
C	100 (0x0064)	60 (0x003C)	ThunRTMain	0x0000DE3E
C	101 (0x0065)	73 (0x0049)	VBDllUnRegisterServer	0x0001BCFC
C	102 (0x0066)	70 (0x0046)	VBDllCanUnloadNow	0x0002C692
C	103 (0x0067)	72 (0x0048)	VBDllRegisterServer	0x000A4A8A
C	104 (0x0068)	71 (0x0047)	VBDllGetClassObject	0x00028FCA
C	105 (0x0069)	69 (0x0045)	UserDllMain	0x0001BBA7
C	106 (0x006A)	13 (0x000D)	DllRegisterServer	0x000D3AD5
C	107 (0x006B)	14 (0x000E)	DllUnregisterServer	0x000D3CB3
C	108 (0x006C)	94 (0x005E)	__vbaAryLock	0x000E24D0

The Dependency Walker tool allows you to see not only the DLLs and their functions that are imported by an executable, whether a .exe or .dll file, but also the functions exported by DLLs. We will discuss the export table a bit more in the next section.

The Dependency Walker tool also has a useful profiling function that allows you to set specific parameters for how a module or application will be profiled, then launch the application to see which modules (DLLs) will be loaded. This allows you to trace the various DLL function calls and returned values as the application runs. This can be useful in detected modules that are dynamically loaded but aren't listed in the import tables of other modules, or to determine why an "application failed to initialize properly" error is reported. However, this falls outside the scope of static analysis, since it requires the file to be run.

Export Table

As DLLs provide functions that other executable files can import, the DLLs themselves maintain a table of functions available in their (you guessed it) export table. These are functions that are available for other executable images (DLLs, EXEs, and the like) to import or use so that application authors do not need to write their own code for everything they want to do on a system. The DLLs act as libraries or repositories of prewritten code that is available for use on the system.

Pedump.exe will dump the export table from DLLs. For example, a portion of the export table for ws2_32.dll is shown here:

```
exports table:
  Name:            WS2_32.dll
  Characteristics: 00000000
  TimeDateStamp:   41107EDA -> Wed Aug 04 02:14:50 2004
  Version:         0.00
```

```
Ordinal base:      00000001
# of functions:    000001F4
# of Names:        00000075
Entry Pt   Ordn   Name
00011028     1    accept
00003E00     2    bind
00009639     3    closesocket
0000406A     4    connect
00010B50     5    getpeername
0000951E     6    getsockname
000046C9     7    getsockopt
00002BC0     8    htonl
00002B66     9    htons
00004519    10    ioctlsocket
00002BF4    11    inet_addr
```

If you have any experience with UNIX and/or Perl socket programming, you will recognize the exported functions as being the core functionality for network-based communications. For example, the *bind()* and *accept()* functions are used by services or daemons that listen for connections (backdoors and so on), and the *connect()* function is used by client utilities that connect to servers, such as Web browsers and IRC bots.

I should point out that DLLs can import functions from other DLLs, in addition to exporting their own functions. For example, using pedump.exe to view the PE information for ws2_32.dll, we see that the executable imports functions from kernel32.dll, ws2help.dll, ntdll.dll, and others. Some DLLs will import functionality from other DLLs to build on the base functionality provided. Tools such as the Dependency Walker will show you these chained or cascading DLL dependencies in a nice GUI format.

Resources

Often a PE file will have a section named .rsrc and a Resource data directory listed as well. This resource section can contain information about things such as dialogs and icons and other useful bits of information that can help you identify a file, but perhaps the most useful thing during analysis of an executable file is file-versioning information.

 The Perl script fvi.pl (located on the accompanying DVD) uses the Win32::File::VersionInfo module to extract file version information from a PE file, if such information is available. Fvi.pl takes a filename (with the full path) as the sole argument and returns the information it finds as follows:

```
C:\Perl>fvi.pl c:\windows\system32\svchost.exe
Filename           : c:\windows\system32\svchost.exe
Type               : Application
OS                 : NT/Win32
Orig Filename      : svchost.exe
File Descriptoin   : Generic Host Process for Win32 Services
File Version       : 5.1.2600.2180 (xpsp_sp2_rtm.040803-2158)
Internal Name      : svchost.exe
Company Name       : Microsoft Corporation
Copyright          : Microsoft Corporation. All rights reserved.
Product Name       : Microsoft« Windows« Operating System
Product Version    : 5.1.2600.2180
Trademarks         :
```

There are a couple of things you need to keep in mind when using tools such as this. First, the Win32::File::VersionInfo module is specific to the Windows platform. Second, neither the module nor the Perl script makes any attempt to verify that the file in question is actually a PE file. This means that if fvi.pl fails to return any information, that does not mean that the file in question is malware. In fact, many malware authors make sure that such information is not compiled into their tools, whereas others include faked file version information to throw off investigators. Some even include file-versioning information simply to amuse themselves and others.

Notes from the Underground…

The RussianTopz Bot

While I was performing analysis of the russiantopz IRCbot, one of the interesting bits of information I discovered about the bot program (named statistics.exe) was that it really wasn't an IRCbot written by anyone from Russia! Looking past the name of the file and delving into the file-versioning information, I found that the file was really a copy of the mIRC32.exe[20] IRC client application. The GUI IRC client was hidden from the desktop by a file called teamscan.exe, which was in reality a copy of Adrian Lopez's hidewndw.exe[21] utility.

Although the use of file-versioning information is not always a conclusive means of analysis, it does provide additional information that will add to the overall picture of your investigation.

Obfuscation

So far, we've used normal, legitimate executable files to illustrate the various structures of PE files. Although these tools and techniques can be used to identify files, malware authors very often put forth effort to disguise or "obfuscate" their files, not only to avoid detection by administrators and investigators but also to hide from antivirus and other security software programs. Often the malware authors use packers and even encryption tools to disguise their software, or they will simply create new versions of their programs.

A number of kinds of utilities , such as binders, packers, and "cryptors," can be used to obfuscate executable files. We'll take a look at each of these in turn.

Binders

Binders are utilities that allow the user to bind one application to another, in essence creating a Trojan application. The idea is that the carrier application will entice the user to launch it; examples include games and other executables. When the victim launches the carrier application, he or she sees the application run, and nothing seems amiss. All the while, however, the Trojan application runs, often behind the scenes, unbeknownst to the victim.

One of the first binders available was EliteWrap,[22] but Silk Rope and SaranWrap[23] became popular when the Cult of the Dead Cow released their Back Orifice utility. Looking at write-ups and descriptions of malware available at antivirus sites (as well as others), it would appear that binders are no longer "in vogue" among malware authors and perhaps not considered "cool" any longer. This could be largely due to the fact that the binders leave behind signatures that have long been detected by antivirus software.

Although there are many binders available under many different names, they all perform the same basic function: to bind one executable to another. EliteWrap is perhaps unique in that it allows the user to configure a script of commands to be run or responses to be provided, allowing some additional functionality in the bound executables.

WARNING

After downloading EliteWrap 1.04 to a Windows XP Pro SP2 system, I tried several times to produce a working, bound package and failed each time. I tried using EliteWrap in interactive mode as well as using a script. Each time I ended up with an output file much smaller than any of the input files, and when I attempted to run the output file, I received a dialog box that stated "Error #57 reading package."

Packers

Packers is another name for programs that allow the user to compress their programs, saving space. Another name for such tools is *compressors*. This is not such an issue due to expanding storage capacity, but compressing the executable file allows it to transit the network quicker and potentially allow it to avoid detection by both host- and network-based antivirus and intrusion protection systems. Packers also make analysis of the executable more difficult. Some legitimate companies pack their programs to make them run faster (there's less to load from disk into RAM) or to protect trade secrets. There are many packers available; popular packing programs include ASPack,[24.] UPX,[25.] and FSG.

ASPack works by compressing the executable image, writing a small decompression routine at the end of the file. The executable's entry point is then changed to point to the beginning of the decompression routine, and the original entry point is saved. When the executable is decompressed into memory, the entry point is reset to the original value. One indication that ASPack has been used is the existence of section names such as .adata, .udata, and .aspack. (Keep in mind, however, that the section names are just that—names—and they can be altered.) Reportedly there are tools available that will allow you to unpack files packed with ASPack.

UPX is another popular packer, and although it can be used as a packer, it can also be used to decompress files that have been packed with UPX—so it's an unpacker for itself as well. One indicator that you've got a file compressed with UPX is the existence of the section names UPX0 and UPX1, but keep in mind that these names can be changed by simply editing the PE file with a hex editor.

These are just a few examples of compression utilities used by malware authors; there are many, many more out there. Depending on the compression utility used, you might find an application or plugin that is meant to decompress that algorithm, reversing the process. You might have to spend some time doing research on the

Internet to see if reversing the compression is an option and whether there is a utility to assist you.

Tools such as ProcDump32[26.] include the ability to unpack common compression algorithms. Figure 6.10 illustrates the Choose Unpacker dialog box for ProcDump32, from which the user can select the algorithm used to pack the executable.

Figure 6.10 Choose Unpacker Dialog Box from ProcDump32

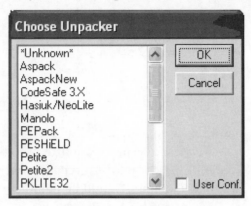

ProcDump32 also includes other functionality, such as allowing the user to dump a running process to disk, unpack or decrypt a PE file using common algorithms, or edit PE headers. We've already seen other tools that allow you to do this, but ProcDump32 does provide some fairly useful functionality and should definitely be included as part of your malware analysis toolkit.

Cryptors

Cryptors is a slang term for programs that allow the user to encrypt programs. Encrypting an executable is another method that is used in an attempt to avoid detection by both host- and network-based antivirus and intrusion protection systems. This actually seems to be a pretty popular method for obfuscating malware, and in some cases, the encryption algorithm or routine might be known or at least discoverable (based on a signature of some kind), whereas in others it could be completely unknown.

As an example of an obfuscated bit of malware, we'll take a look at a file that we know has been obfuscated in some way. The HoneyNet Project provided interesting Scan of the Month (SotM) challenges[27.] for some time, providing a variety of data and scenarios for folks to try their hand at deciphering. The interesting thing about the SotM challenges is that after a period of time, the submissions are judged and posted, so you get to see how the challenges were solved in detail. Ed Skoudis provides similar challenges at his site, CounterHack.net.

The HoneyNet SotM 32 was to analyze a malware binary called RaDa.exe. The icon for the malware binary is illustrated in Figure 6.11.

Figure 6.11 Icon for the RaDa.exe Malware Binary

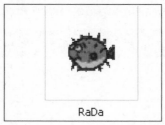

Using pedump.exe and PEview to look at RaDa.exe, we see that it has a pretty normal PE header and that everything seems to translate well. By that I mean that the tools are able to parse the PE header information and from a parsing perspective, it seems to make sense. If it didn't, pointers would be pointing off to strange sections of the file or off the end of the executable file altogether.

Perhaps the most interesting thing we see is that the file has three sections: JDR0, JDR1, and .rsrc. Now, .rsrc is one that we're familiar with, but the other two aren't anything we've seen before in PE files we've looked at so far. Another thing that we notice is that the Imports Table lists only two DLLs, KERNEL32.DLL and MSVBVM60.DLL, as shown here:

```
Imports Table:
  KERNEL32.DLL
  OrigFirstThunk:   00000000 (Unbound IAT)
  TimeDateStamp:    00000000 -> Wed Dec 31 19:00:00 1969
  ForwarderChain:   00000000
  First thunk RVA:  00010BE0
  Ordn  Name
     0  LoadLibraryA
     0  GetProcAddress
     0  ExitProcess


  MSVBVM60.DLL
  OrigFirstThunk:   00000000 (Unbound IAT)
  TimeDateStamp:    00000000 -> Wed Dec 31 19:00:00 1969
  ForwarderChain:   00000000
```

```
First thunk RVA: 00010BF0
Ordn   Name
 618
```

This is odd because we know this is malware, and any malware that actually does anything is going to import more than two DLLs and definitely more than just three functions from KERNEL32.DLL.

TIP

> This is also a great way to spot obfuscated malware quickly. When the Import Table shows just KERNEL32.DLL (or maybe that one and one or two others) and there are only a few imported functions from that DLL that include *LoadLibraryA* and *GetProcAddress*, this is an indicator that the file has been obfuscated in some way.

The other imported module, MSVBVM60.DLL, is a Visual Basic runtime. The output of fvi.pl tells us that the File Description from the resource section of that DLL is "Visual Basic Virtual Machine." From this we can deduce that the malware itself was written using Visual Basic. This deduction is also borne out in the challenge submissions for analyzing this file listed at the HoneyNet site.

Since RaDa.exe has a resource section, we can run fvi.pl against it and in doing so retrieve the following:

```
Filename          : d:\tools\rada.exe
Type              : Application
OS                : Unknown/Win32
Orig Filename     : RaDa
File Description  :
File Version      : 1.00
Internal Name     : RaDa
Company Name      : Malware
Copyright         :
Product Name      : RaDa
Product Version   : 1.00
Trademarks        :
```

Very interesting, and nice to know that the author is letting us know that, yes, this is malware. Don't expect this to happen often, if at all.

Now that we've seen definite signs that this malware is obfuscated (and yes, we cheated a bit by choosing a program that we already knew was obfuscated), we'd like to know *how* it has been obfuscated. Was a packer used? Was compression used, or how about encryption? We can use a handy tool called PEiD[28.] to examine this file and attempt to determine the obfuscation method. Figure 6.12 illustrates RaDa.exe loaded into PEiD.

Figure 6.12 RaDa.exe Loaded into PEiD

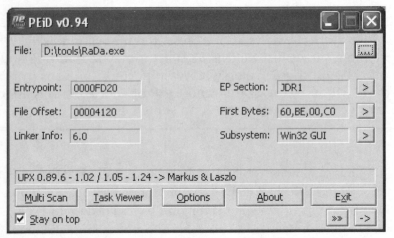

Notice that PEiD detected the obfuscation method as a version of the UPX compression utility. This is interesting because the section names listed by PEview were JDR0 and JDR1 rather than UPX0 and UPX1. As we mentioned earlier, the UPX0 and UPX1 section names are indicative of the UPX compression utility. What this tells us is that if the PEiD information is accurate, the author used an editor to modify those section names.

PEiD detects common packers, cryptors, and compilers by locating the entry point of the application and performing analysis of the bytes at that location, attempting to identify the obfuscation method used. The authors of PEiD have collected signatures for many different obfuscation tools and included them with PEiD. They've also provided some nifty tools along with PEiD, including a task viewer for viewing running processes and the modules they use, a dialog box for extra information about the file (illustrated in Figure 6.13), a dialog box for viewing the PE header, and even a dialog box to view the disassembled binary.

Figure 6.13 PEiD Extra Information Dialog Box with RaDa.exe Loaded

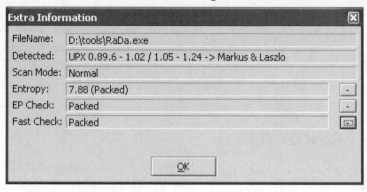

If you do take the opportunity to download both PEiD and the RaDa.exe file, run the disassembler by clicking the button with the right arrow to the right of the First Bytes text field. If you're at all familiar with assembly language programming (and I haven't done it since graduate school, when we programmed the Motorola 68000 microprocessor), the things that might grab your immediate attention are the jump instructions and the many, many add instructions that you see listed. If you're at all curious about the details of the analysis of this binary, take a look at the submissions at the HoneyNet site, particularly the one by Chris Eagle. Chris is a well-known instructor and presenter at BlackHat[29] conferences as well as a Senior Lecturer and Associate Chair for the Department of Computer Science at the Naval Postgraduate School in Monterey, California.

TIP

If you're interested in delving deeper into the inner workings of malware and executable files in general, it would be a good idea to read through the submissions for SotM 32 and 33 at the HoneyNet Challenge site. Not only will you see commonalities between all the analyses, but you will also see information about other tools you can use to go further into your analysis.

Dynamic Analysis

Dynamic analysis involves launching an executable file in a controlled and monitored environment so that its effects on a system can be observed and documented. This is an extremely useful analysis mechanism in that it gives you a more detailed view of what the malware does on and to a system and especially in what order. This is most useful in cases in which the malware is packed or encrypted, since the executable image must be unpacked or decrypted (or both) in memory prior to being run. So not only will we see the tracks in the snow and the broken tree limbs, as it were, but using techniques for capturing and parsing the contents of memory (as discussed in Chapter 3), we can actually see the Abominable Snowman, live and in action.

Testing Environment

If you do intend to perform dynamic analysis of malware, one of your considerations will be the testing or host environment. After all, it isn't a good idea to see what a piece of malware does by dropping it onto a production network and letting it run amok. It's bad enough that these things happen by accident; we don't want to actually do this on purpose.

One way to set up your testing environment is to have a system on a separate network, with no electrical connectivity (notice here that I don't say "logical connection" or "VLAN on a switch") to the rest of your network. There has to be that "air gap" there; I strongly recommend that you don't even mess with having a knife switch to separate your malware "cage" from your infrastructure, because we all know that one day, when you've got something really nasty that you're testing, someone's going to look up and realize that they forgot to throw the switch and separate the networks. Also, if you're undergoing an audit required by any sort of regulatory body, the last thing you want to have is a way for malware that will potentially steal sensitive personal data to get into a network where sensitive personal data lives. If your lab is accredited or certified by an appropriate agency, you can seriously jeopardize that status by running untrusted programs on a live network. Losing that accreditation will make you very unpopular with what is left of your organization. Not only does this apply to labs accredited for forensic analysis work, it can also apply to other regulatory agencies as well.

One of the drawbacks of having "throwaway" system or two is that you have to reinstall the operating system after each test; how else are you going to ensure that you're collecting clean data and that your results aren't being tainted by another piece of malware? One way to accomplish this is with virtualization.

Virtualization

If you don't have a throwaway system that you can constantly reinstall and return to a pristine state (who really wants to do that?), virtualization is another option available to you. A number of freeware and commercial virtualization tools are available to you, such as:

- **Bochs**[30.] Runs on Windows, Linux, and even Xbox. Some users have found this program difficult to set up. It's free and open source but could be difficult to set up and manage.

- **Parallels**[31.] Runs on the Mac platform as well as Windows and Linux.

- **Microsoft's Virtual PC**[32.] Runs on Windows as the host OS; can run DOS, Windows, and OS/2 guest operating systems; and is freely available.

- **VirtualIron**[33.] "Bare metal install" (meaning that it is not installed on a host operating system) and can reportedly run Windows and Linux at near-native speeds.

- **Xen**[34.] Runs on NetBSD and Linux; supports Windows guest operating systems that reportedly run at near-native speeds.

- **Win4Lin**[35.] Runs on Linux; allows you to run Windows applications.

- **VMware** Runs on Windows, Linux, and so on and allows you to host a number of guest operating systems. The VMware Server and VMPlayer products are freely available. VMware is considered by many to be the de facto standard for virtualization products and is discussed in greater detail in the following sections.

This is by no means a complete list, of course. The virtualization option you choose depends largely on your needs, environment (i.e., available systems, budget, and so on), as well as your comfort level in working with various host and guest operating systems. If you're unsure as to which option is best for you, take a look at the Comparison of Virtual Machines page[36.] on Wikipedia. This might help you narrow down your choices based on your environment, budget, and level of effort required to get a virtualization platform up and running.

The benefit of using a virtual system in analyzing malware is that you can create a "snapshot" of that system and then "infect" it and perform all your testing and analysis. Once you've collected all your data, you can revert to the snapshot, returning the system to a pristine, prior-to-infection state. Not only can systems be more easily recovered, but multiple versions of similar malware can be tested against the same identical platform for a more even comparison.

Perhaps the most commonly known virtualization platform is VMware.[37.] VMware provides several virtualization products for free, such as VMPlayer, which allows for playing virtual machines (although not creating them) and VMware

Server. In addition, a number of prebuilt virtual machines or appliances are available for download and use. As of this writing, I saw ISA Server and MS SQL Server virtual appliances available for download.

There is a caveat to using VMware, and that caveat applies to other virtualization environments as well. Not long ago, there were discussions about how software could be used to detect the existence of a virtualization environment. Soon afterward, analysts began seeing malware that would not only detect the presence of a virtualization environment but would actually behave differently or simply would not function at all. On November 19, 2006, Lenny Zeltser posted an ISC handler's diary entry[38] that discussed virtual machine detection in malware through the use of commercial tools. This is something that you should keep in mind and consider when you're performing dynamic malware analysis. Be sure to thoroughly interview any users who witnessed the issue, and determine as many of the potential artifacts as you can before taking your malware sample back to the lab. That way, if you are seeing radically different behavior in the malware when it's running in a virtual environment, you might have found an example of malware that includes this code.

Throwaway Systems

If virtualization is simply not an option due to price, experience, comfort level, or something else, you can opt to go with throwaway systems that can quickly be imaged and rebuilt. Some corporate organizations use tools like Symantec's Norton Ghost[39] to create images for systems that all have the same hardware. That way, a standard build can be used to set up systems, making them easier to manage. Other organizations have used a similar approach with training environments, allowing the IT staff to quickly return all systems to a known state. For example, when I was performing vulnerability assessments, I performed an assessment for an organization that had a training environment. IT staff at that organization proudly told me that using Norton Ghost, they could completely reload the operating systems on all 68 training workstations with a single diskette.

If this is something that you opt to do, you need to make sure that the systems are not attached to a corporate or production network in any way. One might think that this goes without saying, but there have been quality assurance and testing networks that have been taken down due to a rushed administrator or an improperly configured VLAN on a switch. You should ensure that you have more than just a logical gap between your testing platform and any other networks; an actual air gap is best.

Once you've decided on the platform you will use, you can follow the same data collection and analysis processes that you would use in a virtual environment on the throwaway systems; the process really does not differ. On a throwaway system, however, you will need to include some method for capturing the contents of memory on your platform (remember, VMware sessions can simply be suspended), particularly if you are analyzing obfuscated malware.

Tools

There are a variety of tools that you can use to monitor systems when you're testing malware. For the most part, you want to have all your tools in place before you launch your malware sample. Also, you want to be familiar with your tools' capabilities as well as how to use them.

One of the big differences between malware analysis and incident response is that as the person analyzing the malware, you have the opportunity to set up and configure the test system prior to its infection. Although it's true, in theory, that system administrators have this same opportunity, it's fairly rare that you'll find major server systems that have been heavily configured with security, especially incident response, in mind.

When you're testing malware, you need to be aware of some challenges. For example, you do not know what the malware is going to do when it's launched. I know it sounds simplistic, but more than once I've talked to people who've not taken this into account. What I mean is that you don't know if the malware is going to open up and sit there waiting to be analyzed or if instead it's going to do its job quickly and disappear. I've seen malware that opened a port awaiting connections (backdoor), others that have attempted to connect to systems on the Internet (IRCbots), and those that have only taken a fraction of a second to inject their code into another running process and then disappear. When doing dynamic analysis, you have the opportunity to repeat the "crime" over and over again to try to see the details. When we perform incident response activities, we're essentially taking snapshots of the scene, using tools to capture state information from the system at discrete moments in time. This is akin to trying to perform surveillance with a Polaroid camera. During dynamic analysis, we want to monitor the scene with live video, where we can capture information over a continual span of time rather than at discrete moments. That way, hopefully, we'll be able to capture and analyze what goes on over the entire life span of the malware.

So, what tools do we want to use? To start, we want to log any and all network connectivity information, since malware may either attempt to communicate to a remote system, open a port to listen for connections, or both. One way we can do this logging is to run a network sniffer such as WireShark[40.] (formerly known as Ethereal) on the network. If you're using a stand-alone system, you'll want to have the sniffer on another system; if you're using VMware, you'll want to have

WireShark running on the host operating system while the malware is being executed in one of the guest operating systems. The reason we do this will be apparent in a moment.

Another tool that you'll want to install on your system is Port Reporter,[41] which is freely available from Microsoft. Port Reporter runs as a service on Windows systems and records TCP and UDP port activity. On Windows XP and Windows 2003 systems, Port Reporter will record the network ports that are used, the process or service that uses that port, the modules loaded by the process, and the user account that runs the process. Less information is recorded on Windows 2000 systems. Port Reporter has a variety of configuration options, such as where within the file system the log files are created, whether the service starts automatically on system boot or manually (which is the default), and so on. These can be controlled through command-line parameters added to the service launch after Port Reporter has been installed. Before installing Port Reporter, be sure to read through the KnowledgeBase article so that you understand how it works and what information it can provide.

Port Reporter creates three types of log files: an initialization log (such as PR-INITIAL-*.log[42]) that records state information about the system when the service starts; a ports log (such as PR-PORTS-*.log) that maintains information about network connections and port usage, similar to netstat.exe; and a process ID log (such as PR-PIDS-*.log) that maintains process information.

Microsoft also provides a WebCast[43] that introduces the Port Reporter tool and describes its functionality. Microsoft also has the Port Reporter Parser[44] tool available to make parsing the potentially voluminous Port Reporter logs easier and much more practical.

With these monitoring tools in place, you might be wondering why you need to run a network sniffer on another system. Why can't you run it on the same dynamic analysis platform with all your other monitoring tools? The answer has to do with rootkits, which we will discuss in Chapter 7, "Rootkits and Rootkit Detection." However, the short answer is that rootkits allow malware to hide its presence on a system by preventing the operating system from "seeing" the process, network connections, and so on. As of this writing, thorough testing has not been performed using various rootkits, so we want to be sure we collect as much information as possible. By running the network sniffer on another platform, separate from the testing platform, we ensure that part of our monitoring process is unaffected by the malware once it has been launched and is active.

TIP

It might also be useful during dynamic malware analysis to run a scan of the "infected" system from another system. This scan could show a backdoor that is opened on the system but hidden through some means, such as a rootkit (discussed in greater detail in Chapter 7). You can use tools such as *nmap*[45.] or PortQry[46.] to quickly scan the "infected" system and even attempt to determine the nature of the service listening on a specific port. Although issues of TCP/IP connectivity and "port knocking" are beyond the scope of this book, there is always the possibility that certain queries (or combinations of queries) sent to an open port on the "infected" system could cause the process bound to that port to react in some way.

Remember, one of the things we as forensic examiners need to understand is that the absence of an artifact is in itself an artifact. In the context of dynamic malware analysis, this means that if we see network traffic emanating from the testing platform and going out to the Internet (or looking for other systems on the local subnet), but we do not observe any indications of the process or the network traffic being generated via the monitoring tools on the testing platform, we could have a rootkit on our hands.

As a caveat and warning, this is a good opportunity for me to express the need for a thorough and documented dynamic malware analysis process. I have seen malware that does not have rootkit capabilities but instead injects code into another process's memory space and runs from there. This is something that needs to be understood because making the assumption that a rootkit is involved will lead to incorrect reporting as well as incorrect actions in response to the issue. If you document your process and tools that you use, the idea is that someone else will be able to verify your results. After all, using the same tools and the same process and the same malware, someone else should be able to see the same outcome, right? Or that person will be able to look at your process and inquire as to the absence or use of a particular tool, which will allow for a more thorough examination and analysis of the malware.

TIP

In performing dynamic malware analysis, you must plan for as much as you possibly can but at the same time not overburden yourself or load your system down with so many tools that you're spending so much time managing the tools that you've lost track of what you're analyzing.

I was working on a customer engagement once when we found an unusual file. The initial indication of the file was in the Registry; when launched, it added a value to the user's Run key as well as to the RunOnce key. Interestingly enough, it added the value to the RunOnce key by prefacing the name of the file with *; this tells the operating system to parse and launch the contents of the key, even if the system is started in Safe Mode (pretty tricky!). We had to resort to dynamic analysis because static analysis quickly revealed that the malware was encrypted, and PEiD was unable to determine the encryption method used.

After launching the malware on our platform and analyzing the captured data, we could see where the malware would launch the Web browser invisibly (the browser process was running, but the GUI was not visible on the desktop) and then inject itself into the browser's process space. From this we were able to determine that once the malware had been launched, we should be looking for the browser process for additional information. It also explained why during volatile data analysis we were seeing that the browser process was responsible for the unusual network connections and there was no evidence of the malware process running.

It's also a good idea to enable auditing for Process Tracking events in the Event Log, for both success and failure events. The Event Log can help you keep track of a number of different activities on the system, including the use of user privileges, logons, object access (this setting requires that you also configure access control lists on the objects—files, directories, Registry keys—that you specifically want monitored), and so on. Since we're interested in processes during dynamic malware analysis, enabling auditing for Process Tracking for both success and failure events will provide us with some useful data. Using auditpol.exe from the Resource Kit (which we discussed in Chapter 1), we can configure the audit policy of the dynamic analysis platform as well as confirm that it is set properly prior to testing. For example, use the following command line to ensure that proper auditing is enabled:

```
C:\tools>auditpol /enable /process:all
```

To confirm that proper auditing is still enabled prior to testing, simply launch auditpol.exe from the command line with no arguments.

TIP

You might also want to enable auditing of System events, but be sure not to enable too much auditing. There is such a thing as having too much data, which can really slow down your analysis, particularly if the data isn't particularly of use to you. Some people might feel that they want to monitor everything so that they ensure that they don't miss anything, but there's a limit to how much data you can effectively use and analyze. Thoroughly assess what you're planning to do, set up a standard configuration for your testing platform and stick with it, unless there is a compelling reason for changing it. Too much data can be as hazardous to an investigation as too little.

One way to monitor access to files and Registry keys is to, as mentioned earlier, enable Object Access auditing, set access control lists on all the objects we're interested in, and, once we've executed the malware, attempt to make sense out of the contents of the Event Log. Or we could look at two ways to monitor access to files and Registry keys: one is to take before and after snapshots and compare the two, and the other is to use real-time monitoring. When performing dynamic malware analysis, the best bet is to do both, and to do that, we'll need some tools. You can go to the SysInternals Web site and download the FileMon[47.] and RegMon[48.] tools (which let you monitor file system and Registry activity in real time), or you can download Process Monitor.[49.] FileMon and RegMon have been replaced by Process Monitor, which is updated and provides a richer feature set. However, if you'd rather use two separate tools, they are available to you; it's simply a matter of preference. The benefit of using real-time monitoring tools instead of snapshot tools is that you not only see files and Registry keys that were created or modified, but you also get to see files and Registry keys that might have been searched for but were not located. Further, you get to see a timeline of activity, seeing the order in which the files or Registry keys were accessed. This can be an important part of your analysis of the malware.

We will discuss some of the snapshot-based tools that are available in the next section.

Process

The process for setting up your testing platform for dynamic analysis of malware is pretty straightforward and simple; the key is to have a process or a checklist. As with volatile data collection or forensic analysis, you don't want to try to perform dynamic analysis from memory every time, because sometimes you're going to be rushed or you're simply going to forget an important step in the process. We're all capable of and guilty of this error; I've had my share of analysis scenarios in which I had to start all over because I forgot to enable one of my tools. I had to go back and completely clean and refresh the now-infected system, then ensure that my tools were installed and that my system configuration was correct. I'm sure that I don't have to describe how frustrating this can be.

The first thing you want to do is to ensure that you've identified, downloaded, and installed all the tools you're going to need. We've addressed a good number of tools in this chapter, but in the future, there could be other tools that you'll be interested in using. Keep a list of the tools that you're using for dynamic analysis, and keep your list updated. Every now and then, share it with others, and add new tools and remove old ones.

Once you have all your tools in place, be sure that you understand how they are used, and ensure that you know and understand the necessary configuration options. Most of the tools will be started manually, and you need to have a checklist of the order in which you're going to start your tools. For example, tools such as RegShot[50] (illustrated in Figure 6.14) and InControl5[51] (illustrated in Figure 6.15) take snapshots of the system for comparison, so you want to launch the first phase (collect the baseline snapshot) first, then start the real-time monitoring tools.

Figure 6.14 RegShot GUI

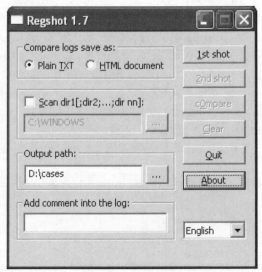

RegShot saves its output in plain text or HTML format. There's a modified version of RegShot available at ParaGlider's PEBuilder plugins[52.] page that saves its output as an NT4 .reg file format. Also, when using snapshot and monitoring tools such as RegShot, you should keep in mind that most tools will only be able to monitor changes within their own user context or below. That means that running the tools within an Administrator account will allow you to monitor changes made at that user context and below but not changes made by SYSTEM-level accounts.

Figure 6.15 Incontrol5 GUI

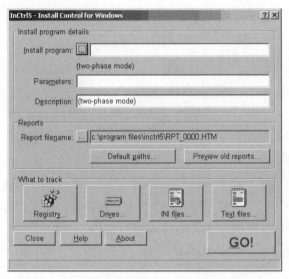

InControl5 provides you with a nice report (HTML, spreadsheet, or text) of files and Registry keys that were added, modified, or deleted. InControl5 will also monitor specific files for changes as well, although the list of files monitored is fairly limited. You can also select an install program, such as an MSI file, for InControl5 to monitor. However, I haven't seen many Trojans or worms propagate as Microsoft installer files.

Once you've launched your malware and collected the data you need, you want to halt the real-time monitoring tools, then run the second phase of the snapshot tools for comparison. At this point, it's your decision as to whether you want to save the logs from the real-time monitoring tools before or after you run the second phase of the snapshot tools. Your testing platform is for your use, and it's not going to be used as evidence, so it's your decision as to the order of these final steps. Personally, I save the data collected by the real-time monitoring tools first and then complete the snapshot tools processes. I know that I'm going to see the newly created files from the real-time monitoring tools in the output of the snapshot tools, and I know when and how those files were created. Therefore, I can easily separate that data from data generated by the malware.

To take things a step further, it's a good idea to create a separate directory for all your log files. This makes separating the data during analysis easier as well as making it easier to collect the data off the system when you've completed the monitoring. In fact, you might even consider adding a USB removable storage device to the system and sending all your log files to that device.

In short, the process looks something like this:

- Ensure that all monitoring tools are updated/installed; refer to tool list.

- Ensure that all monitoring tools are configured properly.

- Create log storage location (local hard drive, USB removable storage, etc.).

- Prepare malware to be analyzed (copy to malware file to the analysis system, document location with the file system).

- Launch baseline phase of snapshot tools.

- Enable real-time monitoring tools.

- Launch malware (document method of launch; scheduled task, double-click via shell, launch from command prompt, etc.).

- Stop real-time monitoring tools, and save their data to the specified location.

- Launch second phase of snapshot tools; save their data to the specified location.

I know this is pretty simple, but you'd be surprised how much important and useful data gets missed when a process like this *isn't* followed. Hopefully, by starting out from a general perspective, we have a process that we can follow, and from there we can drill down and provide the names of the tools we're going to use. These tools may change over time. For example, for quite a while, RegMon and FileMon from SysInternals.com were the tools of choice for monitoring Registry and file system accesses, respectively, by processes. Although those tools are still useful, the author has rolled the functionality of those tools up into the Process Monitor. The Process Monitor toolbar is illustrated in Figure 6.16.

Figure 6.16 The Process Monitor Toolbar, Showing the RegMon and FileMon Icons

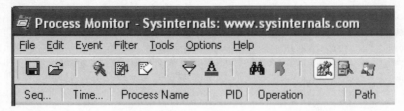

If you've used RegMon or FileMon in the past, the Process Monitor toolbar illustrated in Figure 6.16 should seem familiar; most of the icons are the same ones and in the same order as in the two legacy applications.

When you're using Process Monitor to capture Registry and file system access information, you need to be aware that *all* accesses are captured and that this can make for quite a bit of data to filter through. For example, click the magnifying glass with the red X through it and just sit and watch, without touching the keyboard or mouse. Events will immediately start appearing in the Process Monitor window, even though you haven't done a thing! There's obviously quite a lot that happens on a Windows system every second that you never see. When viewing information collected in Process Monitor, you can click an entry and choose **Exclude | Process Name** to filter out unnecessary processes and remove extraneous data.

TIP

Remember the Image File Execution Options Registry key that we discussed in Chapter 4? Process Monitor is great for showing how the Windows system accesses this key. As a test, open a command prompt, and type the command **net use**, but do not press **Enter**. Open Process Monitor and begin capturing Registry access information. Go back to the command prompt and press **Enter**. Once you see the command complete, halt the Process Monitor capture by clicking the **magnifying glass** so that the red X appears. Figure 6.17 illustrates a portion of the information captured, showing how the net.exe process attempts to determine whether there are any Image File Execution Options for the listed DLLs.

Figure 6.17 Excerpt of Process Monitor Capture Showing Access to the Image File Execution Options Registry Key

```
\Windows NT\CurrentVersion\Image File Execution Options\ntdll.dll     NAME NOT FOUND
\Windows NT\CurrentVersion\Image File Execution Options\kernel32.dll   NAME NOT FOUND
\Windows NT\CurrentVersion\Image File Execution Options\msvcrt.dll    NAME NOT FOUND
\Windows NT\CurrentVersion\Image File Execution Options\RPCRT4.dll    NAME NOT FOUND
\Windows NT\CurrentVersion\Image File Execution Options\ADVAPI32.dll  NAME NOT FOUND
\Windows NT\CurrentVersion\Image File Execution Options\NETAPI32.dll  NAME NOT FOUND
```

One final step to keep in mind is that you might want to dump the contents of physical memory (RAM) using one of the methods discussed in Chapter 3. Not only will you have all the data from dynamic analysis that will tell you what changes the malware made on the system, but in the case of obfuscated malware, you will also have the option of extracting the executable image from the RAM dump, giving you a view of what the malware really looks like, thus enhancing your analysis.

Summary

In this chapter, we've taken a look at two methods we can use to gather information about executable files. By understanding the specific structures of an executable file, we know what to look for as well as what looks odd, particularly when specific actions have been taken to attempt to protect the file from analysis. The analysis methods that we've discussed in this chapter allow us to determine the effects of a piece of software (or malware) on a system as well as the artifacts it leaves behind that indicate its presence. Sometimes this is useful to an investigator, since antivirus software might not detect it, or the antivirus vendor's write-up and description do not provide sufficient detail. As a first responder, these artifacts will help you locate other systems within your network infrastructure that might have been compromised. As an investigator, these artifacts will provide you with a more comprehensive view of the infection as well as what the malware did on the system. In the case of Trojan backdoors and remote access/control software, the artifacts will help you establish a timeline of activities on the system.

Each analysis technique we presented has its benefits and drawbacks, and like any tool, each should be thoroughly justified and documented. Static analysis lets us see the kinds of things that might be possible with the malware, and it will give us clues as to what we can expect when we perform dynamic analysis. However, static analysis often provides only a limited view into the malware. Dynamic analysis can also be called "behavioral" analysis because when we execute the malware in a controlled, monitored environment, we get to see what effects the malware has on the "victim" system, and in what order. However, dynamic analysis has to be used with great care, since we're actually running the malware and if we're not careful we can end up infecting an entire infrastructure.

Even if you're not going to actually perform any analysis of the malware, be sure to fully document it: where you found it within the file system, any other files that are associated with it, compute cryptographic hashes, and so on. Malware authors don't always name their applications with something that stands out as bad, such as syskiller.exe. Often the name of the malware is innocuous, or even intended to mislead the investigator, so fully documenting the malware is extremely important.

Notes

1. For more information go to www.datarescue.com/idabase/index.htm.
2. For a definition of MD5 go to http://en.wikipedia.org/wiki/Md5.
3. For a definition of SHA-1 go to http://en.wikipedia.org/wiki/Sha-1.

4. For more information on Jesse Kornblum's ssdeep tool go to http://ssdeep.source-forge.net/.

5. Jesse Kornblum's paper on the subject is available at www.dfrws.org/2006/pro-ceedings/12-Kornblum.pdf.

6. For more information go to www.microsoft.com/technet/sysinternals/Miscellaneous/Strings.mspx.

7. For more information on the IE0199 virus go to www.mycert.org.my/virus-info/ie0199.htm.

8. To read the first part of Matt Pietrek's two-part series of articles on the Win32 portable executable file format go to http://msdn.microsoft.com/msdnmag/issues/02/02/PE/.

9. Matt Pietrek's second article on the Win32 portable executable file format is available at http://msdn.microsoft.com/msdnmag/issues/02/03/PE2/.

10. For more information on PEview.exec go to www.magma.ca/~wjr/.

11. For more information go to www.microsoft.com/whdc/system/platform/firmware/PECOFF.mspx.

12. For more information on ImageHlp go to http://msdn2.microsoft.com/en-gb/library/ms680198.aspx.

13. To find out more about Mark Zbikowski visit http://en.wikipedia.org/wiki/Mark_Zbikowski.

14. For more information go to http://msdn2.microsoft.com/en-gb/library/ms680313.aspx.

15. For more information go to http://msdn2.microsoft.com/en-gb/library/ms680339.aspx.

16. For more information go to http://msdn2.microsoft.com/en-us/library/ms680305.aspx.

17. For more information go to http://msdn2.microsoft.com/en-us/library/ms680305.aspx.

18. For more information go to http://msdn2.microsoft.com/en-us/library/ms680341.aspx.

19. To use Microsoft Advanced Search go to http://search.microsoft.com/advanced-search.aspx?mkt=en-US&setlang=en-US.

20. For more information go to www.mirc.com/get.html.

21. For more information on the hidewndw.exe utility go to http://premium.caribe.net/~adrian2/creations.html.

22. For more information go to http://homepage.ntlworld.com/chawmp/elitewrap/.

23. For more information go to http://packetstormsecurity.org/trojans/bo/index3.html.

24. For more information visit www.aspack.com/.

25. For more information visit http://upx.sourceforge.net/.

26. For more information go to www.fortunecity.com/millenium/fire-mansam/962/html/procdump.html.

27. For more information visit www.honeynet.org/scans/index.html.

28. For more information on PEiD go to http://peid.has.it/.

29. For more information go to www.blackhat.com.

30. For more information visist http://bochs.sourceforge.net/.

31. For more information go to www.parallels.com/.

32. For more information go to www.microsoft.com/windows/virtualpc/default.mspx.

33. For more information visit www.virtualiron.com/.

34. For more information go to www.xensource.com/xen/.

35. For more information go to www.win4lin.com/.

36. Wikipedia's table for comparing virtual machine packages is available at http://en.wikipedia.org/wiki/Comparison_of_virtual_machines.

37. Visit www.vmware.com for more information on VMware.

38. For more information go to http://isc.sans.org/diary.php?storyid=1871.

39. For more information go to www.symantec.com/home_homeoffice/products/overview.jsp?pcid=br&pvid=ghost 10.

40. For more information visit www.wireshark.org/.

41. To find out more about Port Reporter visit http://support.microsoft.com/kb/837243.

42. The * is replaced by the date and time in 24-hour format for when the log file is created.

43. For more information go to http://support.microsoft.com/kb/840832/.

44. For more information go to http://support.microsoft.com/kb/884289.

45. For more information go to http://insecure.org/nmap/index.html.

46. For more information go to http://support.microsoft.com/kb/832919.

47. For more information go to www.microsoft.com/technet/sysinternals/FileAndDisk/Filemon.mspx.

48. For more information go to www.microsoft.com/technet/sysinternals/SystemInformation/Regmon.mspx.

49. For more information go to www.microsoft.com/technet/sysinternals/ProcessesAndThreads/processmonitor.mspx.

50. For more information go to http://regshot.blog.googlepages.com/regshot.html.
51. For more information go to http://home.planet.nl/~pa0joz/pc_util.html.
52. For more information go to www.paraglidernc.com/6901.html.

Solutions Fast Track

Static Analysis

☑ Documenting any suspicious application or file you find during an investigation is the first step in determining what it does to a system and its purpose.

☑ The contents of a suspicious executable might be incomprehensible to most folks, but if you understand the structures used to create executable files, you will begin to see how the binary information within the file can be used during an investigation.

☑ Do not rely on filenames alone when you're investigating a suspicious file. Even seasoned malware analysts have been known to fall prey to an intruder who takes even a few minutes to attempt to "hide" his malware by giving it an innocuous name.

Dynamic Analysis

☑ A dynamic analysis process will let you see what effects malware has on a system.

☑ Using a combination of snapshot-based and real-time monitoring tools will show you not only the artifacts left by a malware infection but also the order (based on time) in which they occur.

☑ When performing dynamic analysis, it is a good idea to use monitoring tools that do not reside on the testing platform, so information can be collected in a manner unaffected by the malware.

☑ Once dynamic malware analysis has been completed, the testing platform can be subject to incident response as well as post-mortem computer forensic analysis. This not only allows an analyst to hone her skills; it provides additional verification of malware artifacts.

Frequently Asked Questions

The following Frequently Asked Questions, answered by the authors of this book, are designed to both measure your understanding of the concepts presented in this chapter and to assist you with real-life implementation of these concepts. To have your questions about this chapter answered by the author, browse to www.syngress.com/solutions and click on the "Ask the Author" form.

Q: When performing incident response, I found that a file called svchost.exe was responsible for several connections on the system. Is this system infected with malware?

A: Well, the question isn't really whether the system is infected but rather is svchost.exe a malicious piece of software? Reasoning through this, the first question I would ask is, what did you do to view the network connections? Specifically, what is the status of the connections? Are they listening, awaiting connections, or have the connections been established to other systems? Second, what are the ports involved in the network connections? Are they normally seen in association with svchost.exe? Finally, where within the file system did you find the file? The svchost.exe file is normally found in the system32 directory and is protected by Windows File Protection (WFP), which runs automatically in the background. If there are no indications that WFP has been compromised, have you computed a cryptographic hash for svchost.exe and compared it to a known-good exemplar? Often during incident response, a lack of familiarity with the operating system leads the responder down the wrong road to the wrong conclusions.

Q: I found a file during an investigation, and when I open it in a hex editor, I can clearly see the *MZ* signature and the PE header. However, I don't see the usual section names, such as .text, .idata, and .rsrc. Why is that?

A: PE file section header names are not used by the PE file itself for anything in particular and can be modified without affecting the rest of the PE file itself. Although "normal" PE files and some compression tools have signatures of "normal" section header names, these can be easily changed. Section header names act as one small piece of information that you can use to build a "picture" of the file.

Q: I've completed both static and dynamic analysis of a suspicious executable file, and I have a pretty good idea of what it does and what artifacts it leaves on a system. Is there any way I can verify my analysis?

A: Once you've completed you own analysis, it might be a good idea to use an available antivirus software package to scan the malware. In most cases, an investigator will do this first, but this does not always guarantee a result. Many an incident responder has shown up on scene to find a worm clearly running amok on a network, even though there are up-to-date antivirus utilities on all affected systems. If you get no results from the available utilities, try uploading the file to a site such as www.virustotal.com, which will scan the file with over two dozen antivirus engines and return a result. If your results are still limited, submit the file for analysis, including all your documentation, to your antivirus vendor.

Q: I am interested in reading more about executable file and malware analysis. Can you recommend any resources?

A: Depending on the amount of time you have to invest, you could consult a number of resources on the subject of "reverse engineering" executable code. Many of the techniques discussed in these resources pertain equally well to malware analysis. Some such sites include the REblog (http://blogs.msdn.com/geffner/default.aspx) and OpenRCE (www.openrce.org/articles/).

Chapter 7

Rootkits and Rootkit Detection

Solutions in this chapter:

- **Rootkits**
- **Rootkit Detection**

☑ **Summary**

☑ **Solutions Fast Track**

☑ **Frequently Asked Questions**

Introduction

At the RSA Conference in February 2005, Mike Danseglio and Kurt Dillard, both from Microsoft, mentioned the word *rootkit*, and the ensuing months saw a flurry of activity as "experts" pontificated about rootkits and software companies produced tools to detect them. Even though rootkits had been around for years, originating in the UNIX world and then migrating over into the Windows realm, this issue was largely misunderstood and in some corners even ignored, in a "head buried in the sand" sort of way. The mention of rootkits at the 2005 conference resulted in a surge in interest in rootkits, and commercial rootkit detection tools were announced soon after. (There had been several freeware tools and methodologies available for some time.) As detection techniques have improved, rootkit authors have devised new ways of subverting the operating system and even the kernel in attempts to remain undetected.

The rootkit threat is significant; there is no question about that. Rootkits can hide the presence of other tools, such as keyloggers, network sniffers, and remote access backdoors, not only from the user but also from the operating system itself. The insidious nature of rootkits can cause issues when they are actually as well as when they aren't but incident responders assume that they have been, due to lack of knowledge and training. Assuming (without any hard-core data to back it up) that a rootkit has been installed on a system or infrastructure can lead an investigator or incident manager down an incorrect path with regard to reactions and decisions based on the misleading incident assessment. Considerable resources could be invested in unnecessary activities, or systems could be wiped of all data and rein-stalled from clean media, all without determining the root cause, and then become reinfected soon after being put back into service.

Rootkits

So, just what is a rootkit? A Sophos[1] podcast released on August 24, 2006, includes the statement that as a result of a poll conducted by Sophos, 37 percent of respondents did not know the definition of a rootkit. Wikipedia defines a rootkit[2] as "a set of software tools intended to conceal running processes, files, or system data from the operating system." In the first part of their three-part series of articles on rootkits published on SecurityFocus, Jaime Butler, a widely regarded expert in rootkit technologies, and Sherri Sparks define a rootkit as follows:

> ... a program or set of programs that an intruder uses to hide her presence on a computer system and to allow access to the

computer system in the future. To accomplish its goal, a rootkit
will alter the execution flow of the operating system or manipulate the data set that the operating system relies upon for
auditing and bookkeeping. [3.]

Another way of looking at it is that a rootkit is a software program that modifies
the operating system so that it is capable of hiding itself and other objects from
users, administrators, and even the operating system itself.

Rootkits are used to hide processes, network connections, Registry keys, files,
and the like from the operating system, and by extension, the administrator. The
term *rootkit* comes from the UNIX world, where such tools were often used to gain
and/or maintain "root" (akin to the Administrator on Windows) level access to a
system. As similar functionality was developed in malware on Windows, the name
made a similar transition along with the tools.

One of the first rootkits developed for Windows was NTRootkit, written by
Greg Hoglund and released in 1999. NTRootkit consists of a driver and is still available with source code, as illustrated in Figure 7.1.

Figure 7.1 The NTRootkit 0.44 Archive Showing Source Files

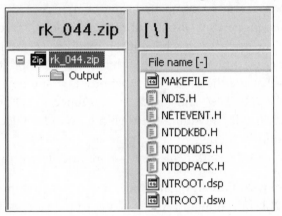

Since then, significant research has gone into the development of rootkits and
rootkit technologies. Hoglund and others have conducted classes at BlackHat[4.] and
other conferences on how to write rootkits, and his Web site, rootkit.com, has
become the preeminent site for Windows rootkit knowledge, development, and
information sharing. Over the years, other rootkits have appeared on the scene, and
development of new rootkit techniques continues unabated. There is also a great
book available on rootkits, the way they are designed, and the way they work:

Rootkits: Subverting the Windows Kernel. This book was written by Greg Hoglund and Jamie Butler and is available on Amazon.com.

Immediately following the RSA Conference in February 2005, there was an explosion in the interest in rootkits and rootkit detection, and as detection techniques became more sophisticated, so did the rootkits themselves. Think of the trend as an ever-escalating battleground, with developments on one side spurring further developments on the other.

There are several different types of rootkit. Early versions of rootkits worked by replacing operating system utilities and applications with Trojan'ed versions so that when the Trojan'ed version of the utility was run, it was programmed not to show specific objects. For example, Trojan'ing the *netstat* command would first remove the attacker's network connections from the file listing and then display the remaining network connections as they would normally appear.

Later came the DLL injection or "user-mode" rootkits. These rootkits install in the security context of the user currently logged into the system and replace, hook, or patch various operating system calls or DLL functions. To put our *netstat* example in the context of a user-mode rootkit, rather than replacing the *netstat* command itself, a user-mode rootkit will hook Windows API function calls so that the functions themselves do not return a complete listing of all network connections. The *netstat* command then proceeds to display all the information it receives from the function call, not knowing that it has been given incomplete and misleading information. Hooking the listed function calls also hides the network connections from any other programs that use the same API functions. User-mode rootkits that hide files will hook the *FindFirstFile()* and *FindNextFile()* function calls so that no program that uses these function calls, including the shell (i.e., Windows Explorer), will see the files that the rootkit is hiding.

Examples of user-mode rootkits include but are not limited to:

- AFX Rootkit 2005 is an open-source rootkit written in Delphi (by Aphex) that uses DLL injection and API hooking to hide a files, Registry keys, processes, and the like.

- Hacker Defender (from hxdef.org, by holy_father) is perhaps the most popular and widespread rootkit available. The F-Secure site describes Hacker Defender as the most widely deployed rootkit in the wild. Hacker Defender also uses port redirection so that traditional means of rootkit detection, such as remote port scans, cannot detect the backdoor implemented by the rootkit. Hacker Defender uses a configuration file, which can be found in the contents of physical memory collected from an infected system. Portions of the configuration file can be found in physical memory; it can't recover the file as a whole. Further, an examination of physical memory sees right through Hacker Defender; the examiner can see all the processes it's been hiding. The examiner has to compare the running processes found during memory analysis to the list presented by the operating system to know which ones were being hidden by the rootkit.

- NTIllusion[5] was designed to be able to infect a system, running under the lowest privileges available, subverting processes owned by the current user.

- Vanquish is a Romanian DLL injection rootkit that can hide files, processes, Registry keys, and the like. Vanquish consists of an autoloader (.exe file) and a DLL, which in turn consists of six submodules. Vanquish requires Administrator privileges to install properly and, according to the readme file that accompanies the distribution, does not work when other rootkits are present on the system.

- Gromozon[6] is a user-mode rootkit that infects a system via a BHO and uses multiple techniques to maintain persistence on the infected system (hides code in EFS files and NTFS alternate data streams, creates a service, creates a reference in the AppInit_DLLs Registry key, and the like). In addition, the rootkit removes the Debug privilege from user accounts to inhibit rootkit detection tools from functioning properly. The Symantec write-up[7] on this rootkit describes it as "spaghetti" due to the various methods of persistence that the authors designed into the code.

TIP

Each of these rootkits is available for download at rootkit.com.

Much more insidious are the "kernel-mode" rootkits, because they subvert the operating system kernel itself. Not only will kernel-mode rootkits intercept low-level API calls, they will also manipulate kernel data structures. One example of a kernel-mode rootkit is FU, developed by Jamie Butler, which uses a technique called *direct kernel object manipulation*, or DKOM, to hide on the system. DKOM is the process of manipulating kernel-level data structures without using the Windows APIs. For example, the Windows kernel maintains a doubly linked circular list of all running processes on the system, and FU will remove requested processes from the list. The processes are still there but are not "seen" by the kernel. The scheduling quantum for the system is a thread, not a process, so the FU thread continues to run while the process is invisible to the system. FU itself uses a driver, named msdirectx.sys by default, to gain access and control the system. The FU program itself, fu.exe, terminates after it loads the driver into memory.

Kernel-mode rootkits may also subvert other kernel structures. The FUTo[8.] rootkit, released as the successor to the FU rootkit, is discussed at great length in volume 3 of the *Uniformed Journal*[9.] (released in January 2006). FUTo extends FU's DKOM capabilities by using assembly language code (vice API calls) to manipulate the *PspCidTable* variable, which is a pointer to the handle table for process and thread client IDs. This handle table is used to keep track of all process identifiers.

Shadow Walker is a proof-of-concept kernel-mode rootkit that was discussed at the BlackHat 2005 conference. Based on the FU rootkit, Shadow Walker contains an additional driver that manipulates the memory manager to hide the existence of the rootkit files. Shadow Walker does this, in short, by ensuring that all hidden pages are in nonpaged memory and by intercepting all accesses to those pages. When the operating system requests to read those pages, the rootkit returns pages of zeros. When the operating system requests to execute those pages, it returns the malicious code. Remember the scene from the *Star Wars* movie in which Obi-Wan Kenobi told the StormTrooper commander, "These are not the droids you are looking for"? Yeah, just like that.

One caveat to kernel-mode rootkits is that they can also cause the system to "blue screen" if they are not properly written. Microsoft support personnel have helped many customers track down repeated BSoDs (the dreaded Blue Screen of Death), only to find that a kernel-mode rootkit was the issue. As mentioned in Chapter 3, a crash dump or BSoD will cause a crash dump file to be written to the hard drive, and support personnel can use this file to diagnose the issue. Often this is the way a rootkit (one that is known, or perhaps a new variant) is discovered on a system.

At times the term *rootkit* is used in a somewhat lazy manner. For example, there is an interesting entry in the Symantec Security Response Web log from September 2006 titled, "The poor man's rootkit." In that entry, the author describes a bit of malware named Trojan.Zonebac that uses a camouflage technique to "hide" its presence on the system. In short, during installation the Trjoan scans the contents of the ubiquitous Run key and selects a commonly used application. It backs up the executable image for the file pointed to by the Registry value and writes itself to the file system using the name of the original file. When the system is started, the Trojan is run automatically, and it then runs the backed-up file as well, so nothing appears amiss. Further, the *LastWrite* time of the Run key is not updated, since no actual changes were made to the key.

Although this is indeed a novel and even ingenious method for hiding on a system, it is not a rootkit. In fact, hiding in plain sight by renaming the malware executable image to something innocuous is a common and effective practice. In fact, it's not uncommon for this sort of technique to be listed under "hack the admin" or "hack the examiner" rather than "hack the server."

WARNING

Relying on nothing more than the name of a file to diagnose an issue can be misleading and could even cause an investigator to completely miss the true root cause of the incident. Too often an administrator will find a suspicious file and Google the filename. He'll then find that there is a legitimate Microsoft file by that name and so declare the incident closed. This does not apply only to administrators; I have seen malware analysts do the same thing. However, I have also seen instances in which malware was installed on a system using the name of a legitimate Microsoft file, such as alg.exe or svchost.exe. In most of the cases that I have been involved with, the administrator has found this "legitimacy" and looked no further. No one noticed that the executable images were not located in the system32 directory, for example. The point is that you cannot rely solely on the filename as a means of identifying a file and the effect it might have on a system or infrastructure.

Rootkits have also been used commercially. Not only have several rootkit authors branched out to provide custom rootkits to whomever was willing to pay their fees, but corporations have used rootkits to hide functionality as well. On October 31, 2005, Mark Russinovich (of SysInternals fame, now with Microsoft) announced on his blog that he'd discovered that Sony Corporation was using a rootkit in an effort to affect digital rights management and protect its property.[10] Among other things, Mark pointed out that not only was the use of this rootkit completely unknown to the person who had purchased the music CD and installed the software on her computer (users were not explicitly warned of the use of the rootkit, nor was it listed in the end–user license agreement), but an attacker who did find this software installed on a system could take advantage of it and install his own tools, which would then be hidden under Sony's umbrella. Since the discovery of this issue and the ensuing furor, Mark has moved on to be employed by Microsoft. Mark's blog entry is archived at the Virus Bulletin site.[11]

Notes from the Underground...

Information Sharing

In his blog entry regarding the Sony rootkit issue (at the Virus Bulletin site), Mark makes the following statement:

Until a few years ago we made the source code to Regmon available publicly, which led to the use of our hooking functions and support routines in the NTRootkit example that's published on www.rootkit.com. The structure of the code in Aries indicates that it's likely to be derived from NTRootkit code.

It's kind of interesting to see how different sources are used to further the development of applications, including malware. In this case, the use of the hooking functions has come full circle.

Mark and others explored the use of rootkits by corporations in their software products, and on January 10, 2006, Symantec released[12] information stating that its Norton Protected Recycle Bin uses rootkit-like functionality as well.

Rootkit Detection

So now that we've seen a little something about what rootkits are and what they can do, how do we go about detecting the presence of a rootkit on a system? To answer this question, let's look at two detection modes, live and post mortem. In live-detection mode, the basic scenario is that we've got a running system and we're going to attempt to determine whether there is a rootkit on the system. In post-mortem detection mode, we're working with an acquired image of the system.

Live Detection

Live detection of rootkits can be a tricky issue to deal with, particularly if the investigator is not knowledgeable about rootkit artifacts and what to look for on a system that might be infected with a rootkit. Often this results in a misdiagnosis and misidentification of the incident, and any further response is taken in the wrong direction.

In the fall of 2006, Jesse Kornblum published a very interesting paper in the *International Journal of Digital Evidence* titled "Exploiting the Rootkit Paradox with Windows Memory Analysis."[13] In that paper, Jesse identified two basic principles that all rootkits attempt to follow; that is, they want to remain hidden, and they want to run. Essentially, to remain hidden on a system, a rootkit has to minimize its footprint and interaction with the system while still interacting with the system in some way. The system itself, specifically the operating system, needs to be able to execute the rootkit, which is trying to remain hidden and persistent across reboots. Therefore, Jesse proposes that if the operating system can find the rootkit, so can an examiner. I might add "a sufficiently knowledgeable examiner" to that statement, but I'm sure that's what Jesse meant to say.

The predominant technique for rootkit detection on a live system is sometimes referred to as *behavioral* or *differential* (or *high/low*) analysis. The basic idea is that by making two different kinds of queries for the same information and looking for differences in the responses, you can detect the presence of a rootkit or of something being hidden by a rootkit. For example, one of the early rootkit detection tools was a Visual Basic Script named rkdetect.vbs[14] that could detect the popular Hacker Defender rootkit by running a remote query to enumerate services using sc.exe, followed by a local query (using psexec.exe and sc.exe), and then looking for anomalies or differences between the two outputs. In my first book,[15] I included a Perl script called rkd.pl that would perform differential analysis against processes, services, and some Registry keys. The script would note differences in output between remote and "local" queries (again, the tools were run locally on a remote system using psexec.exe), but it also included some signature checks—that is, specific checks for specific rootkits. In the book, I demonstrated the use of such tools against the AFX Rootkit 2003.

TIP

Lenny Zeltser,[16] an incident handler with the SANS Internet Storm Center (ISC), posted a diary entry[17] titled "Behavior Analysis of Rootkit Malware" on July 16, 2006. In that diary entry, Lenny provides screen captures and descriptions of several rootkit detection tools (as well as links to others) being tested against some of the rootkits mentioned previously in this chapter.

Over time, rootkits have evolved, using more sophisticated hiding and stealth techniques, and rootkit detection techniques have had to keep up. Differential analysis is still the best way to attempt to detect rootkits, but the items queried are even more granular. For example, some tools will scan the file system using commands similar to *dir /s* and *dir /s /ah* and then compare their output to the contents of the Master File Table (MFT). The idea is to perform a high-level query followed by a very low-level query (as low as possible) and note any differences in the output between the two.

Several freeware and commercial rootkit detection tools are available, yet none of them provide details of *how* they operate. This is done so that the rootkit authors do not have an easy means of determining how the detection tools function and can then add techniques to their rootkits to avoid detection by those tools. However, this does not deter the rootkit authors from downloading the tools and determining how they work for themselves.

RootkitRevealer

RootkitRevealer[18] (illustrated in Figure 7.2) is a rootkit detection tool that appeared on the scene in the spring of 2005. (RootkitRevealer was "slashdotted"[19]—that is, posted to and discussed on the Slashdot.org Web site—on February 23, 2005). Since the initial release, it has gone through some changes to keep up with changes in rootkit techniques.

The author's description of RootkitRevealer specifically states that although the tool is designed to and can detect rootkits that hide files and Registry keys, it does not detect kernel mode rootkits (such as FU) that modify kernel objects.

> ## ! WARNING
>
> When running any tool, you need to be aware of how it works and what it does; this applies to rootkit detection tools as well as any other tool. I worked an engagement once where the customer's incident response was badly managed and uncoordinated. While some administrators were instructed to do specific tasks, several took it upon themselves to run destructive antivirus scans on systems as well as run RootkitRevealer. To perform its scans, RootkitRevealer installed itself as a service, and the executable image had a random name, although the image file itself had random padding (so that the hash of the file was never the same). This was done as an antirootkit detection technique. At one point, an administrator called me to tell me that he had discovered a "massively infected" system that had eight strange services running, and RootkitRevealer had not detected them as rootkits. Well, first of all, if the administrator could "see" the services listed, they probably weren't hidden by a rootkit. Second, all the executable image files had the same icon. Third, all the executable

image files were RootkitRevealer. Due to a lack of coordination and knowledge of the tools being used, incident-response activities resulted in what appeared at first glance to be a massive infection.

Figure 7.2 The RootkitRevealer GUI

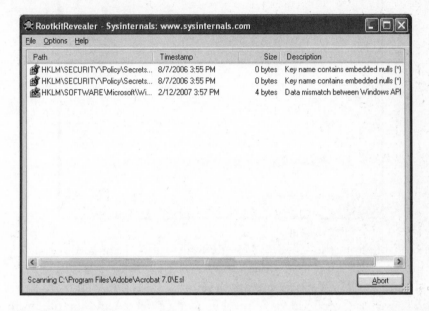

GMER

GMER[20] is a freeware GUI-based rootkit detection application that attempts to detect:

- Hidden processes, files, services, Registry keys, and drivers
- Drivers hooking the system service descriptor table (SSDT), interrupt descriptor table (IDT), or IO request packet (IRP) calls

GMER is also capable of showing NTFS alternate data streams, as illustrated in Figure 7.3.

Figure 7.3 The GMER GUI

Also available from the GMER Web site is a small CLI application called *catchme* that is capable of detecting user-mode rootkits such as Gromozon, Hacker Defender, AFX, and Vanquish. The GMER site has the rootkit detection tool available for download as well as several videos of rootkits being detected and log files from scans where rootkits were detected.

Helios

Helios[21.] is described as an "advanced malware detection system" that uses behavioral analysis and does not employ signatures as a detection mechanism. Although it's described as a malware detection system, Helios is also capable of detecting rootkits. Helios is not open source, but it is free, and (according to the Web site) does have an API that provides access to the product's core functionality. Helios will not only detect rootkits, it will also inoculate against rootkit installation. The Helios GUI is illustrated in Figure 7.4.

TIP

If you are going to download and use Helios, make sure that you install the .NET Framework 2.0. A link to the necessary file is available on the Helios download page.

Figure 7.4 The Helios GUI

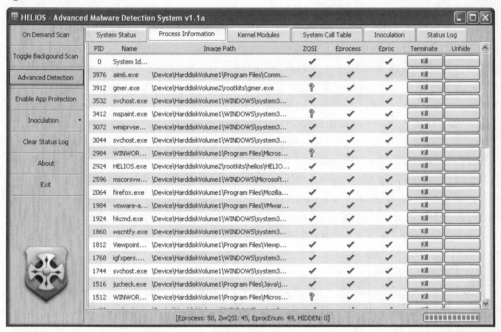

The Helios Web site includes several videos (downloadable or watchable via streaming) that demonstrate the application's use and capabilities.

TIP

Many of the freely available rootkit detection applications that are presented in this chapter are easily downloaded and run from a single directory. Deploying these tools during incident-response activities can be as easy as copying them to a USB thumb drive, then enabling the write-protect switch (if your thumb drive has one) and plugging the thumb drive into the system you want to scan. However, you do need to keep in mind any dependencies and requirements, such as Helios requiring the Microsoft .Net Framework 2.0.

MS Strider GhostBuster

The Microsoft Research Center[22] has devoted significant resources to the study of the detection of rootkits on Windows systems, the result of which is the Strider GhostBuster[23] project, a tool that is designed to detect rootkits that hook or subvert Window API functions. GhostBuster uses a technique that is referred to as "cross-view diff" (which amounts to a technique similar to behavioral or differential analysis). By performing one query on an "infected" system, then booting to "clean" media (a bootable Windows CD that is uninfected) and running the same query, you can then perform a "diff" between the two outputs and determine what is hidden. This is particularly useful with regard to files, but because an exact copy of the entire system (including all applications and patches) must be maintained on the bootable CD/DVD, this technique might not be particularly useful with regard to processes. To locate "hidden" processes using this technique (such as booting the system to separate, "clean" media), the administrator would be required to maintain a complete set of all applications as well as operating system and application patches and configuration settings on the clean media. Any change, even the slightest, would need to be replicated on separate media. This is perhaps too cumbersome for most infrastructures and investigations.

Although the GhostBuster site does contain links to information and papers regarding various aspects of rootkit technologies, as of this writing an actual GhostBuster tool is not available for download and use. However, some of the papers at the site are extremely useful and make for some very good professional reading. For example, a paper presented at Usenix LISA 2004, *Gatekeeper: Monitoring Auto-Start Extensibility Points (ASEPs) for Spyware Management*, provides some excellent insight into Registry autostart locations.

ProDiscover

ProDiscover/IR, from Technology Pathways,[24] includes functionality to assist the investigator in examining systems for rootkits during incident-response activities. Installing the ProDiscover server applet (PDServer.exe) on a system (by either running it from a CD or thumb drive or by installing it remotely over the network), the investigator can then connect to the server and perform a variety of actions, some of which are illustrated in Figure 7.5.

Figure 7.5 ProDiscover Functionality for Rootkit Detection

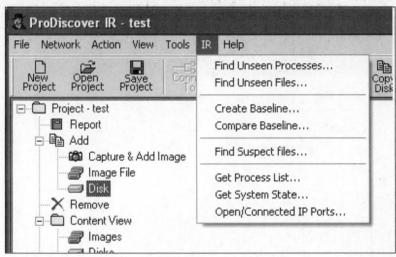

As shown in Figure 7.5, the investigator can attempt to locate unseen processes and files as well as collect some information with regard to the active process list and system state via the menu system in ProDiscover IR. The ProScript API allows a bit more granularity and flexibility in the information that can be collected as well as how it is managed. Attempting to locate unseen processes and files can assist the investigator in locating rootkits on the system.

F-Secure BlackLight

F-Secure is a Finnish company that produces antivirus software (according to the company's blog,[25] its antivirus product was recently incorporated into the VirusTotal.com scanning site), as well as a rootkit elimination product called BlackLight.[26] BlackLight detects objects hidden by rootkit technologies and provides the user with an opportunity to eliminate or remove the offending software.

BlackLight, freely available on a trial basis, comes with both GUI and CLI versions that are available for download from the F-Secure Web site. Figure 7.6 illustrates the BlackLight GUI.

Figure 7.6 BlackLight GUI

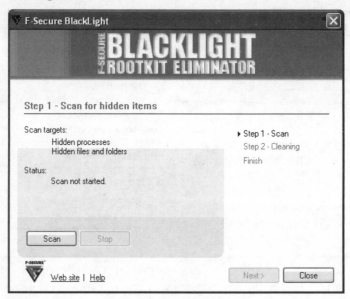

Like many of the other rootkit-detection applications, BlackLight ships as an executable and does not include an installation program (i.e., .msi file); once you download the executable for whichever version you choose, you can run the application immediately.

Sophos Anti-Rootkit

Sophos[27] is another antivirus vendor that also provides antirootkit software. The Sophos Anti-Rootkit product is freely available for download and use, and like the F-Secure BlackLight product, comes in both GUI (illustrated in Figure 7.7) and CLI flavors. The Sophos product can be used to scan the infrastructure, in addition to single hosts, for rootkits, as well as remove them. Anti-Rootkit scans the system for hidden processes, Registry keys, and files on the local hard drives.

TIP

The third article in a three-article series by Jamie Butler and Sherri Sparks, "Windows Rootkits of 2005," was published on SecurityFocus.com on January 5, 2006. This article, which discusses five rootkit-detection techniques and highlights a total of nine rootkits, is well worth reading.

Figure 7.7 Sophos Anti-Rootkit GUI

AntiRootkit.com

F-Secure and Sophos aren't the only antivirus companies that provide rootkit-detection and/or elimination products. Other vendors include the capability to detect rootkits, either as separate products or as integrated components in their antivirus products. The McAfee Rootkit Detective product searches for hidden files, processes, and Registry keys or values on a potentially infected system, as does Trend Micro's RootkitBuster product.

Perhaps the best site available for information on rootkit-detection techniques and products is AntiRootkit.com. The site provides a blog as well as list of free and commercial rootkit-detection/elimination products (products are listed predominantly for Windows, but there are Linux, BSD, and even a Mac OS X product listed) as well as a list of rootkit prevention products that can be used to prevent or inhibit rootkits from installing in the first place. News and articles links provide access to even more information.

Post-Mortem Detection

Post-mortem detection of a rootkit poses its own set of challenges. You're probably thinking, how difficult can this be? After all, you're looking at an image, not a live system … what would you be looking for? Given various techniques available to malware authors, including antiforensics techniques that are discussed and made publicly available (the MetaSploit Project has an entire section of its Web site dedicated to antiforensics techniques), locating the offending malware, even on an image, can be difficult. However, if you understand what you're looking for and where to look for it, you are more likely to be successful in your examination.

One method of post-mortem detection of rootkits is to mount the image as a virtual file system on your analysis system using a tool like Mount Image Pro,[28.] allowing the files to be read as a file system without engaging the operating system from the image to do so. Mount Image Pro mounts the image as read-only, so no changes can be made to the files. From here you can run any number of antivirus tools against the files in the image. The files within the image appear as just that— files. None of the processes and services from the image are running, so the rootkit will not be engaged, and the kernel of the analysis system is not subverted.

WARNING

Using Mount Image Pro to access an acquired image as a file directory structure is great if you want to scan it with antivirus and spyware detection tools, but the available rootkit detection tools will not be of much use to you. The reason is that these tools look for things being hidden—files, Registry keys, processes, and the like—and when an acquired image is mounted as a drive letter, none of the files is hidden.

A method that I use to quickly check for the presence of a rootkit in an acquired image is to access the Registry Viewer within ProDiscover and navigate to the Services key in each available ControlSet, as illustrated in Figure 7.8.

TIP

To determine the *ControlSet* that is marked as "current" or loaded as the *CurrentControlSet* when the system is booted, locate the *Current* value in the System\Select key. The data is a *DWORD* Registry type and tells you which of the available *ControlSets* is marked as "current."

Figure 7.8 An Excerpt from ProDiscover Registry View

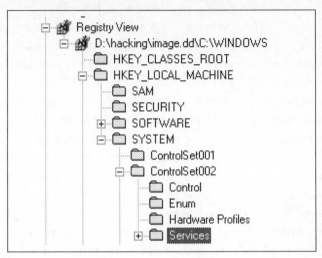

Once I've located the key, I then sort the entries in the right-hand pane based on the *LastWrite* time of each key. Most of the entries in this list will correspond to when the system was originally installed. In some cases, several keys might all have the same *LastWrite* time as a result of a software update that affected all of them, often on the same day. However, when a kernel-mode rootkit driver is installed it will usually stand out with only one or two entries made on one day. This *LastWrite* time doesn't always correspond to the dates provided in an incident report, but in most cases they will stand out like a sore thumb. In addition, they will provide you with a date on which to orient your timeline analysis of activity on the system. Because there does not seem to be any publicly available Windows API for modifying Registry key *LastWrite* times from user-mode applications, you can be sure that the key's *LastWrite* time corresponds to when the rootkit and its driver were installed.

An additional means of rootkit detection that hangs someplace between live and post mortem was discussed in Chapter 3. If the investigator dumps the contents of physical memory and quickly analyzes it, the system might still be running, but the analysis will actually occur on a snapshot of RAM. As Jesse pointed out in his "Paradox" paper, a "smart" rootkit will not interfere with the memory dump process, since doing so could reveal the presence of the rootkit. After all, a rootkit that causes the operating system to crash dump (resulting in the dreaded BSoD) renders the system unusable to both the administrator/user and the intruder. The predominant tool used for obtaining the contents of RAM from a live system, dd.exe, as modified by George M. Garner, Jr., has been demonstrated to be extremely stable in most usage scenarios. If the rootkit were to cause the system to crash dump, the resulting crash dump file could be analyzed to reveal the existence of the rootkit. By collecting the contents of RAM and searching for EPROCESS blocks (refer to Chapter 4 for information regarding searching RAM dumps for process information), you can compare the processes that have not exited with those visible in the active process list to determine which, if any, were hidden by a rootkit.

Another option available to you is to boot the image into VMware[29] using LiveView[30] and examine the live system for a possible rootkit. In Chapter 6 I mentioned that some malware uses software to detect the presence of a virtual environment, and if it does detect that it is running in an environment such as VMware, it can change its behavior to avoid detection. Of course, some rootkits might do this as well, and that secondary behavior could cause issues on the system. You can also scan the virtual system with a port scanner such as *nmap*[31] and then compare the results of the scan to the output of netstat.exe or openports.exe. If you find ports that are open using *nmap* but you don't see those ports in the output of netstat.exe, you might have a live rootkit on the system.

Prevention

We've talked quite a bit about rootkit detection but nothing about actually preventing rootkits from being installed on Windows systems. The first step to rootkit detection is prevention, performed through system configuration, which is beyond the scope of this book. However, suffice it to say that taking a minimalist approach to system configure (for example, not providing a user with Administrator-level access unless he requires it, and then for those instances in which he does require that level of access) can go a long way toward preventing or inhibiting the installation of rootkits. If a rootkit installation is inhibited, the rootkit won't function normally and you'll be able to tell that it's there; in fact, it might be glaringly obvious that a system has been the victim of an attempted rootkit installation due to error messages or simply extremely unusual behavior.

! **WARNING**

Some folks opt not to take a minimalist approach to system configuration. The biggest issue is users having Administrator-level access to their systems and being allowed to install any software they could find. I once worked on a case in which I found a system that had a total of four remote desktop services running, and I determined that the intruder had used one of them to gain access to the system. At first I thought that the intruder had installed some of the remote access software, but the system administrator later told me that all four of the applications were legitimate and had been installed by the IT department; each of the remote access applications was a backup for the others. None of the system administrators had the time or skills to manage all the remote access applications, and the intruder was able to use one of them to gain access to the system.

Summary

Though rootkits have been around for quite a while in both the Linux and Windows worlds, interest in rootkits exploded in February 2005 when the word was mentioned by Microsoft employees at the RSA Conference. Books (Hoglund's *Rootkits: Subverting the Windows Kernel* and even a book called *Rootkits for Dummies* are available on Amazon.com) and training courses (Hoglund has taught rootkit techniques during training sessions at BlackHat conferences) covering rootkit development are available, as are samples of working (albeit in some cases proof-of-concept) rootkits.

Rootkits pose a significant threat to systems and infrastructures, the most serious of which is a lack of education and knowledge on the part of administrators and investigators as to exactly what a rootkit is, what a rootkit is capable of, and how it works. With a stronger understanding of these areas, investigators will be better equipped to address issues of rootkits during both live-response and post-mortem investigations.

Notes

1. For more information go to www.sophos.com.
2. For more information go to http://en.wikipedia.org/wiki/Rootkit.
3. James Butler and Sheri Sparks, "Windows Rootkits of 2005, part one" (www.securityfocus.com/infocus/1850, 2005).
4. For more information go to www.blackhat.com.
5. For more information go to www.securiteam.com/securityreviews/5FP0E0AGAC.html.
6. See http://pcalsicuro.phpsoft.it/gromozon.pdf.
7. For more information go to www.symantec.com/enterprise/security_response/weblog/2006/08/gromozoncom_and_italian_spaghe.html.
8. For more information go to www.uninformed.org/?v=3&a=7.
9. For more information go to www.uniformed.org.
10. For more information go to www.symantec.com/avcenter/security/Content/2006.01.10.htm.
11. For more information go to www.virusbtn.com/virusbulletin/archive/2005/12/vb200512-sonys-rootkit.
12. For more information go to www.symantec.com/avcenter/security/Content/2006.01.10.html.

13. For more information go to www.utica.edu/academic/institutes/ecii/publica-tions/articles/EFE2FC4D-0B11-BC08-AD2958256F5E68F1.pdf.

14. For more information go to www.security.nnov.ru/files/rkdetect.zip.

15. *Windows Forensics and Incident Recovery*, published by Addison-Wesley, July 2004.

16. For more information go to www.zeltser.com/.

17. For more information go to http://isc.sans.org/diary.html?storyid=1487.

18. For more information go to www.microsoft.com/technet/sysinternals/utilities/RootkitRevealer.mspx.

19. For more information go to http://it.slashdot.org/it/05/02/23/1353258.shtml?tid=172&tid=218.

20. For more information on GMER go to www.gmer.net/index.php.

21. For more information on Helios go to http://helios.miel-labs.com/.

22. For more information go to http://research.microsoft.com/.

23. For more information visit http://research.microsoft.com/rootkit/.

24. For more information go to www.techpathways.com/.

25. For more information go to www.f-secure.com/weblog/archives/archive-022007.html#00001106.

26. For more information on Blacklight visit www.f-secure.com/blacklight/.

27. For more information go to www.sophos.com/products/free-tools/sophos-anti-rootkit.html.

28. For more information visit www.mountimage.com.

29. For more information go to www.vmware.com.

30. For more information visit http://liveview.sourceforge.net/.

31. See http://insecure.org/nmap/index.html.

Solutions Fast Track

Rootkits

☑ Rootkits are capable of hiding files, Registry keys, processes, network connections, and other objects from the administrator as well as the operating system.

☑ The use of rootkits and rootkit technologies in malware and cybercrime is increasing.

☑ A better understanding of rootkit function and capabilities will prepare investigators to address the issues of rootkits.

Rootkit Detection

☑ Detecting rootkits on live systems requires the use of differential analysis.

☑ Detecting rootkits on an acquired image of a system can be as straightforward as scanning a mounted image (via Mount Image Pro) with antivirus software or even sorting the Services Registry keys based on their *LastWrite* times.

☑ Rootkits might be detected on live systems by capturing and parsing the contents of physical memory to locate processes that are active but not part of the active process list.

Frequently Asked Questions

The following Frequently Asked Questions, answered by the authors of this book, are designed to both measure your understanding of the concepts presented in this chapter and to assist you with real-life implementation of these concepts. To have your questions about this chapter answered by the author, browse to www.syngress.com/solutions and click on the "Ask the Author" form.

Q: I found some unusual traffic logged in my firewall, with a timestamp from four hours ago. It seems that a system on my network attempted to make a connection out to the Internet on an odd port. I went to the system in question and didn't find any active network connections that would account for that traffic. Do I have a rootkit?

A: The short answer is maybe not. Everything that originates from a system, especially network traffic, must have a process or thread that is responsible for generating it. Services will generally run for as long as the system is running, but processes can be short lived. If you do not continue to see similar firewall log entries, it is likely that the process completed and exited, which is why you do not see it on the system.

Q: How do I prevent rootkits from getting on a system in the first place?

A: Configuration management can go a long way toward preventing or inhibiting rootkit infections. If you take a minimalist approach, such as providing only the minimum services and access necessary for the function of the system, you greatly reduce the attack surface. For example, if users cannot install arbitrary software, they are prevented from installing spyware, rootkits, and the like.

Reducing the number of services running on a system reduces the options an attacker has available for gaining access and installing his tools and rootkit.

Q: I found a rootkit on one of my servers; now what? I'm told that there's no way of telling what happened and that I should just wipe the hard drive and completely reinstall the operating system from "clean" media and then load the data back on from uninfected backups.

A: This is very often the route that most administrators take when they've encountered a rootkit. However, there are several problems with this approach. First, you should conduct a thorough investigation of the system (or hire professionals to do it), since you might be able to tell what occurred (such as theft of data). Next, you need to determine, as much as possible, how the rootkit got on the system in the first place; perform a root cause analysis (RCA). Without this sort of investigation, you're going to put a system right back on the network that might be compromised or infected all over again. Finally, if you're subject to any regulatory oversight (Visa PCI, HIPAA, FISMA, or similar) you might be required (either implicitly or explicitly) to investigate the issue and provide a report, and you need to provide as much information as possible.

Index

Syngress: *The Definition of a Serious Security Library*

Syn·gress (sin-gres): *noun, sing.* Freedom from risk or danger; safety. See *security*.

Syngress IT Security Project Management Handbook

Susan Snedaker

The definitive work for IT professionals responsible for the management of the design, configuration, deployment and maintenance of enterprise-wide security projects. Provides specialized coverage of key project areas including Penetration Testing, Intrusion Detection and Prevention Systems, and Access Control Systems.

ISBN: 1-59749-076-8

Price: $59.95 US $77.95 CAN

Combating Spyware in the Enterprise

Paul Piccard

Combating Spyware in the Enterprise is the first book published on defending enterprise networks from increasingly sophisticated and malicious spyware. System administrators and security professionals responsible for administering and securing networks ranging in size from SOHO networks up to the largest enterprise networks will learn to use a combination of free and commercial anti-spyware software, firewalls, intrusion detection systems, intrusion prevention systems, and host integrity monitoring applications to prevent the installation of spyware, and to limit the damage caused by spyware that does in fact infiltrate their networks.

ISBN: 1-59749-064-4

Price: $49.95 US $64.95 CAN

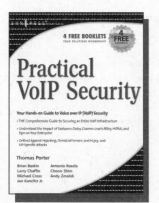

Practical VoIP Security

Thomas Porter

After struggling for years, you finally think you've got your network secured from malicious hackers and obnoxious spammers. Just when you think it's safe to go back into the water, VoIP finally catches on. Now your newly converged network is vulnerable to DoS attacks, hacked gateways leading to unauthorized free calls, call eavesdropping, malicious call redirection, and spam over Internet Telephony (SPIT). This book details both VoIP attacks and defense techniques and tools.

ISBN: 1-59749-060-1

Price: $49.95 U.S. $69.95 CAN

SYNGRESS®

Syngress: *The Definition of a Serious Security Library*

Syn•gress (sin–gres): *noun, sing.* Freedom from risk or danger; safety. See *security.*

Syngress: *The Definition of a Serious Security Library*

Syn·gress (sin–gres): *noun, sing.* Freedom from risk or danger; safety. See *security*.

Syngress: *The Definition of a Serious Security Library*

Syn•gress (sin–gres): *noun, sing.* Freedom from risk or danger; safety. See *security*.

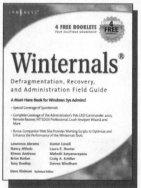

Syngress: *The Definition of a Serious Security Library*

Syn•gress (sin-gres): *noun, sing.* Freedom from risk or danger; safety. See *security*.

Syngress: *The Definition of a Serious Security Library*

Syn•gress (sin-gres): *noun, sing.* Freedom from risk or danger; safety. See *security*.

Syngress: *The Definition of a Serious Security Library*

Syn•gress (sin–gres): *noun, sing.* Freedom from risk or danger; safety. See *security*.

How to Cheat at Managing Windows Server Update Services

Brian Barber

If you manage a Microsoft Windows network, you probably find yourself overwhelmed at times by the sheer volume of updates and patches released by Microsoft for its products. You know these updates are critical to keep your network running efficiently and securely, but staying current amidst all of your other responsibilities can be almost impossible. Microsoft's recently released Windows Server Update Services (WSUS) is designed to streamline this process. Learn how to take full advantage of WSUS using Syngress' proven "How to Cheat" methodology, which gives you everything you need and nothing you don't.

ISBN: 1-59749-027-X

Price: $39.95 US $55.95 CAN

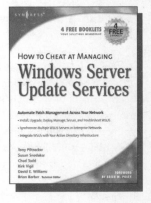

How to Cheat at IT Project Management

Susan Snedaker

Most IT projects fail to deliver – on average, all IT projects run over schedule by 82%, run over cost by 43% and deliver only 52% of the desired functionality. Pretty dismal statistics. Using the proven methods in this book, you'll find that IT project you work on from here on out will have a much higher likelihood of being on time, on budget and higher quality. This book provides clear, concise, information and hands-on training to give you immediate results. And, the companion Web site provides dozens of templates for managing IT projects.

ISBN: 1-59749-037-7

Price: $44.95 U.S. $64.95 CAN

SYNGRESS®

Syngress: *The Definition of a Serious Security Library*

Syn·gress (sin-gres): *noun, sing.* Freedom from risk or danger; safety. See *security*.

Managing Cisco Network Security, Second Edition

Offers updated and revised information covering many of Cisco's security products that provide protection from threats, detection of network security incidents, measurement of vulnerability and policy compliance, and management of security policy across an extended organization. These are the tools that you have to mount defenses against threats. Chapters also cover the improved functionality and ease of the Cisco Secure Policy Manager software used by thousands of small-to-midsized businesses, and a special section on Cisco wireless solutions.

ISBN: 1-931836-56-6

Price: $69.95 USA $108.95 CAN

How to Cheat at Managing Microsoft Operations Manager 2005

Tony Piltzecker, Rogier Dittner, Rory McCaw, Gordon McKenna, Paul M. Summitt, David E. Williams

My e-mail takes forever. My application is stuck. Why can't I log on? System administrators have to address these types of complaints far too often. With MOM, system administrators will know when overloaded processors, depleted memory, or failed network connections are affecting their Windows servers long before these problems bother users. Readers of this book will learn why when it comes to monitoring Windows Server System infrastructure, MOM's the word.

ISBN: 1-59749-251-5

Price: $39.95 U.S. $55.95 CAN